AGAPE
OF
YHVH

ED BRAUER

ISBN 978-1-0980-3865-6 (paperback)
ISBN 978-1-0980-3866-3 (digital)

Christian Faith Publishing, Inc.
832 Park Avenue
Meadville, PA 16335
www.christianfaithpublishing.com

Printed in the United States of America

CONTENTS

(Part One)
MAPS

7	**Ex. 15:2**	Acts 7:55–56
	Ex. 15:11	Acts 4:27
	Ex. 16:4	Jn. 6:48–51
	Ex. 17:6	1 Cor. 10:4
	Ex. 33:19	Jn. 1:14
8	**Lev. 1:1–9**	Eph. 5:2
	Lev. 14:1–3	Lk. 5:14, Heb. 13:13
9	**Lev. 16:15**	Heb. 9:12
	Lev. 16:27	Heb. 13:11
	Lev. 17:11	Mt. 26:28, Mr. 10:45, 1 Jn. 1:7
	Lev. 23:37	Jn. 7:37–38
	Num. 9:12	Jn. 19:33
10	**Num. 20:8**	1 Cor. 10:4
	Num. 21:9	Jn. 3:14–15
	Num. 24:17	Gal. 4:4–5
	Deu. 18:15	Jn. 5:45–47, 6:14, Acts 3:20–23, 7:37
11	**Deu. 18:18–19**	Jn. 8:28–29, Acts 3:22–23
	Deu. 21:23	Jn. 19:38–42, Gal. 3:13
12	**Deu. 32:15**	
	Jos. 5:14–15	Heb. 2:10
	Judg. 13:7	Lk. 1:15
	Ruth 4:10	Eph. 1:5–7
13	**1 Sam. 2:10**	Jn. 12:15
	1 Sam. 2:35–36	Heb. 2:17
	2 Sam. 7:12–14	Mt. 1:1, 2 Pet. 1:11, Lk. 1:32
14	**2 Sam. 7:16**	Rev. 22:16
	2 Sam. 22:2–3	Rom. 11:26
	2 Sam. 22:47	1 Pet. 2:8
	2 Sam. 23:2–4	1 Cor. 10:4
	1 Kg. 19:9, 18	Rom. 11:4
15	**2 Kg. 2:12**	Lk. 24:51
	1 Chr. 17:11–13	Mt. 9:27, Lk. 1:33, Heb. 1:5
	2 Chron. 5:13–14	Mt. 17:1–3, 5
16	**Ezra 3:1–3**	Mt. 1:12, 6:33
	Neh. 9:15	Jn. 6:31
	Esther 5:1–2	Jam. 2:20
17	**Job 9:32–33**	1 Tim. 2:3–6
	Job 19:23–27	Rom. 3:25, 1 Jn. 2:2, 4:10, Jn. 5:24–29

18	**Ps. 2:All**	Acts 4:25–27, Mt. 17:5, Rev. 2:27, 12:5, Jn. 20:31, Rom. 15:12, 2 Cor. 1:9–10 Rev. 19:15
19	**Ps. 8:4**	Heb. 2:6–8
	Ps. 9:7–10	Acts 17:31
	Ps. 16:9–11	Acts 2:31
	Ps. 18:2–3	Lk. 1:68–71
20	**Ps. 18:46**	2 Tim. 3:15
	Ps. 22:All	1 Cor. 5:21, Mt. 27:45–46, 39–44, Lk. 2:7, Jn. 19:6, 19:36, 28, 27:35, Jn. 19:23–24, Lk. 23:46, Jn. 20:17, Col. 1:16, Heb. 10:10–13,
23	**Ps. 23:1**	Jn. 10:11, 1 Pet. 2:25
	Ps. 24:3	Acts 1:11
	Ps. 27:12	Mt. 26:60
	Ps. 30:3	Acts 2:32
	Ps. 31:5	Lk. 23:44–47, Mt. 27:54
	Ps. 31:11–15	Mr. 14:50, Mt. 27:54
24	**Ps. 34:20**	Jn. 19:33–36
	Ps. 35:11	Mt. 26:59–60
	Ps. 35:19	Mr. 14:57–59
	Ps. 38:12–13	Mr. 14:1, Mt. 27:12
25	**Ps. 38:20**	Acts 10:38
	Ps. 40:6–8	Heb. 10:6–10
	Ps. 40:9	Mt. 4:17
	Ps. 40:14	Jn. 18:4–6
	Ps. 41:9	Jn. 13:18
26	**Ps. 45:2**	Jn. 1:17
	Ps. 45:6–7	Heb. 1:8
	Ps. 45:7–8	Lk. 2:11
	Ps. 45:17	Heb. 1:8
	Ps. 49:15	1 Cor. 15:55–57
	Ps. 55:12–14	Jn. 13:18
27	**Ps. 55:15**	Mt. 27:3–5
	Ps. 61:2	1 Cor. 10:4
	Ps. 62:2	1 Cor. 10:4
	Ps. 65:5	Heb. 9:28
	Ps. 68:18	Acts 1:9, 2:33, Eph. 4:8–10

28	**Ps. 69:4**	Jn. 15:25
	Ps. 69:8	Jn. 1:11, 7:5
	Ps. 69:9	Jn. 2:13–17
	Ps. 69:19–21	Mt. 27:29, 26:37, 27:34, Jn. 19:28–30
29	**Ps. 69:22**	Rom. 11:9–10
	Ps. 72:10–11	Mt. 2:1–2, 11
30	**Ps. 72:16–17**	Jn. 12:24, Gal. 3:8
	Ps. 77:15	Lk. 24:21
	Ps. 78:2–3	Mt. 13:34, 7:29
	Ps. 78:20	Lk. 9:16–17
	Ps. 78:35	1 Cor. 10:4
31	**Ps. 80:17**	Mr. 14:61–62
	Ps. 88:All	Lk. 22:44, Rom. 5:9, Lk. 2:49, Mr. 14:65, 15:34, 14:43
32	**Ps. 89:4**	2 Tim. 2:8
	Ps. 89:18	Rev. 17:14
	Ps. 89:26–27	Lk. 23:46, Rom. 8:29
32	**Ps. 89:28–29**	Rev. 3:21
	Ps. 89:34–39	Lk. 1:32–33, Rev. 1:5–6
	Ps. 90:2	Jn. 1:1, 14
	Ps. 91:11–16	Mt. 4:6–7, Lk. 10:19
34	**Ps. 95:1**	Acts 4:12
	Ps. 102:1–11	Mt. 27:39, Jn. 3:14–15
35	**Ps. 102:25–27**	Heb. 1:10–12
	Ps. 105:41	1 Cor. 10:4
	Ps. 109:1–5	Mr. 14:56, Lk. 23:22, Jn. 15:13, Lk. 23:34
	Ps. 109:25	Mr. 15:29
36	**Ps. 110:1–7**	Mt. 22:44–45, Heb. 1:13, Eph. 1:20, Col. 3:1, Heb. 1:3, 1 Cor. 15:25, Eph. 1:22, Heb. 2:8, Isa. 11:1, Heb. 7:21, Zech. 6:12–13, Jn. 12:34, Heb. 2:9, 2 Tim. 1:10, Ps. 16:8, Rom. 2:5, Ps. 68:21
37	**Ps. 111:9**	Acts 4:12
	Ps. 112:4	Mt. 9:36
	Ps. 114:8	
38	**Ps. 118:22–26**	Mr. 12:10–11, Lk. 20:17–18, 1 Pet. 2:3–8
	Ps. 132:11	Lk. 1:32
	Ps. 138:1–3	Mt. 2:1–6

39	**Ps. 144:3**	Heb. 2:6–8
	Ps. 145:19	
	Ps. 147:1–3	Lk. 4:18
40	**Pro. 1:23**	Jn. 16:7
	Prov. 8:1, 22–35	1 Cor. 1:30
	Pro. 30:4	Eph. 4:7–10
41	**Eccl. 12:10–11**	Heb. 13:20–21
	S.O.S. 1:3	Phil. 2:9–10
	S.O.S. 1:12–13	Mr. 14:3, Mt. 2:11
42	**S.O.S. 2:4**	Rev. 19:9
	Isa. 2:3–4	Lk. 24:47–48, Jn. 5:22
	Isa. 4:2	Jer. 23:5–6, Mt. 2:2
	Isa. 5:1–6	Mt. 21:33–40
43	**Isa. 6:1**	Jn. 12:41, Rev. 4:8
44	**Isa. 6:8–10**	Mt. 13:14–16
	Isa. 7:14–16	Lk. 1:35, Mt. 1:18–23, 1 Tim. 3:16
45	**Isa. 8:5–8**	Jn. 9:7, 11, 1:11, Mt. 1:23
	Isa. 8:14	Rom. 9:33, 1 Pet. 2:8
46	**Isa. 9:1–2**	Mt. 4:12–16, Eph. 5:8, 14, Lk. 1:79
	Isa. 9:6, 7	Acts 4:27, 30, Lk. 1:31, Jn. 1:14, Rom. 1:3–4, Rev. 19:16, Mt. 21:15–16, Mt. 13:54, Jn. 6:68, 1 Cor. 1:24, Jn. 8:58, 10:30, 16:33, Lk. 1:32–33 Jn. 5:30, 10:30–32, Mt. 28:18
48	**Isa. 11:1–10**	Heb.7:14, Mt.3:16-17, Acts 10:36, Col.2:3, Lk.6:8, Jn. 2:25, Acts 17:31, Rev. 19:15, 19:11, Jn. 12:20–21, Heb. 4: 9–11
49	**Isa. 12:1–6**	Mt. 1:23, Phil. 2:9–11
50	**Isa. 22:21–25**	Rev. 3:7
	Isa. 25:8	1 Cor. 15:54–58
51	**Isa. 26:19**	Mt. 27:50–54
	Isa. 28:16	1 Pet. 2:3–8
	Isa. 29:13–14	Mt. 15:7–9, 1 Cor. 1:18–31
52	**Isa. 33:22**	1 Tim. 1:16–17
53	**Isa. 34:4–6**	2 Pet. 3:11–12
	Isa. 35:5–6	Mt. 9:27–31, 11:5–6, 12:22–23
	Isa. 40:3–5	Lk. 3:3–6

54	**Isa. 40:9–11**	Jn. 1:34–36, Rev. 22:12, Jn. 10:11–18
55	**Isa. 41:14**	Acts 3:14
	Isa. 42:1–7	Mt. 3:17, Jn. 3:34, Mt. 12:21, Col. 1:16, Lk. 2:32
56	**Isa. 43:3, 10, 11**	2 Cor. 5:19
	Isa. 44:3	Jn. 4:10, 16:7–13
	Isa. 44:6	Jn. 1:49, Rev. 1:8, 22:13
57	**Isa. 44:24**	Eph. 3:9
	Isa. 45:21–25	Phil. 3:20, 2:10–11
	Isa. 46:9–10	Jn. 13:19
	Isa. 48:12	Rev. 1:8, 17–18
58	**Isa. 48:16–17**	Jn. 3:2
	Isa. 49:1–2	Mt. 1:21, Heb. 4:12, Rev. 2:16, Eph. 3:9
	Isa. 49:5–7	Phil. 2:7, Acts 15:16–17, Jn. 1:11
59	**Isa. 49:26**	
	Isa. 50:2–6	Lk. 23:44–45, Mt. 7:29, 26:39, 27:26, 26:67
60	**Isa. 52:7**	Rom. 10:15
	Isa. 52:13–53:12	Eph. 1:19–23, Lk. 18:31–34, Heb. 9:13–14 Rom. 15:21, Jn. 10:38, 12:37–38, Phil. 2:6–8, Lk. 4:28–29, Mt. 27:22–23 Mr. 9:12, Heb. 4:15, Jn. 1:10–11, Mt. 8:17, Rom. 4:25, 2 Cor. 5:21 Heb. 2:9, Col. 1:20, 1 Pet. 2:24, Mt. 9:36, 1 Pet. 2:25, 1 Jn. 2:2 Gal. 1:4, Mt. 27:13–14, Jn. 1:29, 1 Pet. 1:18–19, Jn. 7:27–28 Mt. 27:57–60, 1 Pet. 2:22–23, Mt. 20:28, Rom. 6:9, Phil. 3:8–9 Rom. 5:18–19, Col. 2:15, Mr. 15:28, Rom. 8:34
64	**Isa. 54:5**	Rev. 19:7–8
65	**Isa. 54:8**	Heb. 9:12
	Isa. 55:1	Jn. 7:37–38
	Isa. 55:3–5	Acts 13:34, Jn. 18:37, Heb. 2:10, Acts 3:13

66	Isa. 59:16	Mt. 10:32, Jn. 6:40
	Isa. 59:20	Rom. 11:26–27, Lk. 2:38
	Isa. 60:1–3	Acts 26:23
	Isa. 60:16	Acts 5:31
	Isa. 61:1–3	Lk. 4:18–19, Mr. 1:38, Mal. 4:1–3, 2 Thess. 1:7–10
67	Isa. 61:10	Rev. 21:2
68	Isa. 62:11	Lk. 2:30–32
	Isa. 63:4–5	2 Cor. 5:19
	Isa. 63:8	2 Tim. 1:10
	Isa. 63:16	Gal. 4:6
	Isa. 65:9	Heb. 7:14
69	Isa. 65:17–19	2 Pet. 3:13, Rev. 21:1
	Isa. 66:18–19	Lk. 2:34
	Jer. 14:8	Acts 28:20
	Jer. 23:5–8	Jn. 15:1, Mt. 2:2, Heb. 1:8–9
70	Jer. 30:9	Jn. 18:37
	Jer. 31:15	Mt. 2:16–18
	Jer. 31:21–22	Mt. 1:18
71	Jer. 31:31–32	Mt. 26:28–29
	Jer. 33:14–15	Lk. 2:40
	Jer. 50:34	Lk. 2:25–32
	Jer. 50:1–51:64	Rev. 18:1–24
72	Lam. 3:22–26	Lk. 2:25–32
	Ezek. 17:22–24	Mt. 13:32
73	Ezek. 21:26–27	Lk. 1:52
	Ezek. 34:23–24	1 Pet. 5:4
	Dan. 2:34–35	Acts 4:10–12
	Dan. 2:44–45	Mt. 21:44
74	Dan. 3:25	Mt. 26:63–64
	Dan. 7:13–14	Acts 1:9, Eph. 1:20–22
	Dan. 9:23–27	Gen. 29:27, Gal. 1:3–5, Rom. 5:10, 2 Cor. 5:18–21, Neh. 2:5–8, Jn. 12:12–13 Lk. 19:41–44, Mt. 27:50–54, Heb. 2:9
76	Dan. 10:5–6	Rev. 1:13–16
77	Hos. 3:5	Jn. 18:37, Rom. 11:25–27
	Hos. 11:1	Mt. 2:14–15
	Hos. 13:4	Mt. 2:14–15

78	**Joel 2:28–32**	Acts 2:17–21
	Amos 8:9	Mt. 24:29
79	**Amos 9:11–12**	Acts 15:16–17
	Obad. 1:21	Rev. 19:6
	Jonah 1:17	Mt. 12:40, 16:4
	Mic. 5:2	Mt. 2:6, Jn. 7:42, 1:1–5
80	**Nahum 1:15**	Rom. 10:15
	Hab. 2:4	Rom. 2:16–17
	Hab. 2:14	Rev. 21:23–26
81	**Zeph. 3:14–18**	Jn. 12:13, Heb. 12:12
	Hag. 2:6–9	Heb. 12:26–29
	Hag. 2:23	Mt. 1:12
82	**Zech. 2:10–13**	Rev. 5:13, 19:11–13
	Zech. 3:1–10	Jude 23, Rev. 7:14, Lk. 1:78–79, Heb. 7:27
83	**Zech. 6:12**	Mt. 16:18, Eph. 2:20–22, Heb. 3:3, 8:1
84	**Zech. 9:9**	Mt. 21:8–10, Jn. 12:12–13, Lk. 19:10, Mt. 11:28–30
	Zech. 10:4	Eph. 2:20
	Zech. 11:4–14	Mt. 23:1–4 Mt. 23:37, 9:35–36, 27:3–10
86	**Zech. 12:9–10**	Jn. 19:33–35, 37
	Zech. 13:6–7	Jn. 10:29–30, Mt. 26:31
87	**Zech. 14:4**	Rev. 16:18
	Mal. 3:1–6	Mr. 1:2–4, Mt. 12:6, 3:11–12, Jam. 1:17
88	**Mal. 4:1–6**	2 Thess. 1:8, Lk. 1:78–79, Jn. 1:4, 9, 12:46, Mt. 11:14, Lk. 1:16–17

PREFACE

When one views the most renowned among men (because He was not merely man), it must need be that we do so through the finite; however, through expressed grace granted by the Creator, coupled with faith in Him who maintains all things and His ability to preserve all things, I believe that we can realize the temporal taking hold of the eternal, through the Spirit freely given to those who ask Him. For the edification contained herein we all owe our "Awesome Creator" alone, for any and all omissions or errors, I, as a simple layman accept the responsibility for and ask forgiveness of them, first before the "Perfect Father" and then of my fellow man.

This work is divided into two sections: the first looks at Old Testament, "Messianic, Allegorical, and Prophetic" scriptures, or "MAP," mainly focused on the redemptive plan of YHVH (GOD), including the first and second coming of Christ, God's Judgement, and Eternal Kingdom, with "His" own commentary of New Testament scriptures, which enlighten even obscure writing of the prophets.

The second, "Have I been so long a time with you, and yet hast thou not known Me. Jesus," which is a sequential and harmonic blend of the four gospels and Acts, into a complete account of the earthly life of our blessed Savior Yehowshuwa Masshiyach, Jesus Christ.

Herein is contained the complete Gospel record, penned by the four Apostles whom were foreordained by God, according to His purposes, to bring the world the Grace and Truth contained in His Own Son Jesus. Prophesied and named Emmanuel (God with Us), displaying for all to see, Him for who He is. Glory to God in the highest, and on earth peace, good will toward men. Before us is a scene by scene unveiling of "The One of Whom" is more written than "any other throughout the history of man, because history is His—Story. For this narrative, the Original King James Version is used; may we all fulfill His call to learn of Him.

The correlation of the multitude of scenes in the Life of the Anointed Savior follows the following basic structure. **The Lord inspired me to view the gospels in two ways: first, with the scripture that "not one jot or tittle would pass until all is fulfilled," and within it to diligently view, and secondly, the time and locations statements contained therein.** After much review and search of resources, Luke was chosen as the general base for structure. But where an event is most prolific in another gospel, that gospel was then used. In oversight of "the good news," some main events emerge such as "Jesus Birth, the Sermon on the Mount or on the Plain, the Transfiguration, Jesus's Hour Had Come, the Death on the Cross, The Resurrection, etc…," which aid in correlation. The feasts and feast days described along with their description and duration in Leviticus give added direction. When locations are referenced, then travel time allowance was also considered. When these and various other resources are reviewed, a final structure is determined and reviewed. **Each scene is recorded with all gospel information included,** I wish that every single word were able to be transcribed; however, for narrative continuity, limited "redundancy" exclusions seem necessary, even fewer inclusion not originally scribed are included for verbal clarity and "placed in italics." With this, scriptural sequence lines, of each of the gospels were created and continually consulted. Attempting to keep all this and sometimes more, in consideration, what follows is the result, I have learned so much and will surely continue to understand more as this is read by those more acute to wisdom than I. Before our modern world, The God Whom was in Christ Reconciling the world back unto Himself here again displays before all **the most Abundant of life ever lived,** may each whom reads, truly receive His promise of a more abundant life in Him, both now and forever more, in all things my humble desire is **"To God be the Glory, Great things He has done…"**

Our loving Heavenly Father never pours out blessings sparingly, but always with abundance, in the course of compiling **this greatest of "stories ever told,"** analytics often stretched the mind, but always proved to produce artistry that is only achievable by the One Whom spoke all things into existence from the eternal realm. Here all skeptics discrepancies willingly bow, unto the multiple dimensionality of His genius, His truth, His ultimate work of beauty and love, that of His second Personage, His Son, Jesus the Christ, our savior, the King of Kings and the Lord of lords. All references to the three personages of the Godhead, in both sections of this work are **"Capitalized"** out of honour and awe of **"the Only God"** there are none beside.

It is with complete and perfect confidence, that I commend all whom read and hear, these His eternal and inerrant words, that if unbelief is your position you may prove Him, and find that it is "His goodness that leads you to repentance," and to fellow believers that we all may bow in awe of Him, The Author and finisher of our faith, The One whom first loved us and then gave Himself for us. Amazing Love how can it be that you my King would die for me. For truly it is our joy to honor You. In all that we do...

MESSIANIC, ALLEGORICAL, PROPHETIC SCRIPTURES

(Gen. 1:1) In the beginning God. (Jn. 1:1–2) In the beginning was the Word, and the Word was with God, and the Word was God. The same was in the beginning with God.

(Gen. 1:3) And God said (Jn. 1:1) the Word was God.

(Gen. 3:15) I will put enmity between thee and the woman, and between thy seed and her Seed: it shall bruise thy head, and thou shalt bruise His heel. (Gal. 4:4) But when the fulness of the time was come, God sent forth His Son. Made of a woman, made under the law, to redeem them that were under the law, that we might receive the adoption of sons. (Rom. 16:20) And the God of peace shall bruise Satan under your feet shortly, The grace of our Lord Jesus Christ be with you. Amen. (Heb. 2:14) Forasmuch then as the children are partakers of flesh and blood, He also Himself likewise took part of the same: that through death He might destroy him that had the power of death, that is the devil.

(Gen. 4:4) And Abel, he also brought of the firstlings of his flock (Sheep) and of the fat thereof. And the Lord had respect unto Abel and to his offering. (Num. 18:17) But the firstling of a cow, or the firstling of a sheep, or the firstling of a goat, thou shalt not redeem: they are holy: thou shalt sprinkle their blood upon the alter, and shalt burn their fat *for* an offering made by fire, for a sweet savour unto the Lord. (Heb. 11:4) By faith Abel offered unto God a more excellent sacrifice than Cain, by which he obtained witness that he was righteous, God testifying of his gifts: and by it he being dead yet speaketh.

(Gen. 5:24) And Enoch walked with God: and he *was* not; For God took him. (Mk. 16:19) So then after the Lord had spoken unto them, He was received up into heaven, and sat on the right hand of God. (Heb. 11:5) By faith Enoch was translated that he should not see death; and was not found, because God had translated him: for before his translation he had this testimony, that he pleased God.

(Gen. 12:1–3) Now the LORD had said unto Abram, Get thee out of thy country, and from thy kindred, and from thy father's house, unto a land that I will shew thee: And I will make of thee a great nation, and I will bless thee, and make thy name great; and thou shalt be a blessing: and I will bless them that bless thee, and curse him that curseth thee: and in thee shall all families of the earth be blessed. (Acts 7:2–5)

"Stephen to the council," And he said, Men, brethren, and fathers, harken; The God of glory appeared unto our father Abraham, when he was in Mesopotamia before he dwelt in Charran, and said unto him, Get thee out of thy country, and from thy kindred, and come into the land which I shall shew thee. Then came he out of the land of the Chaldaeans, and dwelt in Charran: and from thence, when his father was dead, he removed him into this land, wherein ye now dwell. And He gave him none inheritance in it, no, not so much as to set his foot on: yet he promised that He would give it to him for a possession, and to his seed after him, when as yet he had no child. (Heb. 11:8) By faith Abraham, when he was called to go out into a place which he should after receive for an inheritance, obeyed, and he went out, not knowing whither he went. (Gal. 3:7–9)

Know ye therefore that they which are of faith, the same are the children of Abraham. And the scripture, foreseeing that God would justify the heathen through faith, preached before the gospel unto

Abraham, saying, In thee shall all nations be blessed. So then they which be of faith are blessed with faithful Abraham.

(Gen. 12:7) And the LORD appeared unto Abram, and said, Unto thy Seed will I give this land: and there builded he an altar unto the LORD, who appeared unto him. (Gal. 3:16) Now Abraham and his Seed were the promises made. He saith not, And to seeds, as of many; but as of one, And to thy Seed, which is Christ.

(Gen. 14:18) And Melchizedek king of Salem brought forth bread and wine: and He was the priest of the most high God. (Heb. 6:20, 7:1) Whither the forerunner is for us entered, *even* Jesus made an high priest, for ever after the order of Melchisedec. For this Melchisedec, king of Salem, priest of the most high God, who met Abraham returning from the slaughter of the kings, and blessed him:

(Gen. 17:19) And God said, Sarah thy wife shall bear thee a son indeed; and thou shalt call his name Isaac: and I will estab-lish My covenant with him for an everlasting covenant, and with his Seed after him. (Heb. 13:20–21) Now the God of peace, that brought again from the dead our Lord Jesus, that Great Shepherd of the sheep, through the blood of the everlasting covenant. Make you perfect in every good work to do His will, working in you that which is well pleasing in His sight, through Jesus Christ; to Whom *be* glory for ever and ever. A-men. (Rom. 9:7) Neither, because they are the seed of Abraham, are they all children: but in Isaac shall thy Seed be called.

(Gen. 22:7–8) And Isaac spake unto Abraham his father, and said, My father: and he said, Here am I, my son. And he said, Behold the fire and the wood: but *where is* the lamb for a burnt offering? And Abraham said, My son, God will provide Himself a Lamb for a burnt offering: so they went both of them together. (Jn. 1:29) The next day John seeth Jesus coming unto him, and saith, Behold the Lamb of God, which taketh away the sin of the world.

(Gen. 24:17) And the servant ran to meet her, and said. Let me, I pray thee, drink a little water of thy pitcher. (Rev. 19:7) Let us be glad and rejoice, and give honour to Him; for the marriage of the Lamb is come, and His wife hath made herself ready.

(Gen. 26:2–5) And the LORD appeared unto him, and said, Go not down into Egypt; dwell in the land which I shall tell thee of: Sojourn in this land, and I will be with thee, and will bless thee; for unto thee, and unto thy seed, I will give all these countries, and I will perform the oath which I sware unto Abraham thy father; and I will make thy seed to multiply as the stars of heaven, and will give unto thy seed all these countries; and in thy Seed shall all the nations of the earth be blessed; Because that Abraham obeyed My voice, and kept My charge, My commandments, My statutes, and My laws. (Heb. 11:18) Of whom it was said, That in Isaac shall thy Seed be called:

(Gen. 28:12) And he dreamed, and behold a ladder set up on the earth, and the top of it reached to heaven: and behold the angels of God ascending and descending on it. (Jn. 1:51) And He said unto him, Verily, verily I say unto you, Hereafter ye shall see heaven open, and the angels of God ascending and descending upon the Son of man.

(Gen. 28:14) And thy seed shall be as the dust of the earth, and thou shalt spread abroad to the west, and to the east, and to the north, and to the south: and in thee and in thy Seed shall all the families of the earth be Blessed. (Gal. 3:8) And the scriptures, foreseeing that God would justify the heathen through faith, preached before the gospel unto Abraham, *saying,* In thee shall all nations be blessed.

(Gen. 49:10) The sceptre shall not depart from Judah, nor a lawgiver from between his feet, until Shiloh come: and unto Him *shall* the gathering of the people *be* (Num. 24:17). I shall behold Him, but not now: I shall see Him, but not nigh: there shall come a

Star out of Jacob, and a Sceptre shall rise out of Israel, and shall smite the corners of Moab, and destroy all the children of Sheth. (Eze. 21:27) I will overturn, overturn, overturn, it: and it shall be *no more*, until He come whose right it is; and I will give it *Him*. (Isa. 2:2) And it shall come to pass in the last days, *that* the mountain of the Lord's house shall be established in the top of the mountains, and shall be exalted above the hills; and all nations shall flow unto it. (Heb. 1:8) But unto the Son *He saith*, Thy throne, O God, *is* for ever and ever: a sceptre of righteousness *is* the sceptre of Thy Kingdom.

(Ex. 3:13–14) And Moses said unto God, Behold, *when* I come unto the children of Israel, and shall say unto them, The God of your fathers hath sent me unto you; and they shall say to me, What *is* his name? What shall I say unto them? And God said unto Moses, I AM THAT I AM: and he said, Thus shalt thou say unto the children of Israel, I AM hath sent me unto you. (Jn. 4:26) Jesus said unto her, I that speak unto thee am *He*. (Jn. 8:58) Jesus said unto them, Verily, verily, I say unto you, Before Abraham was I Am.

(Ex. 12:3) Speak ye unto all the congregation of Israel, saying, In the tenth *day* of this month they shall take to them every man a lamb, according to the house of *their* father's, a lamb for an house: (Jn. 1:29) The next day John seeth Jesus coming unto him, and saith, Behold the Lamb of God, which taketh away the sin of the world.

(Ex. 12:5) Your lamb shall be without blemish, (Heb. 9:14). How much more shall the blood of Christ, who through the eternal Spirit offer Himself without spot to God, purge your conscience from dead works to serve the living God. (1 Pet. 1:19) But with the precious blood of Christ, as of a lamb without blemish and without spot. **A male of the first year: ye shall take *it* out form the sheep, or from the goats:**

(Ex. 12:13) **And the blood shall be to you for a token upon the houses where ye *are*: and when I see the blood, I will pass over *you*, and the plague shall not be upon you to destroy you, when I smite the land of Egypt.** (Rom. 5:8–9) But God commendeth His love toward us, in that, while we were yet sinners Christ died for us. Much more then, being now justified by His blood, we shall be saved from wrath through Him.

(Ex. 12:21–27) **Then Moses called for all the elders of Israel, and said unto them, Draw out and take you a lamb according to your families, and kill the passover.** (1 Cor. 5:7) Purge out therefore the old leaven, that ye may be a new lump, as ye are unleavened. For even Christ our passover is sacrificed for us: **And ye shall take a bunch of hyssop,** (Jn. 19:29). Now there was set a vessel full of vinegar: and they fill a spunge with vinegar, and put *it* upon hyssop, and put *it* to His mouth. **And dip *it* in the blood that *is* in the bason, and strike the lintel and the two side posts with the blood that *is* in the bason; and none of you shall go out at the door of his house until the morning. For the Lord will pass through to smite the Egyptians; and when He seeth the blood upon the lintel, and on the two side posts, the LORD will pass over the door, and will not suffer the destroyer to come in unto your houses to smite *you*. And ye shall observe this thing for an ordinance to thee and to thy sons for ever. And it shall come to pass, when ye be come to the land which the LORD will give you, according as He hath promised, that ye shall keep this service. And it shall come to pass, when your children shall say unto you, What mean ye by this service? That ye shall say, It *is* the sacrifice of the LORD's passover, who passed over the houses of the children of Israel in Egypt, when He smote the Egyptians, and delivered our houses. And the people bowed the head and worshipped.**

(Ex. 12:46) **And in one house shall it be eaten; thou shalt not carry forth ought of the flesh abroad out of the house; neither shall ye break a bone thereof.** (Jn. 19:36) For these things were done, that the scripture should be fulfilled, A bone of Him shall not be broken.

(Ex. 15:2) The Lord *is* my strength and song, and He is become my salvation: He *is* my God, and I will prepare Him an habitation; my father's God, and I will exalt Him. (Acts 7:55–56) But he, being full of the Holy Ghost, looked upstedfastly into heaven, and saw the glory of God, and Jesus standing on the right hand of God, and said, Behold, I see the heavens opened, and the Son of man standing on the right hand of God.

(Ex. 15:11) Who *is* like unto Thee, O LORD, among the gods? who *is* like Thee, glorious in holiness, fearful *in* praises, doing wonders? (Acts 4:27) For of a truth against Thy Holy Child Jesus, Whom Thou hast anointed, both Herod, and Pontius Pilate with the Gentiles, and the people of Israel, were gathered together.

(Ex. 16:4) Then said the LORD unto Moses, Behold, I will rain bread from heaven for you: and the people shall go out and gather a certain rate every day, that I may prove them, whether they will walk in My law, or no. (Jn. 6:48–51) I Am that bread of life. Your fathers did eat manna in the wilderness, and are dead. This is the bread which cometh down from heaven, that a man may eat thereof, and not die. I Am the living bread which came down from heaven: if any man eat of this bread, he shall live for ever: and the bread that I will give is my flesh, which I will give for the life of the world.

(Ex. 17:6) Behold, I will stand before thee there upon the rock in Horeb; and thou shalt smite the Rock, and there shall come water out of it, that the people may drink. And Moses did so in the sight of the elders of Israel. (1 Cor. 10:4) And did all drink the same spiritual drink: for they drank of that spiritual Rock that followed them: and that Rock was Christ.

(Ex. 33:19) And He said, I will make all My goodness pass before thee, and I will proclaim the name of the LORD before thee; and will be gracious to whom I will be gracious, and will shew mercy on whom I will shew mercy. (Jn. 1:14) And the Word was made flesh, and dwelt among us, and we beheld His glory, the glory as of the only begotten of the Father, full of grace and truth.

(Lev. 1:1–9) And the LORD called unto Moses, and spake unto him out of the tabernacle of the congregation, saying, Speak unto the children of Israel, and say unto them, If any man of you bring an offering unto the LORD, ye shall bring your offering of the cattle, *even* of the herd, and of the flock. If his offering *be* a burnt sacrifice of the herd, let him offer a male without blemish: he shall offer it of his own voluntary will at the door of the tabernacle of the congregation before the LORD. And he shall put his hand upon the head of the burnt offering: and it shall be accepted for him to make atonement for him. And he shall kill the bullock before the LORD: and the priests, Aaron's sons, shall bring the blood, and sprinkle the blood round about upon the altar that *is by* the door of the tabernacle of the congregation. And he shall flay the burnt offering, and cut it into his pieces. And the sons of Aaron the priest shall put fire upon the altar, and lay the wood in order upon the fire:
And the priests, Aaron's sons, shall lay the parts, the head, and the fat, in order upon the wood that *is* on the fire which *is* upon the altar: But his inwards and his legs shall he wash in water: and the priest shall burn all on the altar, *to be* a burnt sacrifice, an offering made by fire, of a sweet savour unto the Lord. (Eph. 5:2) And walk in love, as Christ also hath loved us, and hath given Himself for us an offering and a sacrifice to God for a sweetsmelling savour.

(Lev. 14:1–3) And the LORD spake unto Moses, saying, This shall be the law of the leper in the day of his cleansing: He shall be bought unto the priest: (Lk. 5:14) And He charged him to tell no man: but go, and shew thyself to the priest, and offer for thy cleansing, according as Moses commanded, for a testimony unto them. **And the priest shall go forth out of the camp** (Heb. 13:13) Let us go forth therefore unto Him without the camp, bearing His reproach.

(Lev. 16:15) Then shall he kill the goat of the sin offering, that *is* for the people, and bring his blood within the vail (Heb. 9:12) Neither by the blood of goats and calves, but by His own blood He entered in once into the holy place, having obtained eternal redemption *for us.*

(Lev. 16:27) And the bullock *for* the sin offering, and the goat *for* the sin offering, whose blood was brought in to make atonement in the holy *place*, shall *one* carry forth without the camp: (Heb. 13:11) For the bodies of those beasts, whose blood is brought into the sanctuary by the high priest for sin, are burned without the camp.

(Lev. 17:11) For the life of the flesh is in the blood: and I have given it to you upon the altar to make an atonement for your souls: for it is the blood *that* maketh an atonement for the soul. (Mt. 26:28) For this is My blood of the new testament, which is shed for many for the remission of sins. (Mr. 10:45) For even the Son of man came not to be ministered unto, but to minister, and to give His life a ransom for many. (1 Jn. 1:7) But if we walk in the light, as He is in the light, we have fellowship one with another, and the blood of Jesus Christ: His Son cleaneth us from all sin.

(Lev. 23:37) These *are* feasts of the LORD, which ye shall proclaim *to be* holy convocations, to offer an offering made by fire unto the LORD, a brunt offering, and a meat offering, a sacrifice, and drink offerings, every thing upon his day: (Jn. 7:37–38) In the last day, that great *day* of the feast, Jesus stood and cried, saying, If any man thirst, let him come unto Me, and drink. He that believeth on Me, as the scripture hath said, out of his belly shall flow rivers of living water.

(Num. 9:12) They shall leave none of it unto the morning, nor brake any bone of it: according to all the ordinances of the passover they shall keep it. (Jn. 19 :33) But when they came to Jesus, and saw that He was dead already, they brake not His legs.

(Num. 20:8) Take the rod, and gather thou the assembly together, thou, and Aaron thy brother and speak ye unto the Rock before their eyes; and it shall give forth His water, and thou shalt bring forth to them water out of the rock: so thou shalt give the congregation and their beasts drink. (1 Cor. 10:4) And did all drink the same spiritual drink: for they drank of that spiritual Rock that followed them: and that Rock was Christ.

(Num. 21:9) And Moses made a serpent of brass, and put it upon a pole, and it came to pass, that if a serpent had bitten any man, when he beheld the serpent of brass, he lived. (Jn. 3:14–15) And as Moses lifted up the serpent in the wilderness, even so must the Son of man be lifted up: That whosoever believeth in Him should not perish, but have eternal life.

(Num. 24:17) I shall see him, but not now: I shall behold him, but not nigh: there shall come a Star out of Jacob, and a Sceptre shall rise out of Israel, and shall smite the corners of Moab, and destroy all the children of Sheth. (Gal. 4:4–5) But when the fulness of the time was come, God sent forth His Son, made of a woman, made under the law, to redeem them that were under the law, that we might receive the adoption of sons.

(Deu. 18:15) The LORD thy God will raise up unto thee a Prophet from the midst of thee, of thy brethren, like unto me; unto Him ye shall hearken: (Jn. 5:45–47) Do not think that I will accuse you to the Father: There is *one* that accuseth you, *even* Moses, in whom ye trust. For had ye believed Moses, ye would have believed Me: for he wrote of Me. But if ye believe not his writings, how shall ye believe My words? (Jn. 6:14) Then those men, when they had seen the miracle that Jesus did, said, This is of a truth that prophet that should come into the world. (Acts 3:20–23) And He shall send Jesus Christ, which before was preached unto you: Whom the heaven must receive until the times of restitution of all things, which God hath spoken by the mouth of all His holy prophets since the world began. For Moses truly said unto the fathers, A Prophet shall the

Lord your God raise up unto you of your brethren, like unto me; Him shall ye hear in all things whatsoever He shall say unto you. And it shall come to pass, *that* every soul, which will not hear that Prophet, shall be destroyed from among the people. (Acts 7:37) This is that Moses, which said unto the children of Israel, A prophet shall the Lord your God raise up unto you of your brethren, like unto me; Him shall ye hear.

(Deu. 18:18–19) I will raise them up a Prophet from among their brethren, like unto thee, and will put My words in His mouth; and He shall speak unto them all that I shall command Him. And it shall come to pass, *that* whosoever will not hearken unto My words which He shall speak in My name, I will require *it* of him. (Jn. 8:28–29) Then said Jesus unto them, When ye have lifted up the Son of man, then shall ye know that I AM *He*, and *that* I do nothing of Myself; but as my Father hath taught Me, I speak these things. And He that sent Me is with Me: the Father hath not left Me alone; for I do always those things that please Him. (Acts 3:22–23) For Moses truly said unto the fathers, A prophet shall the Lord your God raise up unto you of your brethren, like unto me; Him shall ye hear in all things whatsoever He shall say unto you. And it shall come to pass, *that* every soul, which will not hear that Prophet, shall be destroyed from among the people.

(Deu. 21:23) His body shall not remain all night upon the tree, but thou shalt in any wise bury Him that day; (for he that is hanged *is* accursed of God:) that thy land be not defiled, which the LORD thy God giveth thee *for* an inheritance. (Jn. 19:38–42) And after this Joseph of Arimathaea being a disciple of Jesus but secretly for fear of the Jews, besought Pilate that he might take away the body of Jesus: and Pilate gave *him* leave. He came therefore, and took the body of Jesus. And there came also Nicodemus, which at the first came to Jesus by night, and brought a mixture of myrrh and aloes, about an hundred pound *weight*. Then took they the body of Jesus, and wound it in linen clothes with the spices, as the manner of the Jews is to bury. Now in the place where He was crucified there was a garden; and in the garden a new sepulchre, wherein was never man yet laid. Therefore laid they Jesus therefore because of the Jews preparation *day*; for the sepulchre was nigh at hand. (Gal. 3:13) Christ hath redeemed us from the curse of the law, being made a curse for us: for it is written, Cursed is every one that hangeth on a tree:

(Deu. 32:15) But Jeshurun waxed fat, and kicked: thou art waxen fat, thou art grown thick, thou art covered *with fatness*; then he forsook God *which* made him. And lightly esteemed the Rock of his salvation.

(Jos. 5:14–15) And he said, Nay; but as Captain of the host of the LORD am I now come. And Joshua fell on his face to the earth, and did worship, and said unto him, What saith my lord unto his servant? And the Captain of the LORD's host said unto Joshua, Loose thy shoe from off thy foot; for the place whereon thou standest *is* holy. And Joshua did so. (Heb. 2:10) For it became Him, for whom *are* all things, and by Whom *are* all things, in bringing many sons unto glory, to make the Captian of their salvation perfect through sufferings.

(Judg. 13:7) But he said unto me, Behold, thou shalt conceive, and bear a son; and now drink no wine nor strong drink, neither eat any unclean *thing*: for the child shall be a Nazarite to God from the womb to the day of his death. (Luke 1:15) For he shall be great in the sight of the Lord, and shall drink neither wine nor strong drink; and he shall be filled with the Holy Ghost, even from his mother's womb.

(Ruth 4:10) Moreover Ruth the Moabitess, the wife of Mahlon: have I purchased to be my wife, to raise up the name of the dead upon his inheritance, that the name of the dead be not cut off from among his brethren, and from the gate of his place: ye *are* witnesses this day. (Eph. 1:5–7) Having predestinated us unto the adoption of children by Jesus Christ to Himself, according to the good pleasure of His will. To the praise of the glory of His grace, wherein He hath made us accepted in the beloved. In Whom we have redemption through His blood, the forgiveness of sins, according to the riches of His grace.

(1 Sam. 2:10) The adversaries of the LORD shall be broken to pieces; out of heaven shall He thunder upon them: the LORD shall judge the ends of the earth; and He shall give strength unto His king, and exalt the horn of His anointed. (Jn. 12:15) Fear not, daughter of Sion: behold, Thy King cometh, sitting on an ass's colt.

(1 Sam. 2:35–36) And I will raise Me up a Faithful Priest, that shall do according to *that* **which is in Mine heart and in My mind: and I will build Him a sure house: and He shall walk before Mine Anointed for ever. And it shall come to pass,** *that* **every one that is left in thine house shall come and crouch to Him for a piece of silver and a morsel of bread, and shall say, Put me, I pray thee, into one of the priests offices, that I may eat a piece of bread.** (Heb. 2:17) Wherefore in all things it behoved Him to be made like unto *His* brethren, that He might be a merciful and faithful high priest in things *pertaining* to God, to make reconciliation for the sins of the people.

(2 Sam. 7:12–14) And when thy days be fulfilled, and thou shalt sleep with thy fathers I will set up thy Seed after thee, which shall proceed out of thy bowels, and I will establish His kingdom. (Mt. 1:1) The book of the generation of Jesus Christ, the son of David, the son of Abraham. **He shall build an house for My name, and I will stablish the throne of His kingdom for ever.** (2 Pet. 1:11) For so an entrance shall be ministered unto you abundantly into the everlasting kingdom of our Lord and Saviour Jesus Christ. **I will be His Father, and He shall be My son. If he commit iniquity, I will chasten him with the rod of men, and with the stripes of the children of men.** (Lk. 1:32) He shall be great, and shall be called the Son of the Highest: and the Lord God shall give unto Him the throne of His father David:

(2 Sam. 7:16) And thine house and thy kingdom shall be established for ever before thee: thy throne shall be established for ever. (Rev. 22:16) I Jesus have sent mine angel to testify unto you these things in the churches. I Am the root and the offspring of David, *and* the bright and morning star.

(2 Sam. 22:2–3) And he said, The LORD is my rock, and my fortress, and my deliverer; The God of my rock; in Him will I trust: *He is* **my shield, and the horn of my salvation, my high tower, and my refuge, my saviour; Thou savest me from violence.** (Rom. 11:26) And so all Israel shall be saved: as it is written, There shall come out of Sion the Deliverer, and shall turn away ungodliness from Jacob:

(2 Sam. 22:47) The LORD liveth; and blessed *be* **my rock; and exalted be the God of the rock of my salvation.** (1 Pet. 2:8) And a stone of stumbling, and a rock of offence, *even to them* which stumble at the word, being disobedient: whereunto also they were appointed.

(2 Sam. 23:2–4) The Spirit of the Lord spake by me, and His word *was* **in my tongue. The God of Israel said, the Rock of Israel spake to me, He that ruleth over men** *must be* **just, ruling in the fear of God.** *And he shall be* **as the light of the morning,** *when* **the sun riseth,** *even* **a morning without clouds;** *as* **the tender grass** *springing* **out of the earth by clear shining after rain.** (1 Cor. 10:4) And did all drink the same spiritual drink: for they drank of that spiritual Rock that followed them: and that Rock was Christ.

(1 Kg. 19:9, 18) And he came thither unto a cave, and lodged there; and, behold, the word of the Lord *came* **to him, and he said unto him, What doest thou here Elijah? Yet have I left** *Me* **seven thousand in Israel, all the knees which have not bowed unto Baal, and every mouth which hath not kissed him.**
(Rom. 11:4) But what saith the answer of God unto him? I have reserved to Myself seven thousand men, who have not bowed the knee to *the image of* Baal.

(2 Kg. 2:12) And Elisha saw it, and he cried, My father, my father, the chariot of Israel, and the horsemen thereof. And he saw him no more: and he took hold of his own clothes, and rent them in two pieces. (Lk. 24:51) And it came to pass, while He blessed them, He was parted from them, and carried up into heaven.

(1 Chr. 17:11–13) And it shall come to pass, when thy days be expired that thou must go *to be* with thy fathers, that I will raise up thy Seed after thee, which shall be of thy sons; and I will establish His kingdom. (Mat. 9:27) And when Jesus departed thence, two blind men followed Him, crying, and saying, Thou Son of David, have mercy on us. **He shall build Me an house, and I will stablish His throne for ever.** (Lk. 1:33) And He shall reign over the house of Jacob for ever; and of His kingdom there shall be no end. **I will be His Father, and he shall be My Son and I will not take My mercy away from Him, as I took it from him that was before thee:** (Heb. 1:5) For unto which of the angels said He at any time, Thou art My Son, this day have I begotten thee? And again, I will be to Him a Father, and He shall be to Me a Son?

(2 Chron. 5:13–14) It came even to pass, as the trumpeters and singers *were* as one, to make one sound to be heard in praising and thanking the LORD; and when they lifted up *their* voice with the trumpets and cymbals and instruments of musick, and praised the LORD, *saying,* For *He is* good; for His mercy *endureth* for ever; that then the house was filled with a cloud, *even* the house of the LORD; So that the priests could not stand to minister by reason of the cloud: for the glory of the LORD had filled the house of God. (Mat. 17:1–3, 5) And after six days Jesus taketh Peter, James and John his brother, and bringeth them up into an high mountain apart, and was transfigured before them: and His face did shine as the sun, and His raiment was white as the light. And behold, there appeared unto them Moses and Elias talking with Him. While he yet spake, behold, a bright cloud overshadowed them: and behold a voiceout of the cloud, which said This is My beloved Son, in whom I am well pleased; hear ye Him.

(Ezra 3:1–3) **And when the seventh month was come, and the children of Israel** *were* **in the cities, the people gathered themselves together as one man to Jerusalem. Then stood up Jeshua the son of Jozadak, and his brethren the priests, and Zerubbabel the son of Shealtiel, and his brethren, and builded the altar of the God of Israel,** (Mt. 1:12). And after they were brought to Babylon, Jechonias begat Salathiel, and Salathiel begat Zorobabel; **to offer burnt offerings thereon, as it is written in the law of Moses the man of God. And they set the altar upon his bases; for fear** *was* **upon them because of the people of those countries: and they offered burnt offerings thereon unto the LORD,** *even* **burnt offerings morning and evening.** (Mt. 6:33) But seek ye first the kingdom of God, and His righteousness; and all these things shall be added unto you.

(Neh. 9:15) **And gavest them bread from heaven for their hunger, and broughtest forth water for them out of the rock for their thirst, and promisedst them that they should go in to possess the land which Thou hadst sworn to give them.** (Jn. 6:31–33) Our fathers did eat manna in the desert; as it is written, He gave them bread from heaven to eat. Then Jesus said unto them, Verily, verily, I say unto you, Moses gave you not that Bread from heaven; but My Father giveth you the true Bread from heaven. For the bread of God is He which cometh down from heaven, and giveth life unto the world.

(Esther 5:1–2) **Now it came to pass on the third day, that Esther put on** *her* **royal** *apparel,* **and stood in the inner court of the king's house, over against the king's house: and the king sat upon his royal throne in the royal house, over against the gate of the house. And it was so, when the king saw Esther the queen standing in the court,** *that* **she obtained favour in his sight: and the king held out to Esther the golden sceptre that** *was* **in his hand. So Esther drew near, and touched the top of the sceptre.** (James 2:20) But will thou know, O vain man, that faith without works is dead?

(Job 9:32–33) For He *is* not a man, as I *am, that* I should answer Him, *and* we should come together in judgement. Neither is there any Daysman betwixt us, *that* might lay his hand upon us both.

(1 Tim. 2:3–6) For this *is* good and acceptable in the sight of God our Saviour. Who will have all men to be saved, and to come unto the knowledge of the truth. For there *is* one God, and one Mediator between God and men, the man Christ Jesus; Who gave Himself a ransom for all, to be testified in due time.

(Job 19:23–27) Oh that my words were now written! oh that they were printed in a book! That they were graven with an iron pen and lead in the rock for ever! For I know *that* my Redeemer liveth, and *that* He shall stand at the latter *day* upon the earth: (Rom. 3:25) Whom God hath set forth *to be* a propitiation through faith in His blood, to declare His righteousness for the remission of sins that are past, through the forbearance of God. (1 Jn. 2:2) And He is the propitiation for our sins: and not for ours only, but also for the sins of the whole world. (1 Jn. 4 :10) Herein is love, not that we loved God, but that He loved us, and sent His Son to be the propitiation for our sins. **And *though* after my skin *worms* destroy this *body,* yet in my flesh shall I see God: Whom I shall see for myself, and mine eyes shall behold, and not another; *though* my reins be consumed within me.** (Jn. 5:24–29) Verily, verily, I say unto you, He that heareth My word, and believeth on Him that sent Me, hath everlasting life, and shall not come into condemnation; but is passed from death unto life. Verily, verily, I say unto you, The hour is coming, and now is, when the dead shall hear the voice of the Son of God: and they that hear shall live. For as the Father hath life in Himself; so hath He given to the Son to have life in Himself; And hath given Him authority to execute judgment also, because He is the Son of man. Marvel not at this: for the hour is coming, in the which all that are in the graves shall hear His voice, And shall come forth; they that have done good, unto the resurrection of life; and they that have done evil, unto the resurrection of damnation.

(Ps. 2:All) Why do the heathen rage, and the people imagine a vain thing? The kings of the earth set themselves, and the rulers take counsel together, against the LORD, and against His Anointed, *saying,* **Let us break their bands asunder, and cast away their cords from us.** (Acts 4:25–27) Who by the mouth of thy servant David hast said, Why do the heathen rage, and the people imagine a vain thing? The kings of the earth stood up, and the rulers were gathered together against the Lord, and against His Christ. For of a truth against Thy Holy Child Jesus, whom Thou hast anointed, both Herod, and Pontius Pilate, with the Gentiles, and the people of Israel, were gathered together. **He that sitteth in the heavens shall laugh: the Lord shall have them in derision. Then shall He speak unto them in His wrath, and vex them in His displeasure. Yet have I set My King upon My holy hill of Zion. I will declare the decree: Thou** *art* **My Son: this day have I begotten Thee.** (Mt. 17:5) While he yet spake, behold, a bright cloud overshadowed them: and behold a voice out of the cloud, which said, This is My beloved Son, in whom I am well pleased; hear ye Him. **Ask of Me, and I shall give** *Thee* **the heathen** *for* **Thine inhertance, and the uttermost parts of the earth** *for* **Thy possession. Thou shalt break them with a rod of iron; Thou shalt dash them in pieces like a potter's vessel.** (Rev. 2:27) And He shall rule them with a rod of iron; as the vessels of a potter shall they be broken to shivers: even as I received of My Father. (Rev. 12:5) And she brought forth a man child, who was to rule all nations with a rod of iron: and her Child was caught up unto God, and to His throne. **(Ps. 2:12) Kiss the Son, lest He be angry, and ye perish** *from* **the way, when His wrath is kindled but a little. Blessed are all they that put their trust in Him.** (Jn. 20:31) But these are written, that ye might believe that Jesus is the Christ, the Son of God: and that believing ye might have life through His name. (Rom. 15:12) And again, Esaias saith, There shall be a root of Jesse, and He that shall rise to reign over the Gentiles; in Him shall the Gentiles trust. (2 Cor. 1:9–10) But we had the sentence of death in ourselves, that we should not trust in ourselves, but in God which raises the dead: Who delivered us from so great a death, and doth deliver: in Whom we trust that He will yet deliver *us*; (Rev. 19:15)

And out of His mouth goeth a sharp sword, that with it He should smite the nations: and He shall rule them with a rod of iron: and He treadeth the winepress of the fierceness and wrath of Almighty God.

(Ps. 8:4) What is man, that Thou art mindful of him? And the son of man, that Thou visitest Him? (Heb. 2:6–8) But one in a certain place testified, saying, What is man, that Thou art mindful of him? Or the son of man, that Thou visitest Him? Thou madest Him a little lower than the angels; Thou crownedst Him with glory and honour, and didst set Him over the works of Thy hands; Thou hast put all things in subjection under Him, He left nothing *that is* not put under Him. But now we see not yet all things put under Him.

(Ps. 9:7–10) But the Lord shall endure for ever: He hath prepared His throne for judgment. And He shall judge the world in righteousness, He shall minister judgment to the people in uprightness. The LORD also will be a refuge for the oppressed, a refuge in times of trouble. And they that know Thy name will put their trust in Thee: for Thou, LORD, hast not forsaken them that seek Thee. (Acts 17:31) Because He hath appointed a day, in the which He will judge the world in righteousness by *that* man whom He hath ordained; *whereof* He hath given assurance unto all *men*, in that He hath raised Him from the dead.

(Ps. 16:9–11) Therefore My heart is glad, and My glory rejoiceth: My flesh also shall rest in hope. For Thou wilt not leave My soul in hell; neither wilt Thou suffer Thine Holy One to see corruption. (Acts 2:31) He seeing this before spake of the resurrection of Christ, that His soul was not left in hell, neither His flesh did see corruption. **Thou wilt shew Me the path of life: in Thy presence *is* fulness of joy; at Thy right hand *there are* pleasures for evermore.**

(Ps. 18:2–3) The Lord *is* my rock, and my fortress, and my deliverer; my God my strength, in whom I will trust; my buckler, and the horn of my salvation, *and* my high tower. I will call upon

the Lord, who is worthy to be praised: so shall I be saved from mine enemies. (Lk. 1:68–71) Blessed *be* the Lord God of Israel, for He hath visited and redeemed His people. And hath raised up an horn of salvation for us in the house of His servant David As He spake by the mouth of His holy prophets, which have been since the world began: That we should be saved from the hand of all that hate us.

(Ps. 18:46) The Lord liveth; and blessed *be* my rock; and let the God of my salvation be exalted. (2 Tim. 3:15) And that from a child thou hast known the holy scriptures, which are able to make thee wise unto salvation through faith which is in Christ Jesus.

(Ps. 22:1) My God, my God, why hast Thou forsaken Me? *why art Thou so* **far from helping Me,** *and from* **the words of My roaring?** (2 Cor. 5:21) For He hath made Him, *to be* sin for us, who new no sin; that we might be made the righteousness of God in Him. **O my God, I cry in the daytime, but Thou hearest not; and in the night season, and am not silent.** (Mt. 27:45–46) Now from the sixth hour there was darkness over all the land unto the nineth hour. And about the ninth hour Jesus cried with a loud voice, saying, Eli, Eli, la-ma sa bach tha-ni? That is to say, My God, My God why hast Thou forsaken Me? **But Thou *art* holy, O Thou that inhabitest the praises of Israel. Our fathers trusted in Thee: they trusted, and Thou didst deliver them. They cried unto Thee, and were delivered: they trusted in Thee, and were not confounded. But I *am* a worm, and no man; a reproach of men, and despised of the people. All they that see Me laugh Me to scorn: they shoot out the lip, they shake the head** *saying* (Mat. 27:39–44). And they that passed by reviled Him, wagging their heads. And saying, Thou that destroyest the temple, and buildest *it* in three days, save thyself. If thou be the Son of God, come down from the cross. Likewise also the chief priests mocking *Him,* with the scribes and elders, said. He saved others; Himself He can not save. If he be the King of Israel, let Him now come down from the cross, and we will believe Him. He trusted in God: let Him deliver Him now, if He will have Him: for

He said, I am the Son of God. The thieves also, which were crucified with Him, cast the same in His teeth. **He trusted on the LORD** *that* **He would deliver Him: let Him deliver Him, seeing He delighted in Him. But Thou** *art* **He that took Me out of the womb:**

Thou didst make Me hope *when I was* **upon My mother's breasts. I was cast upon Thee from the womb: Thou** *art* **My God from My mother's belly.** (Lk. 2:7) And she brought forth her first-born son, and wrapped Him in swaddling clothes, and laid Him in a manger; because there was no room for them in the inn. **Be not far from Me; for trouble** *is* **near; for** *there is* **none to help. Many bulls have compassed Me: strong** *bulls* **of Bashan have beset Me round. They gaped upon Me** *with* **their mouths,** *as* **a ravening and a roaring lion.** (Jn. 19:6) When the chief priests therefore and officers saw Him, they cried out, saying, Crucify *Him*, crucify *Him*, Pilate saith unto them, Take ye Him, and crucify *Him*: for I find no fault in Him. **I am poured out like water, and all My bones are out of joint: My heart is like wax; it is melted in the midst of My bowels. My strenght is dried up like a potsherd; and My tongue cleaveth to My jaws; and thou hast brought Me into the dust of death. For dogs have compassed Me: the assembly of the wicked have inclosed Me: they pierced My hands and My feet. I may tell all My bones: they look** *and* **stare upon Me. They part My garments among them, and cast lots upon My vesture.** (Jn. 19:36) For these things were done, that the scripture should be fulfilled, a bone of Him shall not be broken. (Jn. 19:28) After this, Jesus knowing that all things were now accomplished, that the scripture might be fulfilled, saith, I thirst. (Mt. 27:35) And they crucified Him, and parted His garments, casting lots: that it might be fulfilled which was spoken by the prophet, They parted My garments among them, and upon My vesture did they cast lots. (Jn. 19:23–24) Then the soldiers, when they had crucified Jesus, took His garments, and made four parts, to every soldier a part: and also *His* coat: now the coat was without seam, woven from the top throughout. They said therefore among themselves, Let us not rend it, but cast lots for it, whose it shall be: that the scripture might be fulfilled, which saith, They parted my raimnet among them, and for My vesture they did cast lots. These things therefore the soldiers did.

But be not Thou far from Me, O Lord: O my strength, haste Thee to help Me. Deliver My soul from the sword; My Darling from the power of the dog. Save Me from the lion's mouth: for Thou hast heard Me from the horns of the unicorns. (Lk. 23:46) And when Jesus had cried with a loud voice, He said, Father, into Thy hands I commend My spirit: **and having said thus, He gave up the ghost. I will declare Thy name unto My brethren: in the midst of the congregation will I praise Thee.** (Jn. 20:17) Jesus saith unto her, Touch Me not: for I am not yet ascended to My Father: but go to My brethren, and say unto them, I ascend unto My Father, and your Father: and *to* my God. And your God. **Ye that fear the LORD, praise Him; all ye the seed of Jacob, glorify Him; and fear Him, all ye the seed of Israel. For He hath not despised nor abhorred the affliction of the afflicted; neither hath He hid His face from Him; but when He cried unto Him, He heard. My praise *shall* be of Thee in the great congregation: I will pay my vows before them that fear Him. The meek shall eat and be satisfied: they shall praise the LORD that seek Him: your heart shall live for ever. All the ends of the world shall remember and turn unto the LORD: and all the kindreds of the nations shall worship before Thee. For the kingdom *is* the LORD'S and He *is* the governor among the nations.** (Col. 1:16) For by Him were all things created, that are in the heaven, and that are in earth, visible and invisible, wheather they be thrones, or dominions, or principalities, or powers: all things were created by Him, and for Him. **All *they that be* fat upon earth shall eat and worship: all they that go down to the dust shall bow before Him: and none can keep alive his soul. A seed shall serve Him; it shall be accounted to the Lord for a generation. They shall come, and shall declare His righteousness unto a people that shall be born, that He hath done *this*.** (Heb. 10:10–13) By the which will we are sanctified through the offering of the body of Jesus Christ once *for all*. And every priest standeth daily ministering and offering oftentimes the same sacrifices, which can never take away sins. But this Man, after He had offered one sacrifice for sins for ever, sat down on the right hand of God. From henceforth expecting till His enemies be made His footstool.

(Ps. 23:1) The Lord is my shepherd; I shall not want. (Jn. 10:11) I Am the good shepherd: the good sheperd giveth His life for the sheep. (1 Pet. 2:25) For ye were as sheep going astray; but are now returned unto the Shepherd and Bishop of your souls.

(Ps. 24:3) Who shall ascend into the hill of the Lord? or who shall stand in His holy place? (Acts 1:11) Which also said, Ye men of Galilee, why stand ye gazing up into heaven? This same Jesus, which is taken up from you into heaven, shall so come in like manner as ye have seen Him go into heaven.

(Ps. 27:12) Deliver Me not over unto the will of Mine enemies: for false witnesses are risen up against Me, and such as breathe out cruelty. (Mat. 26:60) But found none: yea though many false witnesses came, yet found they none.

(Ps. 30:3) O Lord, thou hast brought up My soul from the grave: thou hast kept Me alive, that I should not go down to the pit. (Acts 2:32) This Jesus hath God raised up, whereof we all are witnesses.

(Ps. 31:5) Into Thine hand I commit My spirit: Thou hast redeemed Me, O LORD God of truth. (Lk. 23:44–47) And it was about the sixth hour, and there was darkness over all the earth until the ninth hour. And the sun was darkened and the veil of the temple was rent in the midst. And when Jesus had cried with a loud voice, He said, Father, into Thy hands I commend My spirit: And having said thus, He gave up the ghost. Now when the centurion saw what was done, he glorified God, saying, Certainly this was a righteous man. (Mt. 27:54) Now when the centurion, and they that were with him, watching Jesus, saw the earthquake, and those things that were done, they feared greatly, saying, truly this was the Son of God.

(Ps. 31:11–15) I was a reproach among all Mine enemies, but especially among My neighbours, and a fear to Mine acquaintance: they that did see Me without fled from Me. (Mk. 14:50) And they all forsook Him, and fled. **I am forgotten as a dead man out of mind: I am like a broken vessel. For I have heard the slander of many: fear *was* on every side: while they took counsel together against Me, they devised to take away My life.** (Mat. 27:1) When the moring was come, all the chief priests and elders of the people took counsel against Jesus to put Him to death: **But I trusted in Thee, O LORD: I said, Thou *art* My God. My times *are* in Thy hand: deliver me from the hand of mine enemies, and from them that persecute Me.**

(Ps. 34:20) He keepeth all His bones: not one of them is broken. (Jn. 19:33) But when they came to Jesus, and saw that he was dead already, they brake not his legs:

(Ps. 35:11) False witnesses did rise up; they laid to My charge *things* that I knew not. (Mt. 26:59–60) Now the chief priests, and elders, and all the council, sought false witness against Jesus, to put Him to death: But found none: yea, though many false witnesses came, *yet* found they none.

(Ps. 35:19) Let not them that are Mine enemies wrongfully (falsely) rejoice over Me: *neither* let them wink with the eye that hate Me without a cause. (Mk. 14:57–59) And there arose certain, and bare false witness against Him, saying, We heard Him say. I will destroy this temple that is made with hands, and within three days I will build another made without hands. But neither so did their witness agree together.

(Ps. 38:12–13) They also that seek after My life lay snares *for Me*: and they that seek My hurt speak mischievous things, and imagine deceits all the day long. But I, as a deaf *man*, heard not; and *I was* as a dumb man *that* openeth not His mouth. (Mr. 14:1) After two days was *the feast of* the passover, and of unleaven bread: and the chief priests and the scribes sought how they might take Him by craft, and put *Him* to death.
(Mat. 27:12) And when He was accused of the chief priests and elders, He answered nothing.

(Ps. 38:20) They also that render evil for good are Mine adversaries; because I follow *the thing that* **good** *is.* (Acts 10 :38) How God anointed Jesus of Nazareth with the Holy Ghost and with power: who went about doing good, and healing all that were oppressed of the devil; for God was with Him.

(Ps. 40:6–8) Sacrifice and offering Thou didst not desire; Mine ears hast thou opened: burnt offering and sin offering hast Thou not required. Then said I, Lo, I come: in the volume of the book *it is* **written of Me, I delight to do Thy will, O My God: yea, Thy law** *Is* **within** *My* **heart.** (Heb. 10:6-10) In burnt offerings and sacrifices for sin Thou hast had no pleasure, Then said I, Lo, I come (in the volume of the book it written of Me,) to do Thy will O God. Above when he said, Sacrifice and offering and burnt offerings and *offering* for sin Thou wouldest not, neither hadst pleasure *therein*; which are offered by the law; Then said He, Lo, I come to do Thy will, O God, He taketh away the first, that He may establish the second. By the which will we are sanctified through the offering of the body of Jesus Christ once for *all.*

(Ps. 40:9) I have preached righteousness in the great con-gregation: lo, I have not refrained My lips, O Lord, Thou know-est. (Mat. 4:17) From that time Jesus began to preach, and to say, Repent: for the kingdom of heaven is at hand.

(Ps. 40:14) Let them be ashamed and confounded together that seek after My soul to destroy it; let them be driven backward and put to shame that wish Me evil. (Jn. 18:4–6) Jesus therefore knowing all things that should come upon Him, went forth, and said unto them, Whom seek ye? They answered Him, Jesus of Nazareth. Jesus saith unto them, I Am *He,* And Judas also, which betrayed Him, stood with them. As soon then as He had said unto them I Am *He,* they went backward, and fell to the ground.

(Ps. 41:9) Yea, Mine own familiar friend, in whom I trusted, which did eat of My bread, hath lifted up *his* **heel against Me.** (Jn.

13:18) I speak not of you all: I know whom I have chosen: but that the scripture may be fulfilled, He that eateth bread with Me hath lifted up his heel against Me.

(Ps. 45:2) Thou art fairer than the children of men: grace is poured into Thy lips: therefore God hath blessed Thee for ever. (Jn. 1:17) For the law was given by Moses, *but* grace and truth come by Jesus Christ.

(Ps. 45:6–7) Thy throne, O God, *is* for ever and ever: the sceptre of Thy kingdom *is* a right sceptre. Thou lovest righteousness, and hatest wickedness: therefore God, Thy God, hath anointed Thee with the oil of gladness above thy fellows. (Heb. 1:8–9) But unto the Son *He saith,* Thy throne O God, *is* for ever and ever: a sceptre of righteousness *is* the sceptre of Thy kingdom. Thou lovest righteousness, and hated iniquity; therefore God, *even* Thy God hath anointed Thee with the oil of gladness above thy fellows.

(Ps. 45:7–8) Thou lovest righteousness, and hatest wickedness: therefore God, Thy God, hath anointed Thee with the oil of gladness above thy fellows. All thy garments *smell* of myrrh, and aloes, and cassia, out of the ivory palaces, whereby they have made Thee glad. (Lk. 2:11) For unto you is born this day in the city of David a Saviour, which is Christ the Lord.

(Ps. 45:17) I will make Thy name to be remembered in all generations: therefore shall the people praise Thee for ever and ever. (Heb. 1:8) But unto the Son *He saith,* Thy throne, 0 God is for ever and ever;

(Ps. 49:15) But God will redeem My soul from the power of the grave: for He shall receive Me. Se-lah. (1 Cor. 15:55–57) O death, where *is* thy sting? O grave, where *is* thy victory? The sting of death *is* sin; and the strength of sin *is* the law. But thanks *be* to God, which giveth us the victory through our Lord Jesus Christ.

(Ps. 55:12–14) For *it was* **not an enemy** *that* **reproached Me; then I could have borne** *it*: **neither** *it* **was he that hated Me** *that* **did magnify** *himself* **against Me; then I would have hid Myself from him: But** *it was* **thou, a man Mine equal, My guide, and Mine acquaintance. We took sweet counsel together,** *and* **walked unto the house of God in company.** (Jn. 13:18) He that eateth bread with Me hath lifted up his heel against Me.

(Ps. 55:15) Let death seize upon them, *and* **let them go down quick into hell: for wickedness is in their dwellings,** *and* **among them.** (Mt. 27:3–5) Then Judas, which had betrayed Him, when he saw that he was condemned, repented himself, and brought again the thirty pieces of silver to the chief priests and elders. Saying I have sinned in that I have betrayed the innocent blood. And they said, What *is that* to us? See thou *to that.* And he cast down the pieces of silver in the temple, and departed, and went and hanged himself.

(Ps. 61:2) From the end of the earth will I cry unto Thee, when my heart is overwhelmed: lead me to the rock *that is* **higher than I.** (1 Cor. 10:4) And did all drink the same spiritual drink: for they drank of that spiritual Rock that followed them: and that Rock was Christ.

(Ps. 62:2) He only *is* **my rock and my salvation;** *He is* **my defence; I shall not be greatly moved.**
(1 Cor. 10:4) And did all drink the same spiritual drink: for they drank of that spiritual Rock that followed them: and that Rock was Christ.

(Ps. 65:5) *By* **terrible things in righteousness wilt Thou answer us, O God of our salvation;** *who art* **the confidence of all the ends of the earth, and of them that are afar off** *upon* **the sea:** (Heb. 9:28) So Christ was once offered to bear the sins of many; and unto them that look for Him shall He appear the second time without sin unto salvation.|

(Ps. 68:18) Thou hast ascended on high, Thou hast led captivity captive: Thou hast received gifts for men; yea, *for* **the rebellious also, that the LORD God might dwell** *among them.* (Acts 1:9) And when He had spoken these things, while they beheld, He was taken up: and a cloud received Him out of their sight. (Acts 2:33) Therefore being by the right hand of God exalted, and having received of the father the promise of the Holy Ghost, He hath shed forth this, which ye now see and hear. (Eph. 4:8–10) Wherefore He saith, When He ascended up on high, He led captivity captive, and gave gifts unto men. (Now that He ascended, what is it but that He also descended first into the lower parts of the earth? He that descended is the same also that ascended up far above all heavens, that He might fill all things.)

(Ps. 69:4) They that hate Me without a cause are more than the hairs of Mine head: they that would destroy Me, *being* **Mine enemies wrongfully, are mighty: then I restored** *that* **which I took not away.** (Jn. 15:25) But *this cometh to pass,* that the word might be fulfilled that is written in their law, They hated Me without a cause.

(Ps. 69:8) I am become a stranger unto my brethren, and an alien unto My mother's children.
(Jn. 1:11) He came unto His own, and His own received Him not. (Jn. 7:5) For neither did His brethren believe in Him.

(Ps. 69:9) For the zeal of Thine house hath eaten Me up; and the reproaches of them that reproached Thee are fallen upon Me. (Jn. 2:13–17) And the Jews Passover was at hand, and Jesus went up to Jerusalem, and found in the temple those that sold oxen and sheep and doves, and the changers of money sitting: and when He had made a sourge of small cords, He drove them all out of the temple, and the sheep, and the oxen; and poured out the changers' money, and overthrew the tables; and said unto them that sold doves, Take these things hence; make not my Father's house an house of merchandise. And his disciples remembered that it was written, The zeal of thine house hath eaten Me up.

(Ps. 69:19–21) Thou hast known My reproach, and My shame, and My dishonour: Mine adversaries *are* all before Thee. Reproach hath broken My heart; and I am full of heaviness: and I looked *for some* to take pity, but *there was* none; and for comforters, but I found none. They gave Me also gall for My meat; and in My thirst they gave Me vinegar to drink. (Mt. 27:29) And when they had plated a crown of thorns, they put *it* upon His head, and a reed in His right hand: and they bowed the knee before Him, and mocked Him, saying, Hail, King of the Jews! (Mt. 26:37) And He took with Him Peter and the two sons of Zebedee, and began to be sorrowful and very heavy. (Mt. 27:34) They gave Him vinegar to drink mingled with gall: and when He had tasted *thereof,* He would not drink (Jn. 19:28–30) After this, Jesus knowing that all things were now accomplished, that the scripture might be fulfilled, saith, I thirst, Now there was set a vessel full of vinegar: and they filled a spunge with vinegar and put *it* upon hyssop, and put *it* to His mouth. When Jesus therefore had received the vinegar He said, It is finished. And He bowed His head, and gave up the ghost.

(Ps. 69:22) Let their table become a snare before them: and *that which should have been* for *their* welfare, *let it become* a trap.

(Rom. 11:9, 10) And David saith, Let their table be made a snare, and a trap, and a stumblingblock, and a recompence unto them: Let their eyes be darkened, that they may not see, and bow down their back alway.

(Ps. 72:10–11) The kings of Tarshish and of the isles shall bring presents: the kings of Sheba and Seba shall offer gifts. Yea, all kings shall fall down before Him: all nations shall serve Him. (Mt. 2:1, 2, 11) Now when Jesus was born in Bethlehem of Judaea in the days of Herod the king, behold, there came wise men from the east to Jerusalem, Saying, Where is He that is born King of the Jews? For we have seen His star in the east, and are come to worship Him. And when they were come into the house, they saw the young child with Mary His mother, and fell down, and worshipped Him:

and when they had opened their treasures, they presented unto Him gifts; gold, and frankincense, and myrrh.

(Ps. 72:16–17) There shall be an handful of corn in the earth upon the top of the mountains; the fruit thereof shall shake like Lebanon: and *they* of the city shall flourish like grass of the earth. His name shall endure for ever: His name shall be continued as long as the sun: and men shall be blessed in Him: all nations shall call Him Blessed. (Jn. 12:24) Verily, verily, I say unto you, Except a corn of wheat fall into the ground and die, it abideth alone: but if it die, it bringeth forth much fruit. (Gal. 3:8) And the scripture, foreseeing that God would justify the heathen through faith, preached before the gospel unto Abraham, *saying*, In Thee shall all nations be blessed.

(Ps. 77:15) Thou hast with *Thine* arm redeemed Thy people, the sons of Jacob and Joseph. Selah.
(Luke 24:21) But we trusted that it had been He which should have redeemed Israel: and beside all this, to day is the third day since these things were done.

(Ps. 78:2–3) I will open My mouth in a parable: I will utter dark sayings of old: Which we have heard and known, and our fathers have told us. (Mt. 13:34) All these thing spake Jesus unto the multitude in parables; and without a parable; spake He not unto them; (Mt. 7:29) For He taught them as *one* having authority, and not as the scribes.

(Ps. 78:20) Behold He smote the rock, that the waters gushed out, and the streams overflowed; can He give bread also? Can he provide flesh for His people? (Lk. 9:16–17) Then He took the five loaves and the two fishes, and looking up to heaven, He blessed them, and brake, and gave to the disciples to set before the multitude. And they did eat, and were all filled: and there was taken up of the fragments that remained twelve baskets.

(Ps. 78:35) And they remembered that God *was* **their rock, and the high God their redeemer.** (1 Cor. 10:4)

And did all drink the same spiritual drink: for they drank of that spiritual Rock that followed them: and that Rock was Christ.

(Ps. 80:17) Let Thy hand be upon the man of Thy right hand, upon the Son of man *whom* **Thou madest strong for Thyself.** (Mr. 14:61–62) But He held His peace, and answered nothing. Again the high priest asked Him, and said unto Him, Art Thou the Christ, the son of the Blessed? And Jesus said, I am: and ye shall see the Son of man sitting on the right hand of power, and coming in the clouds of heaven.

(Ps. 88:All) O LORD God of my salvation, I have cried day *and* **night before Thee: Let my prayer come before Thee: incline Thine ear unto My cry; For My soul is full of troubles: and My life draweth nigh unto the grave.** (Lk. 22:44) And being in agony He prayed more earnestly: and His sweat was as it were great drops of blood falling down to the ground. **I am counted with them that go down into the pit: I am as a man** *that hath* **no strength: Free among the dead, like the slain that lie in the grave, whom Thou rememberest no more: and they are cut off from Thy hand. Thou hast laid me in the lowest pit, in darkness, in the deeps. Thy wrath lieth hard upon Me and Thou hast afflicted** *Me* **with all Thy waves. Selah.** (Rom. 5:9) Much more then, being now justified by His blood, we shall be saved from wrath through Him. **Thou hast put away My aquaintance far from Me;** (Lk. 23:49) And all His aquaintance, and the women that followed Him from Galilee, stood afar off beholding these things. **Thou hast made Me an abomination unto them:** (Mark 14:65) And some began to spit on Him, and to cover His face, and to buffet Him, and to say unto Him, Prophesy: and the servants did strike Him with the palms of their hands. **I am shut up, and I cannot come forth. Mine eye mourneth by reason of affliction: LORD, I have called daily upon Thee, I have stretched out My hands unto Thee. Wilt Thou shew wonders to**

the dead? shall the dead arise *and* praise Thee? Selah. Shall Thy lovingkindness be declared in the grave? *or* thy faithfulness in destruction? Shall thy wonders be known in the dark? and Thy righteousness in the land of forgetfulness? But unto Thee have I cried, O LORD; and in the morning shall My prayer prevent Thee. LORD, why castest Thou off My soul? *Why* hidest Thou Thy face from Me? (Mark 15:34) And at the ninth hour Jesus cried with a loud voice, saying, Eloi, Eloi, lama sabachthani? which is, being interpreted, My God, My God, why hast Thou forsaken Me? I *am* afflicted and ready to die from *My* youth up: *while* I suffer Thy terrors I am distracted. Thy fierce wrath goeth over Me; Thy terrors have cut Me off. They came round about Me daily like water; they compassed Me about together. (Mr. 14:43) And immediately while He yet spake, cometh Judas, one of the twelve, and with him a great multitude with swords and staves, form the chief priests and the scribes and the elders. **Lover and friend hast Thou put far from Me, and Mine acquaintance into darkness.**

(Ps. 89:4) Thy seed will I establish for ever, and build up Thy throne to all generations. Selah. (2 Tim. 2:8) Remember that Jesus Christ of the seed of David was raised from the dead according to my gospel.

(Ps. 89:18) For the Lord *is* our defence; and the Holy One of Israel *is* our king. (Rev. 17:14) These shall make war with the Lamb, and the Lamb shall overcome them: for He is Lord of lords, and King of kings: and they that are with Him *are* called, and chosen, and faithful.

(Ps. 89:26–27) He shall cry unto Me, Thou art my Father, my God, and the rock of my salvation. (Luke 23:46) And when Jesus had cried with a loud voice, He said, Father, into Thy hands I commend My spirit: and having said thus He gave up the ghost. **Also I will make Him *My* firstborn, higher than the kings of the earth.** (Rom. 8:29) For whom He did foreknow, He also did predestinate to be conformed to the image of His Son, that He might be the first-born among many brethren.

(Ps. 89:28–29) My mercy will I keep for Him for evermore, and My covenant shall stand fast with Him. His seed also will I make *to endure* for ever, and His throne as the days of heaven. (Rev. 3:21) To him that overcometh will I grant to sit with Me in My throne, even as I also overcame, and am set down with My Father in His throne.

(Ps. 89:34–38) My covenant will I not break, nor alter the thing that is gone out of My lips. Once have I sworn by holiness that I will not lie unto David. His seed shall endure forever, and his throne as the sun before Me. It shall be established for ever as the moon, and as a faithful witness in heaven. Selah. But Thou hast cast off and abhorred, Thou hast been wroth with thine anointed. (Luke 1:32–33) He shall be great, and shall be called the Son of the Highest: and the Lord God shall give unto Him the throne of His father David: And He shall reign over the house of Jacob for ever; and of his kingdom there shall be no end. (Rev. 1:5–6) And from Jesus Christ, *who is* the faithful witness, *and* the first begotten of the dead, and the prince of the kings of the earth. Unto Him that loved us, and washed us from our sins in His own blood, And hath made us kings *and* priests unto God *and* His Father; to Him *be* glory and dominion for ever and ever. Amen.

(Ps. 90:2) Before the mountains were brought forth, or ever Thou hadst formed the earth and the world, even from everlasting to everlasting, Thou *art* God. (Jn. 1:1, 14) In the beginning was the Word, and the Word was with God, and the Word was God. And the Word was made flesh, and dwelt among us (and we beheld His glory, the glory as of the only begotten of the Father) full of grace and truth.

(Ps. 91:11–16) For He shall give His angels charge over Thee, to keep Thee in all Thy ways. They shall bear Thee up in

their hands, lest Thou dash Thy foot against a stone. (Mt. 4:6–7) And saith unto Him, if Thou be the Son of God, cast Thyself down: for it it written, He shall give His angles charge over Thee: and in *their* hands they shall bear Thee up, lest at any time Thou dash Thy foot against a stone. Jesus said unto him, It is written again, Thou shalt not tempt the Lord thy God. **Thou shalt tread upon the lion and adder: the young lion and the dragon shalt Thou trample under feet**. (Lk. 10:19) Behold, I give unto you power to tread on serpents and scorpions, and over all the power of the enemy: and nothing shall by any means hurt you.

Because He hath set His love upon Me, therefore will I deliver Him: I will set Him on high, because He hath known My name. He shall call upon Me, and I will answer Him: I *will be* with Him in trouble; I will deliver Him, and honour Him. (Jn. 12:26) If any man serve Me, let him follow Me: and where I am, there shall also My servant be: if any man serve Me, him will *My* Father honour. **With long life will I satisfy him, and shew him My salvation.**

(Ps. 95:1) O come, let us sing unto the LORD: let us make a joyful noise to the rock of our salvation.

(Acts 4:12) Neither is there salvation in any other: for there is none other name under heaven given among men, whereby we must be saved.

(Ps. 102:1–11) Hear My prayer, O Lord, and let My cry come unto Thee. Hide not Thy face from Me in the day *when* I am in trouble; incline Thine ear unto Me: in the day *when* I call answer Me speedily. For My days are consumed like smoke, and My bones are burned as an hearth. My heart is smitten, and withered like grass; so that I forget to eat My bread. By reason of the voice of My groaning My bones cleave to My skin. I am like a pelican of the wilderness: I am like an owl of the desert. I watch, and am as a sparrow alone upon the house top. Mine enemies reproach Me all the day; *and* they that are mad against Me are sworn against Me. (Mt. 27:39) And they that passed by reviled Him, wagging their heads. **For I have eaten ashes like bread, and**

mingled My drink with weeping, Because of Thine indignation and Thy wrath: for Thou hast lifted Me up, and cast Me down.
(John 3:14–15) And as Moses lifted up the serpent in the wilderness, even so must the Son of man be lifted up: that whosoever believeth in Him should not perish, but have eternal life. **My days *are* like a shadow that declineth; and I am withered like grass.**

(Ps. 102:25–27) Of old hast Thou laid the foundation of the earth: and the heavens *are* the work of Thy hands. They shall perish, but Thou shalt endure: yea, all of them shall wax old like a garment; as a vesture shalt Thou change them, and they shall be changed: But Thou *art* the same, and Thy years shall have no end.
(Heb. 1:10–12) And, Thou, Lord, in the beginning hast laid the foundation of the earth; and the heavens are the works of Thine hands: They shall perish; but Thou remainest; and they all shall wax old as doth a garment; And as a vesture shalt Thou fold them up, and they shall be changed: but Thou art the same, and Thy years shall not fail.

(Ps. 105:41) He opened the Rock, and the waters gushed out; they ran in the dry places *like* a river.
(1 Cor. 10:4) And did all drink the same spiritual drink: for they drank of that spiritual Rock that followed them: and that Rock was Christ.

(Ps. 109:1–5) Hold not Thy peace, O God of My praise; for the mouth of the wicked and the mouth of the deceitful are opened against Me: they have spoken againt Me with a lying tongue. They compassed Me about also with words of hatred; and fought against Me without a cause. For My love they are My adversaries: but I *give Myself unto* prayer. (Mk. 14:56) For many bare false witness against Him, but their witness agreed not together. (Lk. 23:22) And he said unto them the third time, Why, what evil hath He done? I have found no cause of death in Him: I will therefore chastise Him, and let *Him* go. (Jn. 15:13) Greater love hath no man than this, that a man lay down His life for His friends. (Lk.

23:34) Then said Jesus, Father, forgive them; for they know not what they do. And they parted His raiment, and cast lots.

(Ps. 109:25) I became also a reproach unto them: *when* they looked upon Me they shaked their heads.
(Mark 15:29) And they that passed by railed on Him, wagging their heads, and saying, Ah, Thou that destroyest the temple, and build *it* in three days, Save Thyself, and come down from the cross.

(Ps. 110:1–7) The LORD said unto my Lord, (Mt. 22:44–45) The LORD said unto my Lord, Sit Thou on My right hand, till I make Thine enemies Thy footstool? If David [Mk. 12:36 by the Holy Ghost] then call Him Lord, how is He his son? (Heb. 1:13) But to which of the angels said He at any time, **Sit thou at My right hand,** (Eph. 1:20) when He raised Him from the dead, and set *Him* at His own right hand in the heavenly *places.* (Col. 3:1) If ye then be risen with Christ, seek those things which are above, Where Christ sitteth on the right hand of God. (Heb. 1:3) Who being the brightness of *His* glory and the express image of His person, and upholding all things by the word of His power, when He had by Himself purged our sins, sat down on the right hand of the Majesty on high; **until I make thine enemies Thy footstool.** (1 Cor. 15:25) For He must reign, till He hath put all enemies under His feet. (Eph. 1:22) And hath put all *things* under His feet, and gave Him to be the head over all *things* to the church, Which is His body, the fulness of Him that filled all in all. (Heb. 2:8) Thou hast put all things in subjection under His feet, For in that He put all in subjection under Him, He left nothing *that is* not put under Him. But now we see not yet all things put under Him. **The Lord shall send the Rod of Thy strength out of Zion:** (Isa. 11:1) And there shall come forth a Rod out of the stem of Jesse, and a Branch shall grow out of his roots: **rule thou in the midst of thine enemies. Thy people *shall be* willing in the day of Thy power, in the beauties of holiness from the womb of the morning: Thou hast the dew of Thy youth. The LORD hath sworn, and will not repent, Thou *art* a priest for ever after the order of Melchizedek.** (Heb. 7:21) (For those priest were made without an oath; but this with an oath by Him that said unto Him, The LORD sware and will not repent, Thou *art* a priest for ever after the order of Melchisedec:) (Zech. 6:12–13) And speak unto him, saying, Thus speaketh the LORD of hosts, saying, Behold the man whose name *Is* THE BRANCH; and He shall grow up out of His place, and He shall build the temple of the LORD: Even He shall build the temple of the LORD; and He shall bear the glory, and shall sit and rule upon His throne: and He shall be a priest upon His throne: and the counsel of peace shall be between them both. (Jn. 12:34) The people answered Him, We have heard out of the law that Christ abideth for ever: and how sayest Thou The Son of man must be lifted up? Who is this Son of man? (Heb. 2:9) But we see Jesus, who was made a little lower than the angels for the suffering of death, crowned with glory and honour; that He by the grace of God should taste death for every man. (2 Tim. 1:10) But is now made manifest by the appearing of our Saviour Jesus Christ, who hath abolished death, and hath brought life and immortality to light through the gospel: **The Lord at Thy right hand** (Ps. 16:8) I have set the LORD always Before Me: because *He is* at My right hand, I shall not be moved. **Shall strike through kings in the day of His wrath.** (Rom. 2:5) But after thy hardness and impenitent heart treasurest up unto thyself wrath against the day of wrath and revelation of the righteous judgement of God; **He shall judge among the heathen, He shall fill *the places* with the dead bodies; He shall wound the heads over many countries.** (Ps. 68:21) But God shall wound the head of His enemies, *and* the hairy scale of such an one as goeth on still in his trespasses. **He shall drink of the brook in the way: therefore shall He lift up the head.**

(Ps. 111:9) He sent redemption unto His people: He hath commanded His covenant for ever: holy and reverend *is* His name. (Acts 4:12) Neither is there salvation in any other: for there is none other name under heaven given among men, whereby we must be saved.

(Ps. 112:4) Unto the upright there ariseth light in the darkness: *He is* **gracious, and full of compassion, and righteous.** (Mt. 9:36) But when He saw the multitudes, He was moved with compassion on them, because they fainted, and were scattered abroad, as sheep having no shepherd.

(Ps. 114:8) The God of Jacob; Which turned the rock *into* **standing water, the flint into a fountian of waters.**

(Ps. 118:22–26) The stone *which* **the builders refused is become the head** *stone* **of the corner. This is the LORD'S doing; it** *is* **marvellous in our eyes. This** *is* **the day** *which* **the LORD hath made; we will rejoice and be glad in it. Save now, I beseech Thee, O LORD: O LORD, I beseech Thee, send now prosperity. Blessed** *be* **He that cometh in the name of the LORD: we have blessed You out of the house of the LORD.** (Mk. 12:10–11) And have ye not read this scripture; The stone which the builders rejected is become the head of the corner; This is the Lord's doing, and it is marvellous in our eyes? (Lk. 20:17–18) And He beheld them, and said, What is this then that is written, The stone which the builders rejected, the same is become the head of the be corner? Whosoever shall fall upon that stone shall broken; but on whomsoever it shall fall, it will grind him to powder. (1 Pet. 2:3–8) If so be ye have tasted that the Lord *is* gracious. To whom coming, *as unto* a living stone, disallowed indeed of men, but chosen of God, *and* precious, Ye also, as lively stones, are built up a spiritual house, an holy priesthood, to offer up spiritual sacrifices, acceptable to God by Jesus Christ. Wherefore also it is contained in the scripture, Behold, I lay in Sion a chief corner stone, elect precious: and he that believeth on Him shall not be confounded Unto you therefore which believe *He is* precious: but unto them which be disobedient, the stone which the builders disallowed, the same is made the head of the corner, and a stone of stumbling, and a rock of offence, *even to them* which stumble at the word, being disobedient: whereunto also they were appointed.

(Ps. 132:11) The LORD hath sworn *in* truth unto David; He will not turn from it; Of the fruit of thy body will I set upon thy throne. (Lk. 1:32) He shall be great, and shall be called the Son of the Highest: and the Lord God shall give unto Him the throne of His father David.

(Ps. 138:1–3) I will praise Thee with my whole heart: before the gods will I sing praise unto Thee. I will worship toward Thy holy temple, and praise Thy name for Thy lovingkindness and for Thy truth: for Thou hast magnified Thy word above all Thy name. In the day when I cried Thou answeredst Me, and strengthenedst Me *with* strength in My soul. All the kings of the earth shall praise Thee, O LORD, when they hear the words of Thy mouth. Yea, they shall sing in the ways of the LORD: for great *is* the glory of the LORD. Though the LORD *be* high, yet hath He respect unto the lowly: but the proud He knoweth afar off. (Mt. 2:1–6) Now when Jesus was born in Bethlehem of Judaea in the days of Herod the king, behold, there came wise men from the east to Jerusalem, Saying, Where is He that is born King of the Jews? For we have seen His star in the east, and are come to worship Him. When Herod the king had *heard these* things, he was troubled, and all Jerusalem with him.

(Ps. 144:3) LORD, what *is* man, that Thou takest knowledge of him! *Or* the son of man, that Thou makest account of Him! (Heb. 2:6–8) But one in a certain place testified, saying, What is man, that Thou art mindful of him? Or the son of man, that Thou visitest Him? Thou madest Him a little lower than the angels; Thou crownedst Him with glory and honour, and didst set Him over the works of Thy hands; Thou hast put all things in subjection under His feet, For in that He put all in subjection under Him, He left nothing *that is* not put under Him, But now we see not yet all things put under Him.

(Ps. 145:19) He will fulfil the desire of them that fear Him: He also will hear their cry, and will save them.

(Ps. 147:1–3) Praise ye the Lord: for *it is* good to sing praises unto our God; for *it is* pleasant; *and* praise is comely. The Lord doth build up Jerusalem: He gathereth together the outcasts of Israel. He healeth the broken in heart, and bindeth up their wounds. (Luke 4:18) The Spirit of the Lord *is* upon Me, because He hath anointed Me to preach the gospel to the poor; He hath sent Me to heal the brokenhearted, to preach deliverance to the captives, and recovering of sight to the blind, to set at liberty them that are bruised, To preach the acceptable year of the Lord.

(Pro. 1:23) Turn you at My reproof: behold, I will pour out My spirit unto you, I will make known My words unto you. (Jn. 16:7) Nevertheless I tell you the truth; It is expedient for you that I go away: for if I go not away the Comforter will not come unto you: but if I depart, I will send Him unto you. and understanding put forth her voice?

(Prov. 8:1, 22–35) Doeth not wisdom cry, The Lord possessed me in the beginning of His way, before His works of old. I was set up from everlasting, from the beginning, or ever the earth was. When *there were* no depths, I was brought forth; when *there were* no fountains abounding with water. Before the mountains were settled, before the hills was I brought forth: While as yet He had not made the earth, nor the fields, nor the highest part of the dust of the world. When He prepared the heavens, I *was* there: when He set a compass upon the face of the depth: When He established the clouds above: when He strengthened the fountains of the deep: When He gave to the sea His decree, that the waters should not pass His commandment: when He appointed the foundations of the earth: Then I was by Him, *as* one brought up *with Him*: and I was daily *His* delight, rejoicing always before Him; Rejoicing in the habitable part of His earth; and My delights *were* with the sons of men. Now therefore hearken unto Me, O ye children: for blessed *are they that* keep My ways. Hear instruction, and be wise, and refuse it not. Blessed *is* the man that heareth me, watching daily at my gates, waiting at the posts of my doors. For whoso findeth me findeth life, and shall obtain favour of the LORD. But he that sinneth against Me wrongeth his own soul: all they that hate Me love death. (1 Cor. 1:30) But of Him are ye in Christ Jesus, who of God is made unto us wisdom and righteousness and sanctification, and redemption:

(Pro. 30:4) Who hath ascended up into heaven, or descended? Who hath gathered the wind in His fists? Who hath bound the waters in a garment? Who hath established all the ends of the earth? What *is* His name, and what *is* His Son's name if thou canst tell? (Eph. 4:7–10) But unto every one of us is given grace according to the measure of the gift of Christ. Wherefore He saith, When He ascended up on high, He led captivity captive, and gave gifts unto men. (Now that He ascended, what is it but that He also descended first into the lower parts of the earth? He that descended is the same also that ascended up far above all heavens, that He might fill all things.)

(Eccl. 12:10–11) The preacher sought to find out acceptable words: and *that which was* written *was* upright, *even* words of truth. The words of the wise *are* as goads, and as nails fastened *by* the Master of assemblies, *which* are given from One Shepherd. (Heb. 13:20–21) Now the God of peace, that brought again from the dead our Lord Jesus, that Great Shepherd of the sheep, through the blood of the everlasting covenant. Make you perfect in every good work to do His will, working in you that which is wellpleasing in His sight, through Jesus Christ; to Whom *be* glory for ever and ever Amen.

(S.O.S. 1:3) Because of the savour of Thy good ointments Thy name is as ointment poured forth, therefore do the virgins love thee. (Phil. 2:9–10) Wherefore God also hath highly exalted Him, and given Him a name which is above every name: That at the name of Jesus every knee should bow, of *things* in heaven, and *things* in earth, and *things* under the earth;

(S.O.S. 1:12–13) While the king *sitteth* at His table, my spikenard sendeth forth the smell thereof. A bundle of myrrh *is* My well beloved unto me; He shall lie all night betwixt my breasts. (Mk. 14:3) And being in Bethany in the house of Simon the leper, as He sat at meat, there came a woman having an alabaster box of ointment of spikenard very precious; and she broke the box, and poured *it* on His head. (Mt. 2:11) And when they were come into the house they saw the young child with Mary His mother, and fell down, and worshipped Him: and when they had opened their treasures, they presented unto Him gifts; gold, and frankincense, and myrrh.

(S.O.S. 2:4) He brought me to the banqueting house, and His banner over me was love. (Rev. 19:9) And he saith unto me, Write, Blessed *are* they which are called unto the marriage supper of the Lamb. And he saith unto me, These are the true sayings of God.

(Isa. 2:3–4) And many people shall go and say, Come ye, and let us go up to the mountain of the LORD, to the house of the God of Jacob; and He will teach us of His ways, and we will walk in His paths: for out of Zion shall go forth the law, and the word of the Lord from Jerusalem. (Lk. 24:47–48) And that repentance and remission of sin should be preached in His name among all Nations, beginning at Jerusalem, and ye are witnesses of these things.
And He shall judge among the nations, and shall rebuke many people: and they shall beat their swords into plowshares, and their spears into pruninghooks: nation shall not lift up sword against nation, neither shall they learn war any more. (Jn. 5:22) For the Father judgeth no man, but has committed all judgement unto the Son;

(Isa. 4:2) In that day shall the Branch of the LORD be beautiful and glorious, and the fruit of the earth *shall* be excellent and comely for them that are escaped of Israel. (Jer. 23:5–6) Behold, the days come, saith the LORD, that I will raise unto David a righteous Branch, and a King shall reign and prosper, and shall execute judgement and justice in the earth. In His days Judah shall be saved, and Israel shall dwell safely: and this *is* His name whereby He shall be called, THE LORD OUR RIGHTEOUSNESS.

(Mt. 2:2) Saying, Where is He that is born King of the Jews? For we have seen His star in the east, and are come to worship Him.

(Isa. 5:1–6) Now will I sing to My wellbeloved a song of My beloved touching His vineyard. My wellbeloved hath a vineyard in a very fruitful hill: And He fenced it, and gathered out the stones thereof, and planted it with the choicest vine, and built a tower in the midst of it, and also made a winepress therein: and He looked that it should bring forth grapes, and it brought forth wild grapes. (Mt. 21:33–40) Hear another parable, there was a Certain Householder, which planted a vinyard, and hedge it round about, and digged a winepress in it, and built a tower, and let it out to husbandmen, and went into a far country: And when the time of the fruit drew near, He sent His servants to the husbandmen, that they might receive the fruits of it. And the husbandmen took His servants, and beat one, and killed another, and stoned another. Again, He sent other servants more than the first: and they did unto them likewise.

But last of all He sent unto them His Son, saying, They will reverence My Son.

But when the husbandmen saw the son, they said This is the heir; come, let us kill Him, and let us seize on His inheritance. And they caught Him, and Cast Him out of the vineyard, and slew *Him*. When the Lord therefore of the vinyard cometh, what will He do unto those Husbandman?

And now, O inhabitants of Jerusalem, and men of Judah, judge, I pray you, betwixt Me and My vineyard. What could have been done more to My vineyard, that I have not done in it? wherefore, when I looked that it should bring forth grapes, brought it forth wild grapes? And now go to; I will tell you what I will do to My vineyard: I will take away the hedge thereof, and it shall be eaten up; *and* break down the wall thereof, *and* it shall be trodden down: And I will lay it waste: it shall not be pruned, nor digged; but there shall come up briers and thorns: I will also command the clouds that they rain no rain upon it.

(Isa. 6:1) In the year that king Uzziah died I saw also the Lord sitting upon a throne, high and lifted up, and His train filled the temple. (Jn. 12:41) These things said Esaias, when he saw His glory, and spake of Him. **Above it stood the seraphims: each one had six wings; with twain he covered his face, and with twain he covered his feet, and with twain he did fly.** (Rev. 4:8) And the four beasts had each of them six wings about *him;* And *they were* full of eyes within: and they rest not day and night, saying Holy, holy, holy, Lord God Almighty which, was, and is, and is to come. **And one cried unto another, and said, Holy, holy, holy, *is* the LORD of hosts: the whole earth *is* full of His glory.**

(Isa. 6:8–10) Also I heard the voice of the Lord, saying, Whom shall I send, and who will go for Us? Then said I, Here *am* I; send Me. And He said, Go, and tell this people, Hear ye indeed, but understand not; and see ye indeed, but perceive not. Make the heart of this people fat, and make their ears heavy, and shut their eyes; lest they see with their eyes, and hear with their ears, and understand with their heart, and convert, and be healed. (Mt. 13:14–16) And in them is fulfilled the prophesy of Esaias, which saith, By hearing ye shall not hear, and shall not understand; and seeing ye shall not see, and shall not perceive: For this people's heart is waxed gross, and *their* ears are dull of hearing, and their eyes they have closed; lest at any time they should see with *their* eyes, and hear with *their* ears, and should understand with *their* heart, and should be converted, and I should heal them. But blessed *are your* eyes for they see: and your ears, for they hear.

(Isa. 7:14–16) Therefore the Lord himself shall give you a sign; Behold, a virgin shall conceive, and bear a son, and shall call His name Immanuel. Butter and honey shall He eat, that He may know to refuse the evil, and choose the good. For before the child shall know to refuse the evil, and choose the good, the land that thou abhorrest shall be forsaken of both her kings. (Lk. 1:35) And the angel answered and said unto her, The Holy Ghost shall come upon thee, and the power of the Highest shall overshadow thee:

therefore also that holy thing which shall be born of thee shall be called the Son of God. (Mt. 1:18–23) Now the birth of Jesus Christ was on this wise: When as His mother Mary was espoused to Joseph, before they came together, she was found with child of the Holy Ghost. Then Joseph her husband, being a just *man,* and not willing to make her a publick example, was minded to put her away privily. But while he thought on these things, behold the angel of the Lord appeared unto him in a dream saying, Joseph thou son of David, fear not to take unto thee Mary thy wife: for that which is conceived in her is of the Holy Ghost. And she shall bring forth a son, and thou shalt call His name JESUS: for He shall save His people from their sins. Now all this was done, that it might be fulfilled which was spoken of the Lord by the prophet, saying, Behold, a virgin shall be with child, and shall bring forth a son, and they shall call His name Emmanuel, which being interpreted is, God with us. (1 Tim. 3:16) And without controversy great is the mystery of godliness: God was manifest in the flesh, justified in the Spirit, seen of angels, preached unto the Gentiles, believed on in the world, received up into glory.

(Isa. 8:5–8) The Lord spake also unto me again, saying, Forasmuch as this people refuseth the waters of Shiloah that go softly, and rejoice in Rezin and Remaliah's son; Now therefore, behold, the Lord bringeth up upon them the waters of the river, strong and many, *even* the king of Assyria, and all his glory: he shall come up over all his channels, and go over all his banks: And he shall pass through Judah; he shall overflow and go over, he shall reach *even* to the neck; and the stretching out of his wings shall fill the breadth of thy land, O Immanuel. (Jn. 9:7, 11) And said unto him, Go, wash in the pool of Siloam (which is by interpretation, Sent.) He went his way therefore, and washed, and came seeing. He answered and said, A man that is called Jesus, made clay, and anointed mine eyes and said unto me, Go to the pool Siloam, and wash: and I went and washed, and I received sight. (Jn. 1:11) He came unto His own, and His own received Him not. (Mt. 1:23) Behold, a virgin shall be with child, and shall bring forth a son, and they shall call His name Emmanuel, which being interpreted is, God with us.

(Isa. 8:14) And He shall be for a sanctuary; but for a stone of stumbling and for a rock of offence to both the houses of Israel, for a gin and for a snare to the inhabitants of Jerusalem. (Rom. 9:33) As it is written Behold, I lay in Sion a stumblingstone and rock of offence: and whosoever believeth on Him shall not be ashamed. (1 Pet. 2:8) And a stone of stumbling, and a rock of offence, *even to them* which stumble at the word, being disobedient: whereunto also they were appointed.

(Isa. 9:1–2) Nevertheless the dimness *shall* not *be* such as *was* in her vexation, when at the first he lightly afflicted the land of Zebulun and the land of Naphtali, and afterward did more grievously afflict *her by* the way of the sea, beyond Jordan, in Galilee of the nations. The people that walked in darkness have seen a Great Light: they that dwell in the land of the shadow of death, upon them hath the Light shined.

(Mt. 4:12–16) Now when Jesus had heard that John was cast into prison, He departed into Galilee; And leaving Nazareth, He came and dwelt in Capernaum, which is upon the sea coast, in the borders of Zabulon and Nephthalim: That it might be fulfilled which was spoken by Esaias the prophet, saying, The land of Zabulon, and the land of Nephthalim, *by* the way of the sea, beyond Jordan, Galilee of the Gentiles; The people which sat in darkness saw great light; and to them which sat in the region and shadow of death light is sprung up. From that time Jesus began to preach, and to say, Repent: for the kingdom of heaven is at hand. (Eph. 5:8, 14) For ye were sometimes darkness, but now *are ye* light in the Lord: walk as children of light: Wherefore He saith, Awake thou that sleepest, and arise from the dead, and Christ shall give thee light. (Lk. 1:79) To give light to them that sit in darkness and *in* the shadow of death, to guide our feet into the way of peace.

(Isa. 9:6, 7) For unto us a child is born. (Acts 4:27, 30) For of a truth against Thy Holy child Jesus, whom Thou hast anointed, both Herod, and Pontius Pilate, with the Gentiles, and the people of Israel, were gathered together.

By stretching forth Thine hand to heal; and that signs and wonders may be done by the name of Thy Holy child Jesus, **unto us a Son is given:** (Lk. 1:31) And, behold, thou shalt conceive in thy womb, and bring forth a son, and shalt call His name JESUS. (Jn. 1:14) And the Word was made flesh, and dwelt among us, and we beheld His glory, the glory as of the only begotten of the Father, full of grace and truth. (Rom. 1:3–4) Concerning His Son Jesus Christ our Lord, which was made of the seed of David according to the flesh: and declared *to be* the Son of God with power, according to the Spirit of Hoilness, by the resurrection from the dead: **and the government shall be upon His shoulder:**

(Rev. 19:16) And He hath on *His* vesture and on His thigh a name written, KING OF KINGS, and LORD of LORDS, **And His name shall be called Wonderful,** (Mt. 21:15–16) And when the chief priests and scribes saw the wonderful things that He did, and the children crying in the temple, and saying, Hosanna to the Son of David; they were sore displeased, And said unto Him, Hearest thou what these say? And Jesus saith unto them, Yea; have ye never read, Out of the mouth of babes and sucklings thou hast perfected praise? **Counseller.** (Mat. 13:54) And when He was come into His own country, He taught them in their synagogue, insomuch that they were astonished, and said, Whence hath this *man* this wisdom, and *these* mighty works? (Jn. 6:68) Then Simon Peter answered Him, Lord to whom shall we go? Thou hast the words of eternal life. **The Mighty God,** (1 Cor. 1:24) But unto them which are called, both Jews and Greeks. Christ the power of God, and the wisdom of God. **The Everlasting Father,** (Jn. 8:58) Jesus said unto them, Verily, verily, I say unto you, Before Abraham was, I am. (Jn. 10:30) I and *My* Father are one. **The Prince of Peace.**

(Jn. 16:33) These things I have spoken unto you, that in Me ye might have peace. In the world ye have tribulation: but be of good cheer: I have overcome the world. **Of the increase of *His* government** and peace there *shall be* no end. (Lk. 1:32–33) He shall be great, and shall be called the Son of the Highest: and the Lord God shall give unto Him the throne of His father David: And He shall reign over the house of Jacob for ever; and of His kingdom there shall be no end. **upon the throne of David, and upon his kingdom, to order it, and to establish it with judgment and with justice from henceforth even for ever.** (Jn. 5:30) I can of Mine own self do nothing: as I hear, I judge: and My judgement is just; because I seek not Mine own will, but the will of the Father which hath sent Me. **The zeal of the LORD of Hosts will perform this.** (Jn. 10:30–32) I and my Father are one. The the Jews took up stones again to stone him. Jesus answered them, Many good works have I shewed you from My Father; for which of those works do ye stone Me? (Mt. 28:18) And Jesus came and spake unto them, saying, All power is given unto Me in heaven and in earth.

(Isa. 11:1–10) And there shall come forth a rod out of the stem of Jesse, (Heb. 7:14) For *it is* evident that our Lord sprang out of Juda; of which tribe Moses spake nothing concerning priesthood **and a Branch shall grow out of his roots: And the Spirit of the LORD shall rest upon Him,** (Mt. 3:16–17) And Jesus, when He was baptized, went up straightway out of the water: and, lo, the heavens were opened unto Him, and he saw the Spirit of God descending like a dove, and lighting upon Him: and lo a voice from heaven, saying, This is My beloved Son, in whom I am well pleased.

(Acts 10:38) How God anointed Jesus of Nazareth with the Holy Ghost and with power: Who went about doing good, and healing all that were oppressed of the devil; for God was with Him. **the spirit of wisdom and understanding.** (Col. 2:3) In whom are hid all the treasures of wisdom and knowledge **the spirit of counsel and might, the spirit of knowledge and of the fear of the LORD; And shall make Him of quick understanding in the fear of the LORD: and He shall not judge after the sight of His eyes,** (Lk. 6:8) But He knew their thoughts, and said to the man which had the withered hand, Rise up, and stand forth in the midst. And he arose and stood forth. (Jn. 2:25) And needed not that any should testify of man: for He knew what was in man. **neither reprove after the hearing of His** ears. But with righteousness shall He judge the poor, and reprove with equity for the meek of the earth: (Acts 17:31) Because He hath appointed a day, in which He will judge the world in righteousness by *that* man whom He hath ordained *whereof* He hath given assurance unto all *men,* in that He hath raised Him from the dead. **And He shall smite the earth with the rod of His mouth, and with the breath of His lips shall He slay the wicked.** (Rev. 19:15) And out of His mouth goeth a sharp sword, that with it He should smite the nations: and He shall rule them with a rod of iron: and He treadeth the winepress of the fierceness and wrath of Almighty God. **And righteousness shall be the girdle of His loins, and faithfulness the girdle of His reins.** (Rev. 19:11) And I saw heaven opened, and behold, a white horse; and He that sat upon him was called Faithful and True, and in righteousness He doeth judge and make war. **The wolf also shall dwell with the lamb, and the leopard shall lie down with the kid; and the calf and the young lion and the fatling together; and a little child shall lead them. And the cow and the bear shall feed; their young ones shall lie down together: and the lion shall eat straw like the ox. And the sucking child shall play on the hole of the asp, and the weaned child shall put his hand on the cockatrice' den. They shall not hurt nor destroy in all My holy mountian: for the earth shall be full of the knowledge of the LORD, as the waters cover the sea. And in that day there shall be a root of Jesse, which shall stand for an ensign of the people; to it shall the Gentiles seek:** (Jn. 12:20–21) And there were certain Greeks among them that came up to worship at the feast: The same came therefore to Philip, which was of Bethsaida of Galilee, and desired him, saying, Sir, we would see Jesus, **and His rest shall be glorious.** (Heb. 4:9–11) There remaineth therefore a rest to the people of God. For he that is entered into His rest, he also has hath ceased from his own works, as God *did* from His. Let us labour therefore to enter into that rest, lest any man fall after the same example of unbelief.

(Isa. 12:1–6) And in that day thou shalt say, O LORD, I will praise Thee: though Thou wast angry with me, thine anger is turned away, and Thou comfortedst me. Behold, God *is* my sal-

vation; I will trust, and not be afraid: for the LORD JEHOVAH *is* **my strength and** *my* **song; He also is become my salvation.** (Mt. 1:23) Behold, a virgin shall be with child, and bring forth a son, and they shall call His name Emmanuel, which being interpreted is, God with us **Therefore with joy shall ye draw water out of the wells of salvation. And in that day shall ye say, Praise the LORD, call upon His name, declare His doings among the people, make mention that His name is exalted.**

(Phil. 2:9–11) Wherefore God also hath highly exalted Him, and given Him a name which is above every name: That at the name of Jesus every knee should bow, of *things* in heaven, and *things* in earth, and *things* under the earth; And *that* every tongue should confess that Jesus Christ *is* Lord, to the glory of God the Father. **Sing unto the LORD: for He hath done excellent things: this** *is* **known in all the earth. Cry out and shout, thou inhabitant of Zion: for great** *is* **the Holy One of Israel in the midst of thee.**

(Isa. 22:21–25) I will clothe Him with thy robe, and strengthen Him with thy gridle, and I will commit Thy government into His hand; and He shall be a Father to the inhabitants of Jerusalem, and to the house of Judah. And the key of the house of David will I lay upon His shoulder; so He shall open, and none shall shut; and He shall shut, and none shall open. (Rev. 3:7) And to the angel of the church of Philadelphia write; These things saith He that is holy, He that is true, He that hath the key of David, He that openeth, and no man shutteth; and shutteth, and no man openeth; **And I will fasten Him** *as* **a nail in a sure place; and He shall be for a glorious throne to His father's house. And they shall hang upon Him all the glory of His Father's house, the offspring and the issue, all vessels of small quantity, from the vessels of cups, even to all the vessels of flagons. In that day, saith the Lord of hosts, shall the nail that is fastened in the sure place be removed, and be cut down, and fall; and the burden that was upon it shall be cut off: for the Lord hath spoken** *it.*

(Isa. 25:8) He will swallow up death in victory; and the Lord God will wipe away tears from off all faces; and the rebuke of His people shall He take away from off all the earth: for the LORD hath spoken *it*.

(1 Cor. 15:54–58) So when this corruptible shall have put on incorruption, and this mortal shall have put on immortality, then shall be brought to pass the saying that is written, Death is swallowed up in victory. O death, where *is* thy sting? O grave, where *is* thy victory? The sting of death *is* sin; and the strength of *sin is* the law. But thanks *be* to God, which giveth us the victory through our Lord Jesus Christ. Therefore, my beloved brethren, be ye stedfast, unmovable, always abounding in the work of the Lord, forasmuch as ye know that your labour is not in vain in the Lord.

(Isa. 26:19) Thy dead *men* shall live, *together with* my dead body shall they arise. Awake and sing, ye that dwell in dust: for thy dew *is as* the dew of herbs, and the earth shall cast out the dead. (Mt. 27:50–54)

Jesus when He had cried again with a loud voice, yielded up the ghost. And, behold, the vail of the temple was rent in twain from the top to the bottom; and the earth did quake, and the rocks rent; And the graves were opened; and many bodies of the saints which slept arose, and came out of the graves after His resurrection, and went into the holy city, and appeared unto many. Now when the centurion, and they that were with him, watching Jesus, saw the earthquake, and those things that were done, they feared greatly, saying, Truly this was the Son of God.

(Isa. 28:16) Therefore thus saith the Lord God, Behold, I lay in Zion for a foundation, a stone, a tried *stone,* a precious corner stone, a sure foundation: he that believeth shall not make haste. (1 Pet. 2:3–8) If so be that ye have tasted that the Lord *is* gracious. To whom coming, *as unto* a living stone, disallowed indeed of men, but chosen of God, *and* precious, Ye also, as lively stones, are built up a spiritual house, an holy priesthood, to offer up spiritual sacrifices, acceptable to God by Jesus Christ. Wherefore also it is contained in the scripture, Behold, I lay in Sion a chief corner stone, elect, precious: and he that believeth on Him shall not be confounded. Unto you therefore which believe *He is* precious: but unto them which be disobedient, the stone which the builders disallowed, the same is made the head of the corner, and a stone of stumbling, and a rock of offence, *even to them* which stumble at the word, being disobedient: whereunto also they were appointed.

(Isa. 29:13–14) Wherefore the Lord said, Forasmuch as this people draw near *Me* with their mouth, and with their lips do honour Me, but have removed their heart far from Me, and their fear toward Me is taught by the precept of men: (Mt. 15:7–9) *Ye* hypocrites, well did Esaias prophesy of you, saying, This people draweth nigh unto Me with their mouth, and honoureth Me with *their* lips; but their heart is far from Me. But in vain they do worship Me, teaching *for* doctrine the commandments of men. **Therefore, behold, I will proceed to do a marvellous work among this people, *even* a marvellous work and a wonder: for the wisdom of their wise *men* shall perish, and the understanding of their prudent *men* shall be hid.** (1 Cor. 1:18–31) For the preaching of the cross is to them that perish foolishness: but unto us which are saved it is the power of God. For it is written, I will destroy the wisdom of the wise, and will bring to nothing the understanding of the prudent. Where is the wise? Where is the scribe? Where *is* the disputer of this world? Hath not God made foolish the wisdom of this world? For after that in the wisdom of God the world by wisdom knew not God, it pleased God by the foolishness of preaching to save them that believe. For the Jews require a sign, and the Greeks seek after wisdom: But we preach Christ crucified, unto the Jews a stumbingblock, and unto the Greeks foolishness; But unto them which are called, both Jews and Greeks Christ the power of God, and the wisdom of God. Because the foolishness of God is wiser than men; and the weakness of God is stronger than men. For ye see your calling, brethren how that not many wise men after the flesh, not many mighty, not many noble, *are called:* But God hath chosen the foolish things of the world to confound the wise; and God hath chosen the weak things of the world to confound the things which are mighty; And base things of the world, and things which are despised, hath God chosen, *yea*, and things which are not, to bring to nought things that are: That no flesh should glory in His presence. But of Him are ye in Christ Jesus, who are of God is made unto us wisdom, and righteousness, and sanctification, and redemption: That according as it is written, He that glorieth, let him glory in the Lord.

(Isa. 33:22) For the LORD *is* our judge, the LORD *is* our lawgiver, the LORD *is* our king; He will save us.

(1 Tim. 1:16–17) Howbeit for this cause I obtained mercy, that in me first Jesus Christ might shew forth all longsuffering, for a pattern to them which should hereafter believe on Him to life everlasting. Now unto the King eternal, immortal, invisible, the only wise God, *be* honour and glory for ever and ever Amen.

(Isa. 34:4) And all the host of heaven shall be dissolved, and the heavens shall be rolled together as a scroll: and all their host shall fall down, as the leaf falleth off from the vine, and as a falling *fig* from the fig tree.

(2 Pet. 3:11–12) *Seeing* then *that* all these things shall be dissolved, what manner *of persons* ought ye to be in *all* holy conversation and godliness Looking for and hasting unto the coming of the day of God, wherein the heavens being on fire shall be dissolved, and the elements shall melt with fervent heat.

(Isa. 35:5–6) then the eyes of the blind shall be opened, and the ears of the deaf shall be unstopped. Then shall the lame *man* leap as an hart, and the tongue of the dumb sing: for in the wilderness shall waters break out, and streams in the desert. (Mt. 9:27–31) And when Jesus departed thence, two blind men followed Him, crying, and saying, *Thou* Son of David, have mercy on us. And when He was come into the house, the blind men came to Him: and Jesus saith unto them, Believe ye that I am able to do this? They said unto Him, Yea Lord. Then touched He their eyes, saying, According to your faith be it unto you. And their eyes were opened and Jesus straitly charged them, saying, See *that* no man know *it*. But they, when they were departed, spread abroad His fame in all that country. (Mt. 11:5–6) The blind receive their sight, and the lame walk, the lepers are cleansed, and the deaf hear, the dead are raised up, and the poor have the gospel preached to them. And blessed is *he,* whosoever shall not be offended in Me. (Mt. 12:22–23) Then was brought unto Him one possessed with a devil, blind, and dumb: and He healed him, insomuch that the blind and dumb both spake and saw. And all the people were amazed, and said, Is not this the son of David?

(Isa. 40:3–5) The voice of him that crieth in the wilderness, Prepare ye the way of the LORD, make straight in the desert a highway for our God. Every valley shall be exalted, and every mountain and hill shall be made low: and the crooked shall be made straight, and the rough places plain: (Lk. 3:3–6) And he (John the baptist) came into all the country about Jordan, preaching the baptism of repentance for the remission of sins; As it is written in the book of the words of Esaias the prophet, saying, The voice of one crying in the wilderness, Prepare ye the way of the Lord, make His paths straight. Every valley shall be filled, and every mountain and hill shall be brought low; and the crooked shall be made straight, and the rough ways *shall* be made smooth; And all flesh shall see the salvation of God. **And the glory of the LORD shall be revealed, and all flesh shall see *it* together: for the mouth of the Lord hath spoken *it.***

(Isa. 40:9–11) O Zion, that bringest good tidings, get thee up into the high mountain; O Jerusalem, that bringest good tidings, lift up thy voice with strength; lift *it* up, be not afraid; say unto the cities of Judah, Behold your God! (Jn. 1:34–36) And I saw, and bare record that this is the Son of God. Again the next day after John stood, and two of his disciples: And looking upon Jesus as He walked, he saith, Behold the Lamb of God! **Behold, the Lord GOD will come with strong *hand*, and His arm shall rule for Him: behold, His reward *is* with Him, and His work before Him.**

(Rev. 22:12) And, behold I come quickly; and My reward *is* with Me, to give every man according as his work shall be. **He shall feed His flock like a shepherd: He shall gather the lambs with His arm, and carry *them* in His bosom, *and* shall gently lead those that are with young.** (Jn. 10:11–18) I am the good Shepherd: the good Shepherd giveth His life for the sheep. But he that is an hireling, and not the Shepherd, whose own the sheep are not, seeth the wolf coming, and leaveth the sheep, and fleeth: and the wolf catcheth them, and scattereth the sheep. The hireling fleeth, because he is an hireling, and careth not for the sheep. I am the good Sheperd, and know My sheep, and am known of Mine. As the Father knoweth Me, even so know I the Father: and I lay down My life for the sheep. And other *sheep* I have, which are not of this fold: them also I must bring, and they shall hear My voice; and there shall be one fold, *and* One Sheperd. Therefore doth My Father love Me, because I lay down My life, that I might take it again. No man taketh it from Me. But I lay it down of Myself. I have power to lay it down, and I have power to take it again. This commandment have I received of My Father.

(Isa. 41:14) Fear not, thou worm Jacob, *and* ye men of Israel; I will help thee, saith the LORD, and thy redeemer, the Holy One Of Isreal. (Acts 3:14) But ye denied the Holy One and the Just, and desired a murderer to be granted unto you;

(Isa. 42:1–7) Behold My Servant, whom I uphold; Mine Elect, *in whom* My soul delighteth; (Mt. 3:17) And lo a voice from heaven, saying, This is My beloved Son, in Whom I am well pleased. **I have put My Spirit upon Him:** (Jn. 3:34) For He whom God hath sent speaketh the words of God: for God giveth not the Spirit by measure *unto Him*. **He shall bring forth judgement to the Gentiles. He shall not cry, nor lift up, nor cause His voice to be heard in the street. A bruised reed shall He not break, and the smoking flax shall He not quench: He shall bring forth the judgement unto truth. He shall not fail nor be discouraged, till He have set judgement in the earth: and the isles shall wait for His law.** (Mt. 12:21) And in His name shall the Gentiles trust. **Thus**

saith God the LORD, He that created the heavens, and stretched them out; He that spread forth the earth, and that which cometh out of it;

(Col. 1:16) For by Him were all things created, that are in heaven, and that are in earth, visible and invisible, whether *they be* thrones, or dominions, or principalities, or powers: all things were created by Him, and for Him. **He that giveth breath unto the people upon it, and Spirit to them that walk therein: I the Lord have called Thee in righteousness, and will hold Thine hand, and will keep Thee, and give Thee for a covenant of the people, for a light of the Gentiles;** (Lk. 2:32) A light to lighten the Gentiles and the glory of Thy people Israel. **To open the eyes, to bring out the prisoners from the prison, and them that sit in darkness out of the prison house.**

(Isa. 43:3, 10, 11) For I *am* the LORD thy God, the Holy One of Israel, thy Saviour: I gave Egypt *for* thy ransome, Ethiopia and Seba for thee. Ye *are* My witnesses, saith The LORD, and My Servant whom I have chosen: that ye may know and believe Me, and understand that I *am* He: before Me there was no God formed, neither shall there be after Me. I, *even* I, *am* the LORD; and beside Me *there is* no saviour. (2 Cor. 5:19) To wit, that God was in Christ, reconciling the world unto Himself, not imputing their trespasses unto them; and hath committed unto us the word of reconciliation.

(Isa. 44:3) For I will pour water upon him that is thirsty, and floods upon the dry ground: I will pour My Spirit upon thy seed, and My blessing upon thine offspring: (Jn. 4:10) Jesus Answered and said unto her, If thou knewest the gift of God, and Who it is that saith to thee, Give Me to drink; thou wouldest have asked of Him, and He would have given thee living water. (Jn. 16:7–13) Nevertheless I tell you the truth; It is expedient for you that I go away, the Comforter will not come unto you; but if I depart, I will send Him unto you. And when He is come He will reprove the world of sin and of righteousness, and of judgement: Of sin, because they believe not on Me; Of righteousness, because I go to My Father, and ye see Me no more; Of judgement, because the prince of this world is judged. I have yet many things to say unto you, but ye cannot bear them now. Howbeit when He, the Spirit of truth, is come, He will guide you into all truth: for He shall not speak of Himself; but whatsoever He shall hear, *that* shall He speak: and He will shew you things to come.

(Isa. 44:6) Thus saith the LORD the King of Israel, and His redeemer the LORD of hosts; I *am* the first, and I *am* the last; and beside Me *there* is no God. (Jn. 1:49) Nathanel answered and saith unto Him, Rabbi Thou art the Son of God; Thou art the King of Israel. (Rev. 1:8) I am Alpha and Omega the beginning and the ending, saith the Lord, which is, and which was, and which is to come the Almighty. (Rev. 22:13) I am the Alpha and Omega, the beginning and the end, the first and the last.

(Isa. 44:24) Thus saith the Lord, thy redeemer and He that formed thee from the womb, I *am* the LORD that maketh all *things;* that stretcheth forth the heavens alone; that spreadeth abroad the earth by Myself; (Eph. 3:9) And to make all *men* see what *is* the fellowship of the mystery, which from the beginning of the world hath been hid in God, who created all things by Jesus Christ:

(Isa. 45:21–25) Tell ye, and bring *them* near; yea, let them take counsel together: who hath declared this from ancient time? *who* hath told it from that time? *have* not I the LORD? and *there is* no God else beside me; a just God and a Saviour; *there is* none beside Me. Look unto Me, and be ye saved, all the ends of the earth: for I *am* God, and *there is* none else. (Phil. 3:20) For our conversation is in heaven; from whence also we look for the Saviour, the Lord Jesus Christ: **I have sworn by Myself, the word is gone out of My mouth *in* righteousness, and shall not return, That unto Me every knee shall bow, every tongue shall swear. Surely, shall *one* say, in the LORD have I righteousness and strength: *even* to Him shall men come; and all that are incensed against Him shall**

be ashamed. In the LORD shall all the seed of Israel be justified, and shall glory. (Phil. 2:10–11) That at the name of Jesus every knee should bow, of *things* in heaven, and *things* in earth, and *things* under the earth; and *that* every tongue should confess that Jesus Christ *is* Lord, to the glory of God the Father.

(Isa. 46:9–10) Remember the former things of old: for I *am* God, and *there is* none else; *I am* God, and there *is* none like me, Declaring the end from the beginning, and from ancient times *the things* that are not *yet* done, saying, My counsel shall stand, and I will do all My pleasure: (Jn. 13:19) Now I tell you before it come, that, when it is come to pass, ye may believe that I am *He.*

(Isa. 48:12) Hearken unto me, O Jacob and Israel, My called; I *am* He; I *am* the first, I also *am* the last. (Rev. 1:8, 17–18) I am Alpha and Omega, the beginning and the ending, saith the Lord, which is and which was, and which is to come, the Almighty. And when I saw Him, I fell at His feet as dead, And He laid His right hand upon me, saying unto me, Fear not; I am the first and the last: *I am* He that liveth, and was dead; and, behold, I am alive for evermore, Amen; and have the keys of hell and of death.

(Isa. 48:16–17) Come ye near unto Me, hear ye this; I have not spoken in secret from the beginning; from the time that it was, there *am* I: and now the Lord GOD, and His Spirit, hath sent Me. Thus saith the LORD, thy Redeemer, the Holy One of Israel; I *am* the LORD thy God which teacheth thee to profit, which leadeth thee by the way *that* thou shouldest go. (Jn. 3:2) The same came to Jesus by night, and said unto Him, Rabbi, we know that Thou art a teacher come from God: for no man can do these miracles that Thou doest, except God be with Him.

(Isa. 49:1–2) Listen, O isles, unto Me; and hearken, ye people, from far; The LORD hath called Me from the womb; from the bowels of My mother hath He made mention of My name. (Mt. 1:21) And she shall bring forth a son, and thou shall call His name JESUS, for He shall save His people from their sins. **And He hath made My mouth like a sharp sword; in the shadow of His hand hath He hid Me, and made Me a polished shaft; in His quiver hath He hid Me.** (Heb. 4:12) For the word of God *is* quick, and powerful, and sharper than any two edged sword, piercing even to the dividing asunder of soul and spirit, and the joints and marrow, and *is* a discerner of the thoughts and intents of the heart. (Rev. 2:16) Repent; or else I will come unto thee quickly, and will fight against them with the sword of My mouth. (Eph. 3:9) And to make all *men* see what *is* the fellowship of the mystery, which from the beginning of the world hath been hid in God, who created all things by Jesus Christ:

(Isa. 49:5–7) And now, saith the LORD that formed Me from the womb to *be* His Servant, to bring Jacob again to Him, Though Israel be not gathered, yet shall I be glorious in the eyes of the LORD, and My God shall be My strength. (Phil. 2:7) But made Himself of no reputation, and took upon Him the form of a servant, and was made in the likeness of men: **And he said, it is a light thing that Thou shouldest be My Servant to raise up the tribes of Jacob, and to restore the preserved of Israel: I will also give Thee for a light to the Gentiles, that Thou mayest be My salvation unto the end of the earth.** (Acts 15:16–17) After this I will return, and will build again the tabernacle of David, which is fallen down; and I will build again the ruins thereof, and I will set it up: That the residue of men might seek after the Lord, and all the Gentiles, upon whom My name is called, saith the Lord, who doeth all these things. **Thus saith the LORD, the Redeemer of Israel, *and* His Holy One, to Him whom man despiseth, to Him whom the nation abhorreth, to a servant of rulers, Kings shall see and arise, princes also shall worship, because of the LORD that is faithful, *and* The Holy One of Israel, and He shall choose Thee.** (Jn. 1:11) He came unto his own and His own received Him not.

(Isa. 49:26) And I will feed them that oppress thee with their own flesh; and they shall be drunken with their own blood, as

with sweet wine: and all flesh shall know that I the LORD *am* thy Saviour and thy Redeemer, the mighty One of Jacob.

(Isa. 50:2–6) Wherefore, when I came, *was there* no man? when I called, *was there* none to answer? Is My hand shortened at all, that it cannot redeem? or have I no power to deliver? behold, at My rebuke I dry up the sea, I make the rivers a wilderness: their fish stinketh, because *there is* no water, and dieth for thirst. I clothe the heavens with blackness, and I make sackcloth their covering. (Luke 23:44–45) And it was about the sixth hour, and there was darkness over all the earth until the nineth hour. And the sun was darkened, and the veil of the temple was rent in the midst. The Lord GOD hath given Me the tongue of the learned, that I should know how to speak a word in season to *him that is* weary: he wakeneth morning by morning, He wakeneth mine ear to hear as the learned. (Mt. 7:29) For He taught them as *one* having author- ity, and not as the scribes. The Lord God hath opened mine ear, and I was not rebellious, neither turned away back. (Mat. 26:39) And He went a little further, and fell on His face, and prayed, saying, O My Father, if it be possible, let this cup pass from Me: nevertheless not as I will. But as Thou *wilt*. I gave My back to the smiters, and My cheeks to them that plucked off the hair: I hid not My face from shame and spitting. (Mt. 27:26) Then released he Barabas unto them: and when he had scourged Jesus; he delivered *Him* to be crudifed. (Mt. 26:67) Then did they spit in His face, and buffeted Him; and others smote *Him* with the palms of their hands.

(Isa. 52:7) How beautiful upon the mountains are the feet of Him that bringeth good tidings, that publisheth peace; that brin- geth good tidings of good, that publisheth salvation; that saith unto Zion, Thy God reigneth!

(Rom. 10:15) And how shall they preach, except they be sent! As it is written, How beautiful are the feet of them that preach the gospel of peace, and bring glad tidings of good things?

(Isa. 52:13–53:12) Behold, My Servant shall deal prudently, He shall be exalted and extolled, and be very high. As many were astonied at Thee; His visage was so marred more than any man, and His form more than the sons of men: So shall He sprinkle many nations; the kings shall shut their mouths at Him:

(Eph. 1:19–23) And what *is* the exceeding greatness of His power to usward who believe, according to the working of His mighty power, which He wrought in Christ, when He rasied Him from the dead, and set *Him* at His own right hand in the heavenly *places,* Far above all principality, and power, and might, and dominion, and every name that is named, not only in this world, but also in that which is to come: And hath put all *things* under His feet, and gave Him *to be* the head over all *things* to the church, which is His body, the fulness of Him that filleth all in all.

(Lk. 18:31–34) Then He took *unto Him* the twelve, and said unto them, Behold, we go up to Jerusalem, and all things that are written by the prophets concerning the Son of man shall be accomplished. For He shall be delievered unto the Gentiles, and shall be mocked, and spitefully entreated, and spitted on: and they shall scourge *Him,* and put Him to death: and the third day He shall rise again.

(Heb. 9:13–14) For if the blood of bulls and goats, and the ashes of an heifer sprinkling the unclean, sanctifieth to the purifying of the flesh: How much more shall the blood of Christ, who through the eternal Spirit offered Himself without spot to God, purge your conscience from dead works to serve the living God? **for *that* which had not been told them shall they see; and *that* which they had not heard shall they consider.** (Rom. 15:21) But as it is written, To whom He was not spoken of, they shall see: and they that have not heard shall understand. **Who hath believed our report? And to whom is the arm of the LORD revealed?**

(Jn. 10:38) But if I do, though ye believe not Me, believe the works: that ye may know, and believe, that the Father *is* in Me, and I in Him. (Jn. 12:37–38) But though He had done so many miracles before them, yet they believed not on Him: That the saying of Esaias the prophet might be fulfilled, which he spake, Lord, who hath believed our report? and to whom hath the arm of the Lord been revealed? **For He shall grow up before Him as a tender plant, and as a root out of a dry ground: He hath no form nor comeliness;** (Phil. 2:6–8) Who, being in the form of God, thought it not robbery to be equal with God: But made Himself of no reputation, and took upon Him the form of a servant, and was made in the likeness of men: And being found in fashion as a man, He humbled Himself, and became obedient unto death, even the death of the cross, **and when we shall see Him,** *there is* **no beauty that we should desire Him. He is despised** (Lk. 4:28–29) And all they in the synagogue, when they heard these things, were filled with wrath, and rose up, and thrust Him out of the city, and led Him unto the brow of the hill whereon their city was built, that they might cast Him down head-long, **and rejected of men;** (Mt. 27:22–23) Pilate said unto them, What shall I do then with Jesus which is called Christ? *They* all say unto him, Let Him be crucified. And the governor said, Why, what evil hath He done? But they cried out the more, saying, Let Him be crucified. (Mk. 9:12) And He answered and told them, Elias verily cometh first, and restoreth all things; and how is it written of the Son of man, that He must suffer many things, and be set at nought, **a man of sorrows, and aquainted with grief:** (Heb. 4:15) For we have not an high priest which can not be touched with the feeling of our infirmities; but was in all points tempted like as *we are, yet* without sin. **and we hid as it were our faces from Him; He was despised, and we esteemed Him not.** (Jn. 1:10–11)

He was in the world, and the world was made by Him, and the world knew Him not. He came unto His own, and His own received Him not. **Surely He hath borne** *our* **griefs, carried our sorrows:** (Mt. 8:17) That it might be fulfilled which was spoken by Esias the prophet, saying, Himself took our infirmities, and bare *our* sicknesses. **Yet we did esteem Him stricken, smitten of God and afflicted. But He** *was* **wounded for our transgressions,** (Rom. 4:25) Who was delivered for our offences, and was raised again for our justification.

He was **bruised for our iniquities:** (2 Cor. 5:21) For He hath made Him *to be* sin for us, Who knew no sin; that we might be made the righteousness of God in Him. (Heb. 2:9) But we see Jesus, who was made a little lower than the angels for the suffering of death, crowned with glory and honour; that He by the grace of God should taste death for every man. **the chastisement of our peace was upon Him;** (Col. 1:20) And having made peace through the blood of His cross, by Him to reconcile all things unto Himself; by Him *I say,* whether *they be* things in earth, or things in heaven, **and with His stripes we are healed.** (1 Pet. 2:24) Who His own self bare our sins in His own body on the tree, that we, being dead to sins, should live unto righteousness: **All we like sheep have gone astray;** (Mt. 9:36) But when He saw the multitudes, He was moved with compassion on them, because they fainted, and were scattered abroad, as sheep having no shepherd. (1 Pet. 2:25) For ye were as sheep going astray; but are now returned unto the Shepherd and Bishop of your souls, **we have turned every one to his own way; and the LORD hath laid on Him the iniquity of us all.** (1 Jn. 2:2) And He is the propitiation for our sins: and not for ours only, but also *for the sins of* the whole world. (Gal. 1:4) Who gave Himself for our sins, that He might deliver us from this present evil world, according to the will of God and our Father: to Whom *be* glory for ever and ever. Amen.

He was oppressed, and He was afflicted, yet He opened not His mouth: (Mat. 27:13–14) Then Pilate said unto Him, Hearest thou not how many things they witness against thee? And He answered him to never a word; insomuch that the goveror marvelled greatly. **He is brought as a lamb to the slaughter, and as a sheep before her shearers is dumb, so He openeth not His mouth.** (Jn. 1:29) The next day John seeth Jesus coming unto him, and saith Behold, the Lamb of God, which taketh away the sin of the world. (1 Pet. 1:18–19) Forasmuch as ye know that ye were not redeemed with corruptible things, *as* silver and gold, from your vain conversation *received* by tradition from your fathers; But with the precious blood of Christ, as of a lamb without blemish and without spot: **He was taken from prison and from judgement: and who shall declare His generation?** (Jn. 7:27–28) Howbeit we know this man whence He is: but when Christ cometh, no man knoweth whence He is. Then cried Jesus in the temple as He taught, saying, Ye both know

Me, and ye know whence I am: and I am not come of Myself, but He that sent Me is true, Whom ye know not. **For He was cut off out of the land of the living: for the transgression of My people was He stricken. And He made His grave with the wicked, and the rich in His death;** (Mat. 27:57–60) When even was come, there came a rich man of Arimathea, named Joseph, who also himself was Jesus' disciple: He went to Pilate, and begged the body of Jesus. Then Pilate commanded the body to be delivered. And when Joseph had taken the body, he wrapped it in a clean linen cloth, and laid it in his own new tomb, which he had hewn out in the rock: and he rolled a great stone to the door of the sepulchre, and departed, **because He had done no violence, neither was *any* deceit in His mouth.** (1 Pet. 2:22–23) Who did no sin, neither was guile found in His mouth. Who, when He was reviled, reviled not again; when He suffered, He threatened not; but committed *Himself* to Him that judgeth righteously: **Yet it pleased the LORD to bruise Him; He hath put *Him* to grief: when Thou shalt make His soul an offering for sin,** (Mt. 20:28) Even as the Son of Man came not to be ministered unto, but to minister, and to give His life a ransome for many. **He shall see *His* seed, He shall prolong *His* days,** (Rom. 6:9) Knowing that Christ being raised from the dead dieth no more; death hath no more dominion over Him. **and the pleasure of the LORD shall prosper in His hand. He shall see of the travail of His soul, *and* shall be satisfied: by His knowledge My righteous Servant** (Phil. 3:8–9) Yea doubtless, and I count all things *but* loss for the excellency of the knowledge of Christ Jesus my Lord: for whom I have suffered the loss of all things, and do count them *but* dung, that I may win Christ, and be found in Him, not having mine own righteousness, which is of the law, but that which is through the faith of Christ, the righteousness which is of God by faith: **justify many;** (Rom. 5:18–19) Therefore as by the offence of one *judgement came* upon all men to condemnation; even so by the righteousness of one the *free gift came* upon all men unto justification of life. For as by one man's disobedience many were made sinners, so by the obedience of one shall many be made righteous, **for He shall bear their iniquities. Therefore will I divide Him a *portion* with the great, and He shall divide** the spoil with the strong; (Col. 2:15) And having spoiled principalities and powers, He made a shew of them openly, triumphing over them in it. **because He hath poured out His soul unto death: and He was numbered with the transgressors;** (Mk. 15:28) And the scripture was fulfilled, which saith, And He was numbered with the transgressors, **and He bare the sin of many, and made intercession for the transgressors.** (Rom. 8:34) Who *is* he that condemneth? *It is* Christ that died, yea rather, that is risen again, who is even at the right hand of God, who also maketh intercession for us.

(Isa. 54:5) For Thy maker *is* Thine husband; the LORD of hosts *is* His name: and thy Redeemer the Holy One of Israel; The God of the whole earth shall He be called. (Rev. 19:7–8) Let us be glad and rejoice, and give honour to Him: for the marriage of the Lamb is come, and His wife hath made herself ready. And to her was granted that she should be arrayed in fine linen, clean and white: for the fine linen is the righteousness of saints.

(Isa. 54:8) In a little wrath I hid My face from Thee for a moment; but with everlasting kindness will I have mercy on Thee, saith the Lord thy Redeemer. (Heb. 9:12) Neither by the blood of goats and calves, but by His own blood He entered in once into the holy place, having obtained eternal redemption *for us.*

(Isa. 55:1) Ho, every one that thirsteth, come ye to the waters, and he that hath no money; come ye, buy, and eat; yea, come, buy wine and milk without money and without price. (Jn. 7:37–38) In the last day, that great *day* of the feast, Jesus stood and cried, saying, If any man thirst, let him come unto Me, and drink. He that believeth on Me as the scripture hath said, out of his belly shall flow rivers of living water.

(Isa. 55:3–5) Incline your ear, and come unto Me: hear, and your soul shall live; and I will make an everlasting covenant with you, *even* the sure mercies of David. (Acts 13:34) And as concerning that He raised Him up from the dead, *now* no more to return to corruption, he said on this wise, I will give you the sure mercies of David. **Behold, I have given Him *for* a witness to the people, a leader and commander to the people.** (Jn. 18:37) Pilate therefore said unto Him, Art thou a king then? Jesus answered, Thou sayest that I am a king, To this end was I born, and for this cause came I into the world, that I should bear witness unto the truth, Every one that is of the truth heareth my voice.

(Heb. 2:10) For it became Him, for Whom *are* all things, and by Whom *are* all things, in bringing many sons unto glory, to make the captian of their salvation perfect through sufferings. **Behold, thou shalt call a nation *that* thou knowest not, and nations *that* knew not thee shall run unto thee because of the Lord thy God, and for the Holy One of Israel; for He hath glorified Thee.** (Acts 3:13) The God of Abraham, and Isaac, and of Jacob, the God of our fathers, hath glorified His Son Jesus; whom ye delievered up, and denied Him in the presence of Pilate, when he was determined to let *him* go.

(Isa. 59:16) And He saw that *there was* no man, and wondered that *there was* no intercessor: therefore His arm brought salvation unto Him; and His righteousness, it sustained Him. (Mt. 10:32) Whosoever therefore shall confess Me before men, him will I confess also before My Father which is in heaven. (Jn. 6:40) And this is the will of Him that sent Me, that every one which seeth the Son, and believeth on Him, may have everlasting life: and I will raise him up at the last day.

(Isa. 59:20) And the Redeemer shall come to Zion, and unto them that turn from transgression in Jacob, saith the LORD. (Rom. 11:26–27) And so all Israel shall be saved: as it is written, There shall come out of Sion the Deliverer, and shall turn away ungodliness from Jacob. For this *is My* covenant unto them, when I shall take away their sins. (Lk. 2:38) And she coming in that instant gave thanks likewise unto the Lord, and spake of Him to all them that looked for redemption in Jerusalem.

(Isa. 60:1–3) **Arise, shine; for thy light is come, and the glory of the LORD is risen upon Thee. For, behold, the darkness shall cover the earth, and gross darkness the people: but the LORD shall arise upon Thee, and His glory shall be seen upon Thee. And the Gentiles shall come to Thy light, and kings to the brightness of Thy rising.** (Acts 26:23) That Christ should suffer, and that He should be the first that should rise from the dead, *and* should shew light unto the people, and to the Gentiles.

(Isa. 60:16) **Thou shalt also suck the milk of the Gentiles, and shalt suck the breast of kings: and thou shalt know that I the LORD a***m* **thy Saviour and thy Redeemer, the mighty One of Jacob.** (Acts 5:31) Him hath God exalted with His right hand *to be* a Prince and a Saviour, for to give repentance to Israel, and forgiveness of Sins.

(Isa. 61:1–3) **The Spirit of the Lord GOD** *is* **upon Me; because the LORD hath anointed Me to preach good tidings unto the meek; He hath sent Me to bind up the brokenhearted, to proclaim liberty to the captives, and the opening of the prison to** *them that are* **bound; To proclaim the acceptable year of the LORD.** (Lk. 4:18–19) The Spirit of the Lord *is* upon Me, because He hath anointed Me to preach the gospel to the poor; He hath sent Me to heal the brokenhearted, to preach deliverance to the captives, and recovering of sight to the blind, to set at liberty them that are bruised, To preach the acceptable year of the Lord. (Mk. 1:38) And He said unto them, Let us go into the next towns, that I may preach there also: for therefore came I forth. **And the day of vengeance of our God;** (Mal. 4:1–3) For, behold, the day cometh, that shall burn as an oven; and all the proud, yea, and all that do wickedly, shall be stubble: and the day that cometh shall burn them up, saith the LORD of hosts, that it shall leave them neither root nor branch. But unto you that fear My name shall the Sun of righteousness arise with healing in His wings; and ye shall go forth, and grow up as calves of the stall. And ye shall tread down the wicked; for they shall be ashes under the soles of your feet in the day that I shall do *this*, saith the LORD of hosts.

(2 Thess. 1:7–10) And to you who are troubled rest with us, when the Lord Jesus shall be revealed from heaven with His mighty angels, In flaming fire taking vengeance on them that know not God, and that obey not the gospel of our Lord Jesus Christ: Who shall be punished with everlasting destruction from the presence of the Lord, and from the glory of His power; When He shall come to be glorified in His saints, and to be admired in all them that believe (because our testimony among you was believed) in that day. **To comfort all that mourn; To appoint unto them that mourn in Zion, to give unto them beauty for ashes, and oil of joy for mourning, the garment of praise for the spirit of heaviness; that they might be called trees of righteousness, the planting of the LORD that He might be glorified.**

(Isa. 61:10) I will greatly rejoice in the LORD, my soul shall be joyful in my God; for He hath clothed me with the garments of salvation, He hath covered Me with the robe of righteousness, as a bridegroom decketh *himself* with ornaments, and as a bride adometh *herself* with her jewels. (Rev. 21:2) And I John saw the holy city, new Jerusalem, coming down from God out of heaven, prepared as a bride adorned for her husband.

(Isa. 62:11) Behold, the LORD hath proclaimed unto the end of the world, Say ye to the daughter of Zion, Behold, thy salvation cometh; behold, His reward *is* with Him, and His work before Him. (Lk. 2:30–32) (Simeon) For mine eyes have seen Thy salvation, which Thou hast prepared before the face of all people; a light to lighten the Gentiles, and the glory of Thy people Israel.

(Isa. 63:4–5) For the day of vengeance *is* in Mine heart, and the year of My redeemed is come. And I looked, and *there was* none to help; and I wondered that *there was* none to uphold: therefore Mine own arm brought salvation unto Me; and My fury, it upheld Me. (2 Cor. 5:19) To wit, that God was in Christ, reconciling the world unto Himself, not imputing their trespasses unto them; and hath committed unto us the word of reconciliation.

(Isa. 63:8) **For He said, Surely they *are* My people, children *that* will not lie: so He was their Saviour.**

(2 Tim. 1:10) But is now made manifest by the appearing of our Saviour Jesus Christ, Who hath abolished death, and hath brought life and immortality to light through the gospel:

(Isa. 63:16) **Doubtless Thou *art* our Father, though Abraham be ignorant of us, and Israel acknowledge us not: Thou O LORD, *art* our Father, our redeemer; Thy name *is* from everlasting.** (Gal. 4:6) And because ye are sons, God hath sent forth the Spirit of His Son into your hearts, crying, Abba, Father.

(Isa. 65:9) **And I will bring forth a seed out of Jacob, and out of Judah an inheritor of My mountains: and Mine elect shall inherit it, and My servants shall dwell there.** (Heb. 7:14) For *it is* evident that our Lord sprang out of Juda; of which tribe Moses spake nothing concerning priesthood.

(Isa. 65:17–19) **For, behold, I create new heavens and a new earth: and the former shall not be remembered, nor come into mind.** (2 Pet. 3:13) Nevertheless we, according to His promise, look for new heavens and a new earth, wherein dwelleth righteousness. (Rev. 21:1) And I saw a new heaven and a new earth: for the first heaven and the first earth were passed away; and there was no more sea. **But be ye glad and rejoice for ever *in that* which I create: for, behold, I create Jerusalem a rejoicing, and her people a joy. And I will rejoice in Jerusalem, and joy in My people: and the voice of weeping shall be no more heard in her, nor the voice of crying.**

(Isa. 66:18–19) **For I know their works and their thoughts: it shall come, that I will gather all nations and tongues; and they shall come, and see My glory. And I will set a sign among them.** (Lk. 2:34) And Simeon blessed them, and said unto Mary His mother, Behold, this *child* is set for the fall and rising again of many in Israel; and for a sign which shall be spoken against, **unto the nations, to Tarshish, Pul, and Lud, that draw the bow, to Tubal, and Javan, to** the isles afar off, that have not heard My fame, neither have seen My glory; and they shall declare My glory among the Gentiles.

(Jer. 14:8) O the hope of Israel, the saviour thereof in time of trouble, why shouldest thou be a stranger in the land, and as a wayfaring man *that* turneth aside to tarry for a night? (Acts 28:20) For this cause therefore have I called for you, to see *you*, and to speak with *you*: because that for the hope of Israel I am bound with this chain.

(Jer. 23:5–8) Behold, the days come, saith the LORD, that I will raise unto David a righteous Branch,

(Jn. 15:1) I AM the true vine, and My Father is the husband-man. Every branch in Me that beareth not fruit He taketh away: and every *branch* that beareth fruit, He purgeth it, that it may bring forth more fruit. **and a King shall reign and prosper, and shall execute judgement and justice in the earth.** (Mt. 2:2) Saying, Where is He that is born King of the Jews? For we have seen His star in the east, and are come to worship Him. **In His days Judah shall be saved, and Israel shall dwell safely: and this *is* His name whereby He shall be called, THE LORD OUR RIGHTEOUSNESS.** (Heb. 1:8–9) But unto the Son He *saith* Thy throne, O God, *is* for ever and ever: a sceptre of righteousness *is* the sceptre of Thy kingdom. Thou hast loved righteousness, and hated iniquity; therefore God *even* Thy God hath anointed Thee with the oil of gladness above thy fellows. **Therefore, behold, the days come, saith the LORD, that they shall no more say, The LORD liveth, which brought up the children of Israel out of the land of Egypt; But the LORD liveth, which brought up and which led the seed of the house of Israel out of the north country, and from all countries whither I had driven them; and they shall dwell in their own land.**

(Jer. 30:9) But they shall serve the LORD their God, and David their king, whom I will raise up unto them.

(Jn. 18:37) Pilate therefore said unto Him, Art thou a king then? Thou sayest I am a king. To this end was I born, and for this cause came I into the world, that I should bear witness unto the truth, Every one that is of the truth heareth My voice.

(Jer. 31:15) Thus saith the LORD; A voice was heard in Ramah, lamentation, *and* bitter weeping; Rahel weeping for her children refused to be comforted for her children, because they *were* not. (Mt. 2:16–18) Then Herod when he saw that he was mocked of the wise men, was exceeding wroth, and sent forth, and slew all the children that were in Bethlehem and in all the coasts thereof, from two years old and under, according to the time which he had diligently inquired of the wise men. Then was fulfilled that which Jeremy the prophet, saying, In Rama was there a voice heard, lamentation, and weeping, and great mourning, Rachel weeping *for* her children, and would not be comforted, because they are not.

(Jer. 31:21–22) Set thee up waymarks, make thee high heaps: set thine heart toward the highway, *even* the way *which* thou wentest: turn again, O virgin of Israel, turn again to these thy cities. How long wilt thou go about, O thou backsliding daughter? for the LORD hath created a new thing in the earth, A woman shall compass a man.
(Mt. 1:18) Now the birth of Jesus Christ was on this wise: When as His mother Mary was espoused to Joseph, before they came together, she was found with child of the Holy Ghost.

(Jer. 31:31–32) Behold, the days come, saith the LORD, that I will make a new covenant with the house of Israel, and with the house of Judah: Not according to the covenant that I made with their fathers in the day *that* I took them by the hand to bring them out of the land of Egypt; which My covenant they brake, although I was an husband unto them, saith the LORD:
(Mt. 26:28–29) For this is My blood of the new testament, which is shed for many for the remission of sins. But I say unto you, I will not drink henceforth of this fruit of the vine, until that day when I drink it new with you in My Father's kingdom.

(Jer. 33:14–15) Behold, the days come, saith the LORD, that I will perform that good thing which I have promised unto the house of Israel and to the house of Judah. In those days, and at that time, will I cause the Branch of righteousness to grow up unto David; and He shall execute judgement and righteousness in the land.
(Luke 2:40) And the child grew, and waxed strong in spirit, filled with wisdom: and the grace of God was upon Him.

(Jer. 50:34) Their Redeemer *is* strong; the LORD of hosts *is* His name: He shall throughly plead their cause, that He may give rest to the land, and disquiet the inhabitants of Babylon.
(Lk. 2:40) And the child grew, and waxed strong in spirit, filled with wisdom: and the grace of God was upon Him.

(Jer. 50:1–51:64) Babylon's Judgement. (Rev. 18:1–24) Babylon's fall.

(Lam. 3:22–26) *It is of* the LORD'S mercies that we are not comsumed, because His compassions fail not. *They are* new every morning: great *is* Thy faithfulness. The LORD *is* my portion, saith my soul; therefore will I hope in Him. The LORD *is* good unto them that wait for Him, to the soul *that* seeketh Him. *It is* good that a *man* should both hope and quietly wait for the salvation of the LORD. (Lk. 2:25–32) And behold there was a man in Jerusalem whose name *was* Simeon, and the same man *was* just and devout, waiting for the consolation of Israel and the Holy Ghost was upon him, and it was revealed unto him by the Holy Ghost, that he should not see death, before he had seen the Lord's Christ. And he came by the Spirit into the temple: and when the parents brought in the child Jesus, to do for Him after the custom of the law, Then took he Him up in his arms, and blessed God, and said, Lord, now lettest thou thy servant depart in peace, according to Thy word: For mine eyes have seen Thy salvation, Which Thou hast prepared before the face of all people; A light to lighten the Gentiles, and the glory of Thy people Israel.

(Ezek. 17:22–24) Thus saith the Lord GOD; I will also take of the highest branch of the high cedar, and will set *it***; I will crop off from the top of his young twigs a tender one, and will plant** *it* **upon an high mountain and eminent: In the mountain of the height of Israel will I plant it: and it shall bring forth boughs, and bear fruit, and be a goodly cedar: and under it shall dwell all fowl of every wing; in the shadow of the branches thereof shall they dwell. And all the tress of the field shall know that I the LORD have brought down the high tree, have exalted the low tree, have dried up the green tree, and have made the dry tree to flourish, I the LORD have spoken and have done** *it***.** (Mt. 13:31–32) Another parable put He forth unto them, saying, The kingdom of heaven is like to a grain of mustard seed, which a man took, and sowed in in his field: Which indeed is the least of all seeds: but when it is grown, it is the greatest among herbs, and becometh a tree, so that the birds of the air come and lodge in the branches thereof.

(Ezek. 21:26–27) Thus saith the Lord GOD; Remove the diadem, and take off the crown: this *shall* **not be the same: exalt** *Him that is* **low, and abase** *him that is* **high. I will overturn, over-turn, overturn, it: and it shall be no** *more* **until He come whose right it is; and I will give it** *Him***.** (Lk. 1:52) He hath put down the mighty from *their* seats, and exalted them of low degree.

(Ezek. 34:23–24) And I will set up One Shepherd over them, and He shall feed them, *even* **my servant David; he shall feed them, and he shall be their shepherd. And I the LORD will be their God, and my servant David a prince among them; I the LORD have spoken** *it***.** (1 Pet. 5:4) And when the Chief Shepherd appears, ye will receive the crown of glory that does not fade away.

(Dan. 2:34–35) Thou sawest till that a Stone was cut out without hands, which smote the image upon his feet *that were* **of iron and clay, and brake them to pieces. Then was the iron, the clay, the brass, the silver, and the gold, broken to pieces together, and became like the chaff of the summer threshingfloors; and**

the wind carried them away, that no place was found for them: and the Stone that smote the image became a great mountain, and filled the whole earth. (Acts 4:10–12) Be it known unto you all, and to all the people of Israel, that by the name of Jesus Christ of Nazareth, whom *ye* crucified, whom God rasied from the dead, *even* by Him doth this man stand here before you whole. This is the Stone which was set at nought of you builders, which is become the head of the corner. Neither is there salvation in any other: for there is none other name under heaven given among men whereby we must be saved.

(Dan. 2:44–45) And in the days of these kings shall the God of heaven set up a kingdom, which shall never be destroyed: and the kingdom shall not be left to other people, *but* it shall break in pieces and consume all these kingdoms, and it shall stand for ever. Forasmuch as thou sawest that the Stone was cut out of the mountain without hands, and that it brake in pieces the iron, the brass, the clay, the silver, and the gold; the great God hath made known to the king what shall come to pass hereafter: and the dream *is* certain, and the interpretation thereof sure. (Mt. 21:44) And whosoever shall fall on this Stone shall be broken: but on whomsoever it shall fall, it will grind him to powder.

(Dan. 3:25) He answered and said, Lo, I see four men loose, walking in the midst of the fire, and they have no hurt; and the form of the forth is like the Son of God. (Mt. 26:63–64) But Jesus held His peace, and the high priest answered and said unto Him, I adjure Thee by the living God, that Thou tell us whether Thou be the Christ, the Son of God. Jesus saith unto him, Thou hast said: nevertheless I say unto you, Hereafter shall ye see the Son of man sitting on the right hand of power, and coming in the clouds of heaven.

(Dan. 7:13–14) I saw in the night visions, and, behold, *one* like the Son of man came with the clouds of heaven, (Acts 1:9) And when He had spoken these things, while they beheld, He was taken up; and a cloud received Him out of their sight, **and came**

to the Ancient of days, and they brought him near before him. And there was given Him dominion, (Eph. 1:20–22) Which He wrought in Christ, when He raised Him from the dead, and set *Him* at His own right hand in the heavenly *places*. Far above all principality, and power, and might, and dominion, and every name that is named, not only in this world, but also in that which is to come: And hath put all *things* under His feet, and gave Him *to be* the head over all *things* to the church, **and glory, and a kingdom, that all people, nations, and languages, should serve Him: His dominion *is* an everlasting dominion, which shall not pass away, and His kingdom *that* which shall not be destroyed.**

(Dan. 9:23–27) At the beginning of thy supplications the commandment came forth, and I am come to shew *thee*; for thou *art* greatly beloved: therefore understand the matter, and consider the vision. Seventy weeks are (Gen. 29:27) Fulfil her (Rachel) week, and we will give thee this also for the service which thou shalt serve with me yet seven years, **determined upon Thy people and upon Thy holy city, to finish the transgression, and to make an end of sins.** (Gal. 1:3–5) Grace *be* to you and peace from God the Father, and *from* our Lord Jesus Christ, Who gave Himself for our sins, that He might deliver us from this present evil world, according to the will of God and our Father: To Whom *be* glory for ever and ever Amen. **And to make reconciliation for iniquity, and to bring in everlasting righteousness and to seal up the vision** (Rom. 5:10) For if, when we were enemies, we were reconciled to God by the death of his Son, much more, being reconciled, we shall be saved by His life. (2 Cor. 5:18–20) And all things *are* of God, Who has reconciled us to Himself by Jesus Christ, and hath given to us the ministry of reconciliation: To wit, that God was in Christ, reconciling the world unto Himself, not imputing their trespasses unto them: and hath committed unto us the word of reconciliation. Now then we are ambassadors for Christ, as though God did beseech *you* by us: we pray *you* in Christ's stead, be ye reconciled to God. For He hath made Him *to be* sin for us, Who knew no sin; that we might be made the righteousness of God in Him. **And prophecy, and to anoint the most Holy. Know therefore**

and understand, *that* **from the going forth of the commandment to restore and to build Jerusalem** (Neh. 2:5–8) And I said unto the king, if it please the king, and if thy servant have found favour in thy sight, that thou wouldest sent me unto Judah, unto the city of my fathers' sepulchres, that I may build it. And the king said unto me (the queen also sitting by him) For how long shall thy journey be? And when wilt thou return? So it pleased the king to send me: and I set him a time. Moreover I said unto the king, If it please the king, let letters be given me to the governors beyond the river, that they may convey me over till I come into Judah; And a letter unto Asaph the keeper of the king's forest, that he may give me timber to make beams for the gates of the palace which *appertained* to the house, and for the wall of the city, and for the house that I shall enter into. And the King granted me, according to the good hand of my God upon me. **unto the Messiah the Prince** *shall be* **seven weeks, and threescore and two weeks:** (Jn. 12:12–13) On the next day much people that were come to the feast, when they heard that Jesus was coming to Jerusalem. Took branches of palm trees, and went forth to meet Him, and cried, Hosanna: Blessed *is* the King of Israel that cometh in the name of the Lord. (Lk. 19:41–44) And when He was come near, He beheld the city, and wept over it, Saying, If thou hast known, even thou, at least in this thy day, the things *which belong* unto thy peace! But now they are hid from thine eyes. For the days shall come upon thee, that thine enemies shall cast a trench about thee, and compass thee round, and keep thee in on every side. And shall lay thee even with the ground, and thy children within thee; and they shall not leave in thee one stone upon another; because thou knewest not the time of thy visitation. **The street shall be built again, and the wall, even in troublous times. And after threescore and two weeks shall Messiah be cut off, but not for Himself:** (Mt. 27:50–54) Jesus when He had cried again with a loud voice, yielded up the ghost. And, Behold, the veil of the temple was rent in Twain from the top to the bottom; and the earth did quake, and the rocks rent; And the graves were opened; and many bodies of the saints which slept arose, And came out of the graves after His resurrection, and went into the holy city, and appeared unto many. Now when the centurion, and they that were with him, watching Jesus, saw the earthquake and those things that were done, they feared greatly, saying, Truly this was the Son of God. (Heb. 2:9) But we see Jesus, who was made a little lower than the angels for the suffering of death, crowned with glory and honour; that He by the grace of God should taste death for every man. **and the people of the prince that shall come shall destroy the city and the sanctuary; and the end thereof *shall be* with a flood, and unto the end of the war desolations are determined. And he shall confirm the covenant with many for one week: and in the midst of the week he shall cause the sacrifice and the oblation to cease, and for the overspreading of adominations he shall make *it* desolate, even until the cosummation, and that determined shall be poured upon the desolate.**

(Dan. 10:5–6) Then I lifted up mine eyes, and looked, and behold a certain man clothed in linen, Whose loins *were* girded with fine gold of Uphaz: His body also *was* like the beryl, and His face as the appearance of lightning, and His eyes as lamps of fire, and His arms and His feet like in colour to polished brass, and the voice of His words like the voice of a multitude. (Rev. 1:13–16) And in the midst of the seven candlesticks *one* like unto the Son of man, clothed with a garment down to the foot, and girt about the paps with a golden girdle. His head and *His* hairs *were* white like wool, as white as snow; and His eyes *were* as a flame of fire; And His feet like unto fine brass, as if they burned in a furnace; and His voice as the sound of many waters. And He had in His right hand seven stars: and out of His mouth went a sharp two edge sword: and His countenance was as the sun shineth in his strength.

(Hos. 3:5) Afterward shall the children of Israel return, and seek the LORD their God, and David their king; and shall fear the LORD and His goodness in the latter days. (Jn. 18:37) Pilate therefore said unto Him, Art Thou a king then? Jesus answered, Thou sayest I am a king, To this end was I born, and for this cause came I into the world, that I should bear witness unto the truth, Every one that is of the truth heareth My voice. (Rom. 11:25–27)

For I would not, brethren, that ye should be ignorant of this mystery, lest ye should be wise in your own conceits; that blindness in part is happened to Israel, until the fulness of the Gentiles be come in. And so all Israel shall be saved: as it is written, There shall come out of Sion the Deliverer, and shall turn away ungodliness from Jacob: For this *is*, My covenant unto them, when I shall take away their sins.

(Hos. 11:1) When Israel *was* a child, then I loved him, and called My Son out of Egypt. (Mt. 2:14–15) When he arose, he took the young child and His mother by night, and departed into Egypt: And was there until the death of Herod: that it might be fulfilled which was spoken of the Lord by the prophet, saying, Out of Egypt have I called My Son.

(Hos. 13:4) Yet I *am* the LORD thy God from the land of Egypt, and thou shalt know no god but Me: for *there is* no saviour beside Me. (Mt. 2:14–15) When he arose, he took the Young Child and His mother by night, and departed into Egypt: And was there until the death of Herod: that it might be fulfilled which was spoken of the Lord by the prophet, saying, Out of Egypt have I called My Son.

(Joel 2:28–32) And it shall come to pass afterward, *that* I will pour out My Spirit upon all flesh; and your sons and your daughters shall prophesy, your old men shall dream dreams, your young men shall see visions: And also upon the servants and upon the handmaids in those days will I pour out My Spirit. And I will shew wonders in the heavens and in the earth, blood, and fire, and pillars of smoke. The sun shall be turned into darkness, and the moon into blood, before the great and the terrible day of the LORD come. And it shall come to pass *that* whosoever shall call on the name of the LORD shall be delivered: for in mount Zion and in Jerusalem shall be deliverance, as the LORD hath said, and in the remnant whom the LORD shall call. (Acts 2:17–21) And it shall come to pass in the last days, saith God, I will pour out of My Spirit upon all flesh: and your sons and your daughters shall prophesy, and your young men shall see visions, and your old men shall dream dreams: and on My servants and on My handmaidens I will pour out in those days of My Spirit; and they shall prophesy: And I will shew wonders in the heaven above, and signs in the earth beneath; blood, and fire, and vapour of smoke: The sun shall be turned into darkness, and the moon into blood, before that great and notable day of the Lord come: And it shall come to pass, *that* whosoever shall call on the name of the Lord shall be saved.

(Amos 8:9) And it shall come to pass in that day, saith the Lord God, that I will cause the sun to go down at noon, and I will darken the earth in the clear day: (Mt. 24:29) Immediately after the tribulation of those days shall the sun be darkened, and the moon shall not give her light, and the stars shall fall from heaven, and the powers of the heavens shall be shaken: (Acts 2:20) The sun shall be turned into darkness, and the moon into blood, before that great and notable day of the Lord come: (Rev. 6:12) And I beheld when He had opened the sixth seal, and, lo, there was a great earthquake; and the sun became black as sackcloth of hair, and the moon became as blood:

(Amos 9:11–12) In that day will I raise up the tabernacle of David that is fallen, and close up the breaches thereof; and I will raise up his ruins, and I will build it as in the days of old: That they may possess the remnant of Edom, and of all the heathen, which are called by My name, saith the LORD that doeth this. (Acts 15:16–17) After this I will return, and will build again the tabernacle of David, which is fallen down; and I will build again the ruins thereof, and I will set it up: That the residue of men might seek after the Lord, and all the Gentiles, upon whom My name is called, saith the Lord, who doeth all these things.

(Obad. 1:21) And saviours shall come up on mount Zion to judge the mount of Esau; and the kingdom shall be the LORD'S. (Rev. 19:6) And I heard as it were the voice of a great multitude, and as the voice of many waters, and as the voice of mighty thunderings, saying, Alleluia: for the Lord God omnipotent reigneth.

(Jonah 1:17) Now the LORD had prepared a great fish to swallow up Jonah. And Jonah was in the belly of the fish three days and three nights. (Mt. 12:40, 16:4) For as Jonas was three days and three nights in the whale's belly; so shall the Son of man be three days and three nights in the heart of the earth. A wicked and adulterous generation seeketh after a sign; and there shall no sign be given unto it, but the sign of the prophet Jonas, And He left them, and departed.

(Mic. 5:2) But thou, Bethlehem Ephratah, *though* thou be little among the thousands of Judah, *yet* out of thee shall He come forth unto Me *that is* to be ruler in Israel; whose going forth *have been* from of old, from everlasting. (Mt. 2:6) And thou Bethlehem, *in* the land of Juda, art not the least among the princes of Juda: for out of thee shall come a Governor, that shall rule My people Israel. (Jn. 7:42) Hath not the scripture said, That Christ cometh of the seed of David, and out of the town of Bethlehem, where David was? (Jn. 1:1–5) In the beginning was the Word, and the Word was with God, and the Word was God. The same was in the beginning with God.

All things were made by Him; and without Him was not anything made that was made. In Him was life; and the life was the light of men. And the light shineth in darkness; and the darkness comprehended it not.

(Nahum 1:15) Behold upon the mountains the feet of Him that bringeth good tidings, that publisheth peace! O Judah, keep thy solemn feasts, perform thy vows: for the wicked shall no more pass through thee; he is utterly cut off. (Rom. 10:15) And how shall they preach, except they be sent? As it it written, How beautiful are the feet of them that preach the gospel of peace, and bring glad tidings of good things!

(Hab. 2:4) Behold, his soul *which* is lifted up is not upright in him: But the just shall live by his faith.

(Rom. 2:16–17) For I am not ashamed of the gospel of Christ: for it is the power of God unto salvation to every one that believeth; to the Jew first, and also to the Greek. For therein is the righteousness of God revealed from faith to faith: as it is written, The just shall live by faith.

(Hab. 2:14) For the earth shall be filled with the knowledge of the glory of the LORD, as the waters cover the sea.

(Rev. 21:23–26) And the city had no need of the sun, neither of the moon, to shine in it: for the glory of God did lighten it, and the Lamb is the light thereof. And the nations of them which are saved shall walk in the light of it: and the kings of the earth do bring their glory and honour into it. And the gates of it shall not be shut at all by day: for there shall be no night there. And they shall bring the glory and honour of the nations into it.

(Zeph. 3:14–18) Sing, O daughter of Zion; shout, O Israel; be glad and rejoice with all the heart, O daughter of Jerusalem. The LORD hath taken away thy judgements, He hath cast out thine enemy: the King of Israel, *even* the LORD, *is* in the midst of thee: (Jn. 12:13) Took branches of palm trees, and went forth to meet Him, and cried, Hosanna: Blessed *is* the King of Israel that cometh in the name of the Lord. **thou shalt not see evil any more. In that day it shall be said to Jerusalem, Fear thou not; *and to* Zion, Let not thine hands be slack.** (Heb. 12:12) Wherefore lift up the hands which hang down, and the feeble knees; And make straight paths for your feet, lest that which lame be turned out of the way; but let it rather be healed. **The LORD thy God in the midst of thee *is* mighty: He will save, He will rejoice over thee with joy; He will rest in His love, He will joy over thee with singing. I will gather *them that are* sorrowful for the solemn assembly, *who* are of thee, *to whom* the reproach of it *was* a burden.**

(Hag. 2:6–9) For thus saith the LORD of hosts; Yet once, it *is* a little while, and I will shake the heavens, and the earth, and the sea, and the dry *land*; (Heb. 12:26–29) Whose voice then shook the earth: but now He hath promised, saying, Yet once more I shake not the earth only, but also heaven. And this *word,* Yet once more, signifieth the removing of those things that are shaken, as of things that are made, that those things which cannot be shaken may remain. Wherefore we receiving a kingdom which cannot be moved, let us have grace, whereby we may serve God acceptably with reverence and godly fear: For our God is a consuming fire. **And I will shake all nations, and the desire of all nations shall come: and I will fill this house with glory, saith the LORD of hosts. The silver *is* Mine, and the gold *is* Mine, saith the LORD of hosts. The glory of this latter house shall be greater than of the former, saith the LORD of hosts: and in this place will I give peace, saith the LORD of hosts.**

(Hag. 2:23) In that day, saith the LORD of hosts, will I take thee, O Zerubbabel, My servant, the son of Shealtiel, saith the LORD, and will make thee as a signet: for I have chosen thee, saith the LORD of hosts. (Mt. 1:12) And after they were taken to Babylon, Jeconias begat Salathiel, and Salathiel begat Zorobabel.

(Zech. 2:10–13) Sing and rejoice, O daughter of Zion: for, lo, I come, and I will dwell in the midst of thee, saith the LORD. (Rev. 5:13) And every creature which is in heaven, and on the earth, and under the earth, and such are in the sea, and all that are in them, heard I saying, Blessing, and honour, and glory, and power, *be* unto Him that sitteth upon the throne, and unto the Lamb for ever and ever. **And many nations shall be joined to the LORD in that day, and shall be My people: and I will dwell in the midst of thee, and thou shalt know that the LORD of hosts hath sent Me unto thee. And the LORD shall inherit Judah His portion in the holy land, and shall choose Jerusalem again. Be silent, O all flesh, before the LORD: for He is raised up out of His holy habitation.** (Rev. 19:11–13) And I saw heaven opened, and behold a white horse; and He that sat upon him *was* called Faithful and True, and in righteousness He doth judge and make war. His eyes *were* as a flame of fire, and on His head *were* many crowns; and He had a name written, that no man knew, but He Himself. And He was clothed with a vesture dipped in blood: and His name is called The Word of God.

(Zech. 3:1–10) And shew me Joshua the high priest standing before the angel of the LORD, and Satan standing at His right hand to resist Him. And the LORD said unto Satan, The LORD rebuke thee O Satan; even the Lord that hath chosen Jerusalem rebuke thee: *is* **not this a brand plucked out of the fire?**

(Jude 23) And others save with fear, pulling *them* out of the fire; hating even the garment spotted by the flesh. **Now Joshua was clothed with filthy garments, and stood before the angel. And he answered and spake unto those that stood before him, saying, Take away the filthy garments from him.** (Rev. 7:14) And I said unto him, Sir, thou knowest. And he said unto me, These are they which came out of great tribulation, and have washed their robes, and made them white in the blood of the Lamb. **And unto him he said, Behold, I have caused thine iniquity to pass from thee, and I will clothe thee with change of raiment. And unto him he said, Behold, I have caused thine iniquity to pass from thee, and I will clothe thee with change of raiment. And I said, Let them set a fair mitre upon his head. So they set a fair mitre upon his head, and clothed him with garments. And the angel of the LORD stood by. And The Angel of the LORD protested unto Joshua, saying, Thus saith the Lord of hosts; If thou wilt walk in My ways, and if thou wilt keep My charge, then thou shalt also judge My house, and shalt also keep My courts, and I will give thee places to walk among these that stand by. Hear now, O Joshua the high priest, thou, and thy fellows that sit before thee: for they** *are* **men wondered at: for, behold, I will bring forth My servant the BRANCH.** (Lk. 1:78–79) Through the tender mercy of our God; whereby the dayspring from on high hath visited us, to give light to them that sit in darkness and *in* the shadow of death, to guide our feet into the way of peace. **For behold the stone that I have laid before Joshua; upon one stone shall** *be* **seven eyes: behold, I will engrave the**

graving thereof, saith the LORD of hosts, and I will remove the iniquity of that land in one day. (Heb. 7:27) Who needeth not daily, as those high priests, to offer up sacrifice, first for his own sins, and then for the people's: for this He did once, when He offered up Himself. **In that day, saith the LORD of hosts, shall ye call every man his neighbour under the vine and under the fig tree.**

(Zech. 6:12) And spake unto him, saying, Thus speaketh the LORD of hosts, saying, Behold the man whose name *is* **The BRANCH; and He shall grow up out of His place, and He shall build the temple of the LORD:**
(Mt. 16:18) And I say also unto thee, That thou art Peter, and upon this Rock I will build My church; and the gates of hell shall not prevail against it. (Eph. 2:20–22) And are built upon the foundation of the apostles and prophets, Jesus Christ himself being the chief corner *stone*; In whom all the building fitly framed together groweth unto an holy temple in the Lord: In Whom ye also are builded together for an habitation of God through the Spirit. (Heb. 3:3) For this *Man* was counted worthy of more glory than Moses, inasmuch as He who hath builded the house hath more honour than the house. **Even He shall build the temple of the LORD; and He shall bear the glory, and shall sit and rule upon His throne; and He shall be a priest upon his throne: and the counsel of peace shall be between them both.** (Heb. 8:1) Now of the things which we have spoken *this is* the sum: We have such an high priest, who is set on the right hand of the throne of the Majesty in the heavens:

(Zech. 9:9) Rejoice greatly, O daughter of Zion; shout, O daughter of Jerusalem: (Mt. 21:8–10) And a very great multitude spread their garments in the way; others cut down branches from the trees, and strawed *them* in the way. And the multitudes that went before, and that followed, cried, saying, Hosanna to the Son of David: Blessed *is* He that cometh in the name of the Lord; Hosanna in the highest. And when He was come into Jerusalem, all the city was moved, saying, Who is this? **behold thy King cometh unto thee:** (Jn. 12:12–13) On the next day much people that were come to the feast, when they heard that Jesus was coming to Jerusalem. Took branches of palm trees, and went forth to meet Him, and cried, Hosanna Blessed *is* the King of Israel that cometh in the name of the Lord. **He *is* just, and having salvation;** (Lk. 19:10) For the Son of man is come to seek and save that which was lost. **lowly, and riding upon an ass,** (Mt. 11:28–30) Come unto Me, all *ye* that labour and are heavy laden, and I will give you rest. Take My yoke upon you, and learn of Me: for I am meek and lowly in heart: and ye shall find rest unto your souls. For My yoke *is* easy, and My burden *is* light. **and upon a colt the foal of an ass.**

(Zech. 10:4) Out of him came forth the corner, out of him the nail, out of him the battle bow, out of him every oppressor together. (Eph. 2:20) And are built upon the foundation of the apostles and prophets, Jesus Christ himself being the chief corner *stone;*

(Zech. 11:4–14) Thus saith the LORD my God; Feed the flock of the slaughter; Whose possessors slay them, and hold themselves not guilty: and they that sell them say, Blessed *be* the LORD; for I am rich: and their own shepherds pity them not. (Mt. 23:1–4) Then spake Jesus to the multitude, and to His disciples, Saying, The scribes and the Pharisees sit in Moses seat: All therefore whatsoever they bid you observe, *that* observe and do: but do not ye after their works: for they say, and do not. For they bind heavy burdens and grievous to be borne, and lay *them* on men shoulders; but they *themselves* will not move them with one of their fingers. (Mt. 23:37) O Jerusalem, Jerusalem, *thou* that killest the prophets, and stonest them which are sent unto thee, how often would I have gathered thy children together, even as a hen gathereth her chickens under *her* wings, and ye would not! **For I will no more pity the inhabitants of the land, saith the LORD: but, lo, I will deliver the men every one into his neighbour's hand and into the hand of his king: and they shall smite the land, and out of their hand I will not deliver *them*. And I will feed the flock of slaughter, *even* you, O poor of the flock.** (Mt. 9:35–36) And Jesus went about all the cities and villages, teaching in their synagogues, and preaching the gospel of the kingdom, and healing every sickness and every disease among the people. But when He saw the multitudes, He was moved with compassion on them, because they fainted, and were scattered abroad, as sheep having no shepherd. **And I took unto me two staves; the one I called Beauty** (favour, grace), **and the other I called Bands** (union); **and I fed the flock. Three shepherds also I cut off in one month; and my soul lothed them, and their soul also abhorred Me. Then said I, I will not feed you: that that dieth, let it die; and that that is to be cut off, let it be cut off; and let the rest eat every one the flesh of another. And I took my staff,** *even* **Beauty, and cut it assunder, that I might break My covenant which I had with all the people. And it was broken in that day: and so the poor of the flock that waited upon Me knew that it** *was* **the word of the LORD. And I said unto them, If ye think good, give** *me* **My price; and if not, forbear. So they weighed for My price thirty** *pieces* **of silver. And the LORD said unto me, Cast it unto the potter: a goodly price that I was prised at of them. And I took the thirty** *pieces* **of silver.** (Mt. 27:3–10) Then Judas, which had betrayed Him, when he saw that he was condemned, repented himself, and brought again the thirty pieces of silver to the chief priests and elders. Saying, I have sinned in that I have betrayed the innocent blood. And they said, What *is that* to us? See thou *to that*. And he cast down the pieces of sliver in the temple, and departed, and went and hanged himself. And the chief priests took the silver pieces, and said, It is not lawful for to put them into the tresury, because it is the price of blood. And they took counsel, and bought with them the potter's field to bury strangers in. Wherefore that field was called, The field of blood, unto this day. Then was fulfilled that which was spopken by Jeremy the prophet, saying, And they took the thirty pieces of silver, the price of Him that was value; And gave them for the potter's field, as the Lord appointed me. **and cast them to the** potter in the house of the **LORD. Then I cut asunder mine other staff, even Bands, that I might break the brotherhood between Judah and Israel.**

(Zech. 12:9–10) **And it shall come to pass in that day, *that* I will seek to destroy all the nations that come against Jerusalem. And I will pour upon the house of David, and upon the inhabitants of Jerusalem, the spirit of grace and of supplications: and they shall look upon Me whom they have pierced, and they shall mourn for Him, as one mourneth for *His* only *son,* and shall be in bitterness for Him, as one that is in bitterness for *His* firstborn.** (Jn. 19:33–35) But when they came to Jesus, and saw that He was dead already, they brake not His legs: But one of the soldiers with a spear pierced His side, and forthwith came there out blood and water. And he that saw *it* bare record, and his record is true: and he knoweth that he saith true, that ye might believe.

(Jn. 19:37) And again another scripture saith, They shall look on Him whom they pierced.

(Zech. 13:6–7) **And *one* shall say unto Him, What *are* these wounds in Thine hands? Then He shall answer, *Those* with which I was wounded *in* the house of My friends. Awake, O sword, against My Shepherd, and against the man *that* is My fellow, saith the LORD of hosts: smite the Shepherd, and the sheep shall be scattered: and I will turn Mine hand upon the little ones.** (Jn. 10:29–30) My Father, which gave *them* Me, is greater than all; and no *man* is able to pluck *them* out of My Father's hand. I and *My* Father are one. (Mt. 26:31–32) Then saith Jesus unto them, All ye shall be offended because of Me this night: for it is written, I will smite the shepherd, and the sheep of the flock shall be scattered abroad. But after I am risen again, I will go before you into Galilee.

(Zech. 14:4) **And His feet shall stand in that day upon the mount of Olives, which *is* before Jerusalem on the east, and the mount of Olives shall cleave in the midst thereof toward the east and toward the west, *and there shall be* a very great valley; and half of the mountain shall remove toward the north, and half of it toward the south.** (Rev. 16:18) And there were voices, and thunders, and lightnings; and there was a great earthquake, such as was not since men were upon the earth, so mighty an earthquake, *and* so great, And the great city was divided into three parts, and the cities of the nations fell: and great Babylon came in rememberance before God, to give unto her the cup of the wine of the fierceness of His wrath.

(Mal. 3:1–6) Behold, I will send My messenger, and he shall prepare the way before Me: (Mr. 1:2–4) As it is written in the prophets Behold, I send My messenger before Thy face, which shall prepare Thy way before Thee. The voice of one crying in the wilderness, Prepare ye the way of the Lord, make His paths straight. John did baptize in the wilderness, and preach the baptism of repentance for the remission of sins. **and the Lord, whom ye seek, shall suddenly come to His temple, even the Messenger of the covenant, whom ye** (Mt. 12:6) But I say unto you, That in this place is *One* greater than the temple **delight in: behold, He shall come, saith the LORD of hosts. But who may abide the day of His coming? and who shall stand when He appeareth? for He *is* like a refiner's fire, and like fuller's soap: And He shall sit** (Mt. 3:11–12) I indeed baptize you with water unto repentance: but he that cometh after me is mightier than I, whose shoes I am not worthy to bear: He shall baptize you *with* the Holy Ghost, and with fire: Whose fan *is* in His hand, and He will throughly purge His floor, and gather His wheat into the garner; but He will burn up the chaff with unquenchable fire, ***as* a refiner and purifier of silver: and He shall purify the sons of Levi, and purge them as gold and silver, that they may offer unto the LORD an offering in righteousness. Then shall the offering of Judah and Jerusalem be pleasant unto the LORD, as in the days of old, and as in former years. And I will come near to you to judgment; and I will be a swift witness against the sorcerers, and against the adulterers, and against false swearers, and against those that oppress the hireling in *his* wages, the widow, and the fatherless, and that turn aside the stranger *from his right,* and fear not Me, saith the LORD of hosts. For I am the LORD, I change not;** (Jam. 1:17) Every good gift and every perfect gift is from above, and cometh down from the Father of lights, with Whom is no variableness, neither shadow of turning, **therefore ye sons of Jacob are not consumed.**

(Mal. 4:1–6) For, behold, the day cometh, that shall burn as an oven; and all the proud, yea, and all that do wickedly, shall be stubble: and the day that cometh shall burn them up, saith the LORD of hosts, that it shall leave them neither root nor branch. (2 Thes. 1:8) In flaming fire taking vengeance on them that know not God, and that obey not the gospel of our Lord Jesus Christ: **But unto you that fear My name shall the Sun of righteousness arise with healing in His wings; and ye shall go forth, and grow up as calves of the stall.** (Luke 1:78–79) Through the tender mercy of our God: whereby the dayspring from on high hath visited us, To give light to them that sit in darkness and *in* the shadow of death, to guide our feet into the way of peace. (Jn. 1:4, 9) In Him was life; and the life was the light of men. *That* was the true light, which lighteth every man that cometh into the world. (Jn. 12:46) I am come a light into the world, that whosoever believeth on Me should not abide in darkness. **And ye shall tread down the wicked; for they shall be ashes under the soles of your feet in the day that I shall do *this*, saith the LORD of hosts. Remember ye the law of Moses My servant, which I commanded unto him in Horeb for all Israel, *with* the statutes and judgments. Behold, I will send you Elijah the prophet before the coming of the great and dreadful day of the LORD:** (Mt. 11:12–14) And from the days of John the Baptist until now the kingdom of heaven suffereth violence, and the violent take it by force. For all the prophets and the law prophesied until John. And if ye will receive *it*, this is Elias, which was for to come. **And he shall turn the heart of the fathers to the children, and the heart of the children to the fathers.** (Lk. 1:16–17) And many of the children of Israel shall He turn to the Lord their God. And he shall go before Him in the spirit and power of Elias, to turn the hearts of the fathers to the children, and the disobedient to the wisdom of the just; to make ready a people prepared for the Lord. **Lest I come and smite the earth with a curse.**

Have I been so long a time with you, and yet hast thou not known Me. Jesus

Part Two
Contents

256 The Resurrection

Jesus Appears to His
Disciples Ascension

Lk. 24:2–53, Mt. 28:2–20,
Mr. 16:3–20,
Jn. 20:2–21:25
Acts 1:1–11

Have I been so long a time with you, and
yet hast thou not known Me. *Jesus*

(Part Two)
References

(1) Overall # of event, in this volume, Gold Type

(1) Ordered # of, Blends of a scene from multiple scripture, Purple Type

(1) Ordered # of, Individual scene from a scripture, Green Type

The narrative is in black type.

The words of Jesus are in red type.

Time statements are in blue type.

Statements of location are in brown type.

In the narrative of "Have I been so long time with you, and yet hast thou not known Me," the most exhaustive Gospel is used as the bases for showing a scene of His life, with all additional information in the remaining gospels included, but labeled by bracketing as follows:

Matthew = ()
Mark = {}
Luke = []
John = <>

Standard brackets are used in the KJV, in each gospel, therefore they are brought into this work, so not all standard brackets refer to Matthew.

The references to the other gospels, are labeled at the right-hand side, of the Main scriptural title beginning each new scene.

This book also includes all references to Jesus being capitalized, He is part of the Godhead!

The review of this work brings, the humble servant into greater love for his Lord, the young believer to a fuller maturity, the student of the Saviour to understanding of His majesty, the Pastor the clarity of His Glory, and the Scholar the grace to stand fast in the Word of God becoming flesh. All will be blessed, except those whom chose denial over faith, for without faith it is impossible to please Him.

*Have I been so long a time with you,
and yet hast thou not known me. Jesus*

(1) (1) <John 1:1–5>

<In the beginning was the Word, and the Word was with God, and the Word was God. The same was in the beginning with God. All things were made by Him; and without Him was not anything made that was made. In Him was life; and the life was the light of men. And the light shineth in darkness; and the darkness comprehended it not.>

(2) (2) [Luke 1:1–4]

[Forasmuch as many have taken in hand to set forth in order a declaration of those things which are most surely believed among us, even as they delivered them unto us, which from the beginning were eyewitnesses, and ministers of the word; it seemed good to me also, having had perfect understanding of all things from the very first, to write unto thee in order, most excellent Theophilus, That thou might know the certainty of those things, wherein thou hast been instructed.]

(3) (3) [Luke 1:5–80]

[There was in the days of Herod, the king of Judaea, a certain priest named Zacharias, of the course of Abia: and his wife *was* of the daughters of Aaron, and her name *was* Elisabeth. And they were both righteous before God, walking in all the commandments and ordinances of the Lord blameless. And they had no child, because that Elisabeth was barren, and they both were *now* well stricken in years. And it came to pass, that while he executed the priest's office before God in the order of his course, according to the custom of the priest's office, his lot was to burn incense when he went into the temple of the Lord. And the whole multitude of the people were praying without at the time of incense, and there appeared unto him an angel of the Lord standing on the right side of the alter of incense. And when Zacharias saw *him*, he was troubled, and fear fell upon him. But the angel said unto him, fear not, Zacharias: for thy prayer is heard; and thy wife Elisabeth shall bear thee a son, and thou shall call his name John. And thou shalt have joy and gladness; and many shall rejoice at his birth. For he shall be great in the sight of the Lord, and shall drink neither wine or strong drink; and he shall be filled with the Holy Ghost, even from his mother's womb, and many of the children of Israel shall he turn to the Lord their God. And he shall go before him in the spirit and power of Elias, to turn the hearts of the fathers to the children, and the disobedient to the wisdom of the just; to make ready a people prepared for the Lord. And Zacharias said unto the angel, Whereby shall I know this? For I am an old man, and my wife well stricken in years. And the angel answering said unto him, I am Gabriel, that stands in the presence of God; and am sent to speak, unto thee, and to shew thee these glad tidings. And behold, thou shall be dumb, and not able to speak until the day that these things shall be performed, because thou believest not my words, which shall be fulfilled in their season. And the people waited for Zacharias, and marveled that he tarried so long in the temple. And when he came out, he could not speak unto them: and they perceived that he had seen a vision in the temple: for he beckoned unto them, and remained speechless. And it came to pass, that, as soon as the days of his ministration were accomplished, he departed to his own house. And after those days his wife Elisabeth conceived, and hid herself five months, saying, Thus hath the Lord dealt with me in the days wherein He looked on *me*, to take away my reproach among men.

In the sixth month the angel Gabriel was sent from God unto a city of Galilee, and Nazareth, to a virgin espoused to a man whose name was Joseph, of the house of David; and the virgin's name *was* Mary. And the angel came in unto her, and said, Hail, *thou that art* highly favored, the Lord, *is* with thee: blessed *art* you among women. And when she saw *him,* she was troubled at his saying, and cast in her mind what manner of salutation this should be. And the angel said unto her, Fear not, Mary: for thou hast found favor with God. And behold, thou shalt conceive in thy womb, and bring forth a son, and shalt call His Name JESUS. He shall be great, and shall be called the Son of the Highest: And the Lord God shall give unto Him the throne of His father David: and He shall reign over the house of Jacob forever; and of His kingdom there shall be no end. Then said Mary unto the angel, how shall this be, seeing I know not a man? And the angel answered, and said unto her, the Holy Ghost shall come upon thee, and the power of the Highest shall overshadow thee: Therefore also that holy thing which shall be born of thee shall be called the Son of God. And behold, your cousin Elizabeth, she hath also conceived a son in her old age: and this is the sixth month with her, who was called barren. For with God nothing shall be impossible. And Mary said, Behold the handmaid of the Lord; be it unto me according to thy word. And the angel departed from her.

Mary arose in those days, and went into the hill country with haste, into a city of Juda: and entered into the house of Zacharias, And saluted Elisabeth. And it came to pass, that, when Elisabeth heard the salutation of Mary, the babe leaped in her womb; and Elisabeth was filled with the Holy Ghost: and she spoke out with a loud voice, and said, Blessed *art* thou among women, and blessed *is* the fruit of thy womb. And whence *is* this to me, that the mother of my Lord should come to me? For, lo, as soon as the voice of thy salutation sounded in my ears, the babe leaped in my womb for joy. And *blessed is* she that believed: for there shall be a performance of those things which were told her from the Lord. And Mary said, My soul does magnify the Lord, and my spirit hath rejoiced in God my Savior. For He hath regarded the low estate of His handmaiden: For, behold, from henceforth all generations shall call me blessed. For He that *is* mighty hath done to me great things; and Holy is His name. And His mercy *is* on them that fear Him from generation to generation. He hath shewed strength with His arm; He hath scattered the proud in the imagination of their hearts. He hath put down the mighty from *their* seats, and exalted them of low degree. He has filled the hungry with good things; and the rich He hath sent empty away. He hath holpen His servant Israel, in remembrance of *His* mercy; as He spoke to our fathers, to Abraham, and to his seed forever. And Mary abode with her about three months, and returned to her own house. Now Elisabeth's full time came that she should be delivered: and she brought forth a son. And her neighbors and her cousins heard how the Lord had shewed great mercy upon her; and they rejoiced with her. And it came to pass, that on the eight day they came to circumcise the child; and they called him Zacharias, after the name of his father. And his mother answered and said, not *so;* but he shall be called John. And they said unto her, there is none of your kindred that is called by this name. And they made signs to his father, how he would have him called. He asked for a writing tablet, and he wrote, saying, his name is John. And they marvelled all. His mouth was opened immediately, and his tongue *loosed*, and he spake, and praised God. Fear came on all that dwelt round about them: and all these sayings were noised abroad throughout all the hill country of Judaea. And all they that hear *them* laid *them* in their hearts, saying, What manner of child shall this be! And the hand of the Lord was with him.

And his father Zacharias was filled with the Holy Ghost and prophesied, saying, Blessed *be* the Lord God Of Israel; for He hath visited and redeemed His people, and hath raised up an horn of salvation for us in the house of His servant David; as He spake by the mouth of His holy prophets, which have been since the world began: that we should be saved from our enemies, and from the hand of all that hate us; to perform the mercy *promised* to our fathers and to remember His holy covenant; the oath which He swore to our father Abraham, that He would grant unto us, that we being delivered out of the hand of our enemies might serve Him without fear, in holiness and righteousness before Him, all the days of our life. And thou child, shalt be called the prophet of the Highest: for you shall go before the face of the Lord to prepare His ways; to give knowledge of salvation unto His people by the remission of their sins, through the tender mercy of our God; whereby the dayspring from on high hath visited us, to give light to them that sit in darkness and *in* the shadow of death, to guide our feet into the way of peace. And the child grew, and waxed strong in spirit, and was in the deserts till the day of his shewing unto Israel.]

(4) (4) **(Matthew 1:18–25)**

(Now the birth of Jesus Christ was on this wise: When as his mother Mary was espoused to Joseph, before they came together, she was found with child of the Holy Ghost. Then Joseph her husband, being a just *man*, and not willing to make her a publick example, was minded to put her away privily. But while he thought on these things, behold, the angel of the Lord appeared unto him in a dream, saying, Joseph, thou son of David, fear not to take unto thee Mary your wife: for that which is conceived in her is of the Holy Ghost. And she shall bring forth a son, and thou shalt call His name JESUS: for He shall save His people from their sins. Now all this was done, that it might be fulfilled which was spoken of the Lord by the prophet, saying, Behold, a virgin shall be with child, and shall bring forth a son, and they shall call His name Emmanuel, which being interpreted is, God with us. Then Joseph being raised from sleep, did as the angel of the Lord had bidden him, and took unto him his wife: and knew her not till she had brought forth her firstborn son: and he called His name JESUS.)

(5) (5) **[Luke 2:1–40]**

[And it came to pass in those days, that there went out a decree from Caesar Augustus, that all the world should be taxed. (*And* this taxing was first made when Cyrenius was governor of Syria.) And all went to be taxed; every one into his own city. And Joseph also went up from Galilee, out of the city of Nazareth; into Judaea, unto the city of David, which is called Bethlehem; (because he was of the house and lineage of David;) to be taxed with Mary his espoused wife, being great with child. And so it was, that, while they were there, the days were accomplished that she should be delivered. And she brought forth her firstborn son, and wrapped Him in swaddling clothes, and laid Him in a manger, because there was no room for them in the inn.

And there were in the same country sheperds abiding in the field, keeping watch over their flock by night. And lo, the angel of the Lord came unto them, and the glory of the Lord shone around them: and they were sore afraid. And the angel said unto them, Fear not: for, behold, I bring you good tidings of great joy, which shall be to all people. For unto you is born this day in the city of David a Saviour, which is Christ the Lord. And this *shall be* a sign unto you; Ye shall find the babe wrapped in swaddling clothes, lying in a manger. And suddenly there was with the angel a multitude of heavenly host praising God, and saying, Glory to God in the highest, and on earth peace, good will toward men. And it came to pass, as the angels were gone away from them into heaven, the shepherds said one to another, Let us now go even unto Bethlehem, and see this thing which is come to pass, which the Lord hath made known unto us. And they came with haste, and found Mary, and Joseph, and the babe lying in a manger. And when they had seen *it*, they made known abroad the saying which was told them concerning this child. And all they that heard *it* wondered at those things which were told them by the shepherds. But Mary kept all these things, and pondered *them* in her heart And the shepherds returned, glorifying and praising God for all the things that they had heard and seen, as it was told unto them.

When eight days were accomplished for the circumcising of the child, His name was called JESUS, which was so named of the angel before He was conceived in the womb. And when the days of her purification according to the law of Moses were accomplished, they brought Him to Jerusalem, to present *Him* to the Lord; (As it is written in the law of the Lord, Every male that openeth the womb shall be called holy to the Lord;) And to offer a sacrifice according to that which is said in the law of the Lord, A pair of turtledoves, or two young pigeons.

And, Behold, there was a man in Jerusalem, whose name *was* Simeon; and the same man *was* just and devout, waiting for the consolation of Israel: and the Holy Ghost was upon him. And it was revealed unto him by the Holy Ghost, that he should not see death, before he had seen the Lord's Christ. And he came by the Spirit into the temple: and when the parents brought in the child Jesus, to do for Him after the custom of the law, then took he Him up in his arms, and blessed God and said, Lord, Now lettest Thou Thy servant depart in peace, according to your word: for mine eyes have seen Thy salvation, which thou hast prepared before the face of all people; a light to lighten the Gentiles, and the glory of Thy people Israel. And Joseph and His mother marvelled at those things which were spoken of Him. And Simeon blessed them, and said unto Mary His mother, Behold, this *child* is set for the fall and rising again of many in Israel; and for a sign which shall be spoken against (Yea a sword shall pierce through thy own soul also) that the thoughts of many hearts may be revealed.

And there was one Anna, a Prophetess, the daughter of Phanuel, of the tribe of Aser: she was of a great age, and had lived with a husband seven years from her virginity; and she *was* a widow of about fourscore and four years, which departed not from the temple, but served God with fastings and prayers night and day. And she coming in that instant gave thanks likewise unto the Lord, and spake of Him to all them that looked for redemption in Jerusalem. And when they had performed all things according to the law of the Lord, they returned into Galilee, to their own city Nazareth. And the Child grew and waxed strong in spirit, filled with wisdom: and the grace of God was upon Him.]

(6) (6) **(Matthew 2:1–12)**

(Now when Jesus was born in Bethlehem of Judaea in the days of Herod the King, behold, there came wise men from the east to Jerusalem, saying, Where is He that is born King of the Jews?

For we have seen His star in the east, and are come to worship Him. When Herod the King had heard, *these things*, he was troubled, and all Jerusalem with him. And when he had gathered all the chief priests and scribes of the people together, he demanded of them where Christ should be born. And they said unto him, In Bethlehem of Judaea: for thus it is written by the prophet, and thou Bethlehem, *in* the land of Juda, art not the least among the princes of Juda, for out of thee shall come a Governor, that shall rule My people Israel.

Then Herod, when he had privily called the wise men, inquired of them diligently what time the star appeared. And he sent them to Bethlehem, and said, Go and search diligently for the young child; and when ye have found *Him*, bring me word again, that I may come and worship Him also. When they had heard the King they departed;

and, lo, the star, which they saw in the east, went before them, till it came and stood over where the young child was. When they saw the star, They rejoiced with exceeding great joy. And when they were come into the house, they saw the young child with Mary His mother, and fell down, and worshipped Him: and when they had opened their treasures, they presented unto Him gifts; gold, and frankincense, and myrrh. And being warned of God in a dream that they should not return to Herod, they departed into their own country another way.)

Kingly Line, of the Jews, Through Joseph
(7) (1) (Matthew 1:1–6)

(The book of the generation of Jesus Christ, the son of David, the son of Abraham.

Legal Line, of Humanity, Through Mary
[Luke 3:38–23]

[Adam which was *the son* of God,
Seth, which was *the son* of
Enos, which was *the son* of
Cainan, which was *the son* of
Maleleel, which was *the son* of
Jared, which was *the son* of
Enoch, which was *the son* of
Mathusala, which was *the son* of
Lamech, which was *the son* of
Noe, which was *the son* of
Sem, which was *the son* of
Arphaxad, which was *the son* of
Cainan, which was *the son* of
Sala, which was *the son* of
Heber, which was *the son* of
Phalec, which was *the son* of
Ragau, which was *the son* of
Saruch, which was *the son* of
Nachor, which was *the son* of
Thara, which was *the son* of
Abraham, which was *the son* of

begat Isaac and	Isaac, which was *the son of*
begat Jacob and	Jacob, which was *the son of*
begat Judas and his brethren:	Juda, which was *the son of*
begat Phares and Zara of Thamar	Phares, which was *the son of*
begat Esrom and	Esrom, which was *the son of*
begat Aram and	Aram, which was *the son of*
begat Aminadab and	Aminadab which was *the son of*
begat Naasson and	Naasson which was *the son of*
begat Salmon and	Salmon which was *the son of*
begat Booz of Rachab and	Booz which was *the son of*
begat Obed of Ruth and	Obed which was *the son of*
begat Jesse and	Jesse which was *the son of*
begat David the King and	David which was *the son of*
the King begat Solomon of her	
that had been the wife of Urias)	

(8) (2) (Matthew 1:7–16)   [Luke 3:23–31]

(and Solomon   [Nathan which was *the son of*
begat Roboam and Roboam   **Legal Heir**

Mattatha which was *the son of*

begat Abia and Abia
begat Asa and Asa

Menan which was *the son of*

begat Jehoshaphat
and Jehoshaphat

Melea which was *the son of*
Eliakim which was *the son of*

begat Joram and Joram

Jonan which was *the son of*
Joseph which was *the son of*
Juda which was *the son of*
Simeon which was *the son of*

begat Ozias and Ozias
begat Joatham and Joatham   Levi which was *the son* of
begat Achaz and Achaz   Matthat which was *the son* of
begat Ezekias and Ezekias

                        Jorim which was *the son* of

begat Manasses and Manasses

                Eliezer which was *the son* of
                  Jose which was *the son* of
                    Er which was *the son* of

begat Amon and Amon

              Elmodam which was *the son* of

begat Josias and Josias

                  Cosam which was *the son* of
                    Addi which was *the son* of

begat Jechonias and his brethren
about the time they were carried   Melchi which was *the son* of
away to Babylon: and after they   Neri which was *the son* of
were brought to Babylon Jechonias
    begat Salathiel and   Salathiel   which was *the son* of
    begat Zorobabel and   Zorobabel   which was *the son* of
                  Rhesa which was *the son* of

begat Abiud and Abiud

                Joanna which was *the son* of
                  Juda which was *the son* of

begat Eliakim and Eliakim

                Joseph which was *the son* of

begat Azor and Azor

                Semei which was *the son* of
          Mattathias which was *the son* of

begat Sadoc and Sadoc

                Maath which was *the son* of
                Nagge which was *the son* of

begat Achim and Achim

                  Esli which was *the son* of
                Naum which was *the son* of

begat Eliud and Eliud

Amos which was *the son* of

Mattathias which was *the son* of

begat Eleazar and Eleazar

Joseph which was *the son*

Janna which was *the son* of

Begat Matthan and Matthan

Melchi which was *the son* of

Levi which was *the son* of

begat Jacob and Jacob

Matthat which was *the son* of

Heli which was *the son* of

begat Joseph which was *the son* of

the husband of Mary, of whom

was born who is called Jesus being (as was supposed)

Christ.) the son of]

Adoptive Son

(9) (7) **(Matthew 1:17)**

(So all the generations from Abraham to David *are* fourteen generations; and from David until the carrying away into Babylon *are* fourteen generations; and from the carrying away into Babylon unto Christ *are* fourteen generations.)

(10) (8) **(Matthew 2:13–23)**

(And when they were departed, behold, the angel of the Lord appeareth to Joseph in a dream, saying, arise, and take the young child and His mother, and flee into Egypt, and be thou there until I bring you word: for Herod will seek the young child to destroy Him. When he arose, he took the young child, and His mother by night, and departed into Egypt: and was there until the death of Herod: that it might be fulfilled which was spoken of the Lord by the prophet, saying, Out of Egypt I have called My Son.

Then Herod, when he saw that he was mocked of the wise men, was exceedingly wroth, and sent forth and slew all the children that were in Bethlehem, and in all the coasts thereof, from two years old and under, according to the time which he had diligently inquired of the wise men. Then was fulfilled that which was spoken by Jeremy the prophet, saying, in Rama was there a voice heard lamentation, and weeping, and great mourning, Rachel weeping *for* her children, and would not be comforted, because they are not.

But when Herod was dead, Behold, an angel of the Lord appeareth in a dream, to Joseph in Egypt, saying, Arise, take the young child and His mother, and go into the land of Israel: for they are dead which sought the young child's life. He arose, and took the young child and His mother, and came into the land of Israel. But when he heard that Archelaus did reign in Judaea in the room of his father Herod, he was afraid to go thither: notwithstanding, being warned of God in a dream, he turned aside into the parts of Galilee: and he came and dwelt in a city called Nazareth: that it might be fulfilled which was spoken by the prophets He shall be called a Nazarene.)

(11) (9) **[Luke 2:41–52]**

[Now His parents went to Jerusalem every year at the feast of the Passover. And when He was twelve years old, they went up to Jerusalem after the custom of the feast. And when they had fulfilled the days, as they returned, the child Jesus tarried behind in Jerusalem; and Joseph and His mother knew not *of it*. But they, supposing Him to have been in the company, went a days journey; and they sought Him among *their* kinsfolk and acquaintance. And when they found Him not, they turned back again to Jerusalem, seeking Him. It came to pass, that after three days they found Him in the temple, sitting in the midst of the doctors, both hearing them, and asking them questions. And all that heard Him were astonished at His understanding and answers. And when they saw Him, they were amazed: and His mother said unto Him, Son, why hast thou thus dealt with us? Behold, thy father and I have sought thee sorrowing. And He said unto them, "How is it that ye sought me? Wist ye not that I must be about My Father's business?" And they understood not the saying which He spake unto them. And He went down with them, and came to Nazareth, and was subject unto them: but His mother kept all these sayings in her heart. And Jesus increased in wisdom and stature, and in favor with God and man.]

(12) (10) **<John 1:6–18>**

<There was a man sent from God, whose name was John. The same came for a witness, to bear witness of the Light. That all *men* through him might believe, he was not that Light, but *was sent* to bear witnessof that Light. *That* was the true Light, which lighteth every man that cometh into the world. He was in the world, and the world was made by Him, and the world knew Him not. He came unto His own, and His own received Him not. But as many as received Him, to them gave He power to become the sons of God, *even* to them that believe on His name: which were born, not of blood, nor of the will of the flesh, nor of the will of man, but of God.

And the Word was made flesh, and dwelt among us (and we beheld His glory, the glory as of the only begotten of the Father) full of grace and truth. John bear witness of Him, and cried, saying, This was He of whom I spake, He that comes after me is preferred before me: for He was before me. And of His fulness have all we received, and grace for grace. For the law was given by Moses, *but* grace and truth came by Jesus Christ. No man has seen God at any time; the only begotten Son, which is in the bosom of the Father, He hath declared *Him*.>

(13) (3) **[Luke 3:1–18]**, (Math. 3:1–12), {Mark 1:2–8}, <John 1:19–28>

[Now <this is the record of John> in the fifteenth year of the reign of Tiberus Caesar, Pontius Pilate being governor of Judaea, and Herod being tetrarch of Galilee, and his brother Philip tetrarch of Ituraea and of the region of Trachonitus, and Lysanis the tetrarch of Abilene, Annas and Caiaphas being the high priests. (In those Days) the word of God came unto John (the Baptist) the son of Zacharias (preaching) in the wilderness (of Judaea). (Saying, Repent ye: for the kingdom of heaven is at hand.) And he came into all the country about Jordan, preaching the baptism of repentance for the remission of sins; (For this is he that was spoken of) As it is written in the book of the words of Esaias the prophet, saying, {behold I send My messenger before Thy face, which shall prepare Thy way before Thee.} <When the Jews sent priests and Levites from Jerusalem to ask him who art thou? And he confessed, and denied not: but confessed, I am not the Christ. And they asked him, What then? Art thou Elias? And he saith, I am not. Art thou that prophet? And he answered, No. Then said they unto him, Who art thou? That we may give an answer to them that sent us. What sayest thou of thyself? He said, I *am*> The voice of one crying in the wilderness, Prepare ye the way of the Lord, make His paths straight. Every valley shall be filled, and every mountain and hill shall be brought low; and the crooked shall be made straight, and the rough ways *shall be* made smooth; and all flesh shall see the salvation of God. <And they which were sent were of the Pharisees.> (And the same John had his raiment of camel's hair, and a leathern gridle {of skin} about his lions; and his meat {he did eat} was locust and wild honey.) Then {there} went out {un} to him Jerusalem, and all {the land of} Judaea, and all the region round about Jordan, {and were all baptized of him in the river of Jordan,} confessing their sins. But when he saw many of the Pharisees and Sadducees come to his baptism, he said (unto them) to the multitude that came forth to be baptized of him, O generation of vipers, who hath warned you to flee from the wrath to come? Bring forth therefore fruits worthy (meet for) of repentance, and begin (and think) not to say within yourselves, We have Abraham to *our* father: for I say unto you, That God is able of these stones to raise up children unto Abraham. And now also the axe is laid unto the root of the trees; every tree therefore which bringeth not forth good fruit is hewn down, and cast into the fire. And the people asked him, saying, What shall we do then? He answereth and saith unto them, He that hath two coats, let him impart to him that hath none: and he that hath meat, let him do likewise. Then came also publicans to be baptized, and said unto him, Master, what shall we do? And he said unto them, Exact no more than that which is appointed you. And the soldiers likewise demanded of him, saying, And what shall we do? And he said unto them, Do violence to no man, neither accuse *any* falsely;

and be content with your wages. And as the people were in expectation, and all men mused in their hearts of John, whether he were the Christ, or not; <the Pharisees asked him, and said unto him, Why baptizest thou then, if thou be not that Christ, nor Elias, neither that prophet?> John answered, <them> {and preached} saying unto them all, <there standeth one among you, whom ye know not:> I indeed baptize you with water; (unto repentance:) but (He <it is> that) one mightier than I cometh (after me) <is preferred before me>, the latchet of whose shoes I am not worthy to {stoop down} (bear) unloose: He shall baptize you with the Holy Ghost and with fire: Whose fan is in His hand, and He will throughly purge His floor, and will gather the wheat into His garner; but the chaff He will bum (up) with fire unquenchable. <These things were done in Bethabara beyond Jordan, where John was baptizing.>]

(14) (4) **(Mathew 3:13–17)** [Luke 3:21–23] {Mark 1:9–11}
({And} Then {it} cometh {to pass [when all the people were baptized] in those days, that} Jesus {came} from {Nazareth of} Galilee to Jordan unto John, to be baptized of him, But John forbad Him, saying, I have need to be baptized of Thee, and comest Thou to me? And Jesus answering said unto him, Suffer it to be so now: for thus it becometh us to fulfil all righteousness. Then he suffered Him. And Jesus when He was baptized {of John in Jordan} [and praying], went up {and} straightway {coming up} out of the water: and, lo, the heavens were opened unto Him, and he saw the Spirit of God [the Holy Ghost] descending [in a bodily shape] like a dove, and lighting upon Him: and lo {there came} a voice from heaven, saying, This is {thou art} My beloved Son, in whom [Thee] I am well pleased.)

(15) (5) **[Luke 4:1–13]** (Mathew 4:1–11) {Mark 1:12–13}
[And Jesus being full of the Holy Ghost returned from Jordan; and {immediately} (then was Jesus) led {driveth} by the Spirit into the wilderness, being forty days tempted of the devil.{And was with the wild beasts;} And in those days He did eat nothing: and when they were ended, He afterward hungered. And the devil (the tempter came to Him) said unto Him, If Thou be the Son of God, command this stone that it

be made bread. And Jesus answered him saying, It is written, That man shall not live by bread alone, but by every word (that proceedeth out of the mouth) of God. And the devil, taking Him up into an high mountain, shewed unto Him all the kingdoms of the world (and the glory of them) in a moment in time. And the devil said unto Him, All this power (and these things) will I give Thee, and the glory of them: for that is delivered unto me; and to whosoever I will give it. If Thou therefore wilt worship me, all shall be Thine. And Jesus answered and said unto him, Get thee behind me. Satan, for it is written. Thou shalt worship the Lord thy God, and Him only shalt thou serve. And he brought Him to Jerusalem (the holy city), and set Him on a pinnacle of the temple, and said unto Him, If Thou be the Son of God, cast Thyself down from hence: For it is written, He shall give His angels charge over (concerning) Thee, to keep Thee; And in *their* hands they shall bear Thee up, lest at any time Thou dash Thy foot against a stone, And Jesus answering said unto him, It is said, thou shalt not tempt the Lord thy God. And when the devil had ended all the temptation, he departed from Him for a season (and behold, angels came and ministered unto Him.)]

(16) (11) <John 1:29–4:42>

<The next day John seeth Jesus coming unto him, and saith, Behold the Lamb of God, which taketh away the sin of the world. This is He of whom I said, After me cometh a man which is preferred before me: for He was before me. And I knew Him not: but that He should be made manifest to Israel, therefore am I come baptizing with water. And John bare record, saying, I saw the Spirit descending from heaven like a dove, and it abode upon Him. And I knew Him not: but He that sent me to baptize with water, the same said unto me, Upon whom thou shalt see the Spirit descending and remaining on Him, the same is He which baptizeth with the Holy Ghost. And I saw, and bare record that this is the Son of God.

Again the next day after John stood, and two of his disciples; and looking upon Jesus as He walked, he saith, Behold the Lamb of God! And the two disciples heard him speak, and they followed Jesus. Then Jesus turned, and saw them following, and saith unto them, What seek ye? They said unto Him, Rabbi (which is to say, being interpreted,

Master) where dwellest Thou? He saith unto them, Come and see They came and saw where He dwelt, and abode with Him that day: for it was about the tenth hour. One of the two which heard John *speak*, and followed Him, was Andrew, Simon Peter's brother. He first findeth his own brother Simon, and saith unto him, We have found the Messias, which is, being interpreted, the Christ. And he brought him to Jesus. And when Jesus beheld him, He said, Thou art Simon the son of Jona: thou shalt be called Cephas, which is by interpretation, A stone.

The day following Jesus would go forth into Galilee, and findeth Philip, and saith unto him, Follow Me. Now Philip was of Bethsaida, the city of Andrew and Peter. Philip findeth Nathanael, and saith unto him, We have found Him, of whom Moses in the law, and the prophets, did write, Jesus of Nazareth, the son of Joseph. And Nathanael said unto him, Can there any good thing come out of Nazareth? Philip saith unto him, Come and see. Jesus saw Nathanael coming to Him, and saith of him, Behold an Israelite indeed, in whom is no guile! Nathanael saith unto Him, Whence knowest Thou me? Jesus answered and said unto him, Before that Philip called thee, when thou wast under the fig tree, I saw thee. Nathanael answered and saith unto Him, Rabbi, Thou art the Son of God; Thou art the King of Israel. Jesus answered and said unto him, Because I said unto thee, I saw thee under the fig tree, believest thou? Thou shalt see greater things than these. And He saith unto him, Verily, verily, I say unto you, Hereafter ye shall see heaven open, and the angels of God ascending and descending upon the Son of Man.

And The third day there was a marriage in Cana of Galilee: and the mother of Jesus was there; And both Jesus was called, his disciples, to the marriage. When they wanted wine, the mother of Jesus saith unto Him, They have no wine. Jesus saith unto her, Woman, what have I to do with thee? Mine hour is not yet come. His mother saith unto the servants, Whatsoever He saith unto you do *it*. And there were set there six waterpots of stone, after the manner of the purifying of the Jews, containing two or three firkins apiece. Jesus saith unto them Fill the waterpots with water. They filled them up to the brim. And He saith unto them, Draw out now, and bear unto the Governor of the feast. And they bare *it*. When the ruler of the feast had tasted the water that was made wine, and knew not whence it was: (but the servant which drew the water knew;) the governor of the feast called the bridegroom, and saith unto him, Every man at the beginning doeth set forth good wine; and when men have well drunk, then that which is worse: *but* thou hast kept the good wine until now. This beginning of miracles did Jesus in Cana of Galilee, and manifested forth His glory; and His disciples believed on Him.

After this He went down to Capernaum, He, and His mother, and His brethren, and His disciples: and they continued there not many days.

The Jews' passover was at hand, and Jesus went up to Jerusalem, and found in the temple those that sold oxen and sheep and doves, and the changers of money sitting: And when He had made a scourge of small cords, He drove them all out of the temple, and the sheep, and the oxen; and poured out the changers' money: and overthrew the tables; and said unto them that sold doves, Take these things hence; make not My Father's house an house of merchandise. His disciples remembered that it was written, The zeal of Thine house hath eaten Me up.

Then answered the Jews and said unto Him, What sign shewest Thou unto us, seeing that Thou doest these things? Jesus answered and said unto them, Destroy this temple, and in three days I will raise it up. Then said the Jews, Forty and six years was this temple in building, and wilt Thou rear it up in three days? But He spoke of the temple of His body. When therefore He was risen from the dead, His disciples remembered that He said this unto them; and they believed the scripture, and the word which Jesus had said.

Now when He was in Jerusalem at the Passover, in the feast *day*, many believed in His name, when they saw the miracles which He did. But Jesus did not commit Himself unto them, because He knew all *men*, and needed not that any should testify of man: for He knew what was in man.

There was a man of the Pharisees, named Nicodemus, a ruler of the Jews: The same came to Jesus by night, and said unto Him, Rabbi, we know that Thou art a teacher come from God: for no man can do these miracles that Thou doest, except God be with Him.

Jesus answered and said unto him, Verily, verily, I say unto thee, Except a man be born again, he cannot see the kingdom of God. Nicodemus saith unto Him, How can a man be born when he is old? Can he enter the second time into his mother's womb, and be born? Jesus answered, Verily, verily, I say unto thee, Except a man be born of water and of the Spirit, he cannot enter into the kingdom of God. That which is born of the flesh is flesh; and that which is born of the Spirit is spirit. Marvel not that I said unto thee, Ye must be born again. The wind bloweth where it listeth, and thou hearest the sound thereof, but canst not tell whence it cometh, and whither it goeth; so is every one that is born of the Spirit. Nicodemus answered and said unto Him, How can these things be? Jesus answered and said unto him, Art thou a master of Israel, and knowest not these things? Verily, verily, I say unto thee, We speak that we do know, and testify that we have seen; and ye receive not our witness.

If I have told you earthly things, and ye believe not, how shall ye believe, if I tell you *of* heavenly things? And no man has ascended up to heaven, but He that came down from heaven, *even* the Son of man which is in heaven.

As Moses lifted up the serpent in the wilderness, even so must the Son of man be lifted up;

That whosoever believes in Him should not perish, but have eternal life.

For God so loved the world, that He gave His only begotten Son, that whosoever believeth in Him should not perish, but have everlasting life. For God sent not His Son into the world to condemn the world; but that the world through Him might be saved.

He that believeth on Him is not condemned: but he that believeth not is condemned already, because he has not believed in the name of the only begotten Son of God. This is the condemnnation, that light is come into the world, and men loved darkness rather than light, because their deeds were evil. For every one that doeth evil hateth the light, neither cometh to the light, lest his deeds should be reproved. But he that doeth truth cometh to the light, that his deeds may be made manifest, that they are wrought in God.

After these things came Jesus and His disciples into the land of Judaea and there He tarried with them, and baptized.

And John was also baptizing in Aenon near Salim, because there was much water there: and they came, and were baptized. For John was not yet cast into prison.

Then there arose a question between *some* of John's disciples and the Jews about purifying. And they came unto John, and said unto him, Rabbi, He that was with thee beyond Jordan, to whom thou barest witness, behold, the same baptizeth, and all *men* come to Him. John answered and said, A man can receive nothing, except it be given him from heaven. Ye yourselves bear me witness, that I said, I am not the Christ, but that I am sent before Him. He that hath the bride is the bridegroom: but the friend of the bridegroom, which standeth and heareth Him, rejoiceth greatly because of the bridegroom's voice: this my joy therefore is fulfilled. He must increase, but I *must* decrease. He that cometh from above is above all: he that is of the earth is earthly, and speaketh of the earth: He that cometh from heaven is above all. And what He hath seen and heard, that He testifieth; and no man receiveth His testimony. He that hath received his testimony has set to His seal that God is true. For He whom God hath sent speaketh the words of God: for God giveth not the Spirit by measure *unto Him*. The Father Loveth the Son, and hath given all things into His hand.

He that believeth on the Son hath everlasting life: and he that believeth not the Son shall not see life; but the wrath of God abideth on him.

When therefore the Lord knew how the Pharisees had heard that Jesus made and baptized more disciples than John. (Though Jesus Himself baptized not, but His disciples) He left Judaea, and departed again into Galilee. And He must needs go through Samaria. Then cometh He to a city of Samaria, which is called Sychar, near to the parcel of ground that Jacob gave to his son Joseph. Now Jacob's well was there. Jesus therefore, being wearied with *His* journey, sat thus on the well: and it was about the sixth hour. There cometh a woman of Samaria to draw water: Jesus saith unto her, Give Me to drink. (For His disciples were gone away unto the city to buy meat.)

Then saith the woman of Samaria unto Him, How is it that Thou, being a Jew, askest drink of me which am a woman of Samaria? For the Jews have no dealings with the Samaritans. Jesus answered and said unto her, If thou knewest the gift of God, and who it is that saith to thee. Give Me to drink: thou wouldest have asked of Him, and He would have given thee living water. The woman saith unto Him, Sir thou hast nothing to draw with, and the well is deep: from whence then hast Thou that living water? Art Thou greater than our father Jacob, which gave us the well, and drank thereof himself, and his children, and his cattle? Jesus answered and said unto her, Whosoever drinketh of this water shall thirst again: But whosoever drinketh of the water that I shall give him shall never thirst; but the water that I shall give him shall be in him a well of water springing up into everlasting life. The woman saith unto Him, Sir, give me this water, that I thirst not, neither come hither to draw. Jesus saith unto her, Go, call thy husband, and come hither. The woman answered and said, I have no husband. Jesus said unto her, Thou hast well said, I have no husband: For thou hast had five husbands; and he whom thou now hast is not thy husband: in that saidst thou truly. The woman saith unto Him, Sir, I perceive that Thou art a prophet. Our fathers worshipped in this mountain; and ye say, that in Jerusalem is the place where men ought to worship. Jesus saith unto her, Woman, believe Me, the hour cometh, when ye shall neither in this mountain, nor yet at Jerusalem, worship the Father. Ye worship ye know not what: we know what we worship; for salvation is of the Jews. But the hour cometh, and now is, when the true worshippers shall worship the Father in Spirit and in truth: For the Father seeketh such to worship Him. God *is* a Spirit: and they that worship Him must worship *Him* in Spirit and truth. The woman saith unto Him, I know that Messias cometh, which is called Christ: when He is come, He will tell us all things. Jesus saith unto her, I that speak unto thee am *He.*

And upon this came His disciples, and marvelled that He talked with the woman: yet no man said, What seekest Thou? Or, why talkest Thou with her? The woman then left her waterpot, and went her way into the city, and saith to the men, come, see a man, which told me all things that ever I did: is not this the Christ? Then they went out of the city, and came unto Him.

In the mean while His disciples prayed Him, saying, Master, eat. But He said unto them, I have meat to eat that ye know not of. Therefore said the disciples one to another, Hath any man brought Him *ought* to eat? Jesus saith unto them, My meat is to do the will of Him that sent Me, and finish His work. Say not ye, There are yet four months, and *then* cometh harvest? Behold, I say unto you, Lift up your eyes, and look on the fields: for they are white already to harvest. And he that reapeth receiveth wages, and gathereth fruit unto life eternal: that both he that soweth and he that reapeth may rejoice together. And herein is that saying true, One soweth, and another reapeth. I sent you to reap that whereon ye bestowed no labour: other men laboured, and ye are entered into their labours. And many of the Samaritans of that city believed on Him, for the saying of the woman, which testified, He told me all that ever I did. So when the Samaritans were come unto Him, they besought Him that He would tarry with them: and He abode there two days. And many more believed because of His own word; And said unto the woman, Now we believe, not because of thy saying: for we have heard *Him* ourselves, and know that this is indeed the Christ, the Saviour of the world.>

(17) (12) **[Luke 3:19–20]**

[But Herod the tetrarch, being reproved by him for Herodias his brother Philip's wife, and for all the evils which Herod had done, added yet this above all, that he shut up John in prison.]

(18) (6) **<John 4:43–45>** (Matthew 4:12) {Mark 1:14–15} [Luke 4:14–15]

<Now after two days (when) Jesus [returned in the power of the Spirit] and had heard that John was cast into prison. He departed thence, and went into Galilee, {preaching the gospel of the kingdom of God. The time is fulfilled, and the kingdom of God is at hand: repent ye. and believe the gospel.} For Jesus Himself testified, that a prophet hath no honour in His own country. Then when He was come into Galilee, the Galilaeans received Him,[And there went out

a fame of Him through all the region round about and He taught in their synagogues, being glorified of all,] having seen all the things that He did at Jerusalem at the feast: for they also went unto the feast.>

(19) (7) **[Luke 4:16–30]** (Matthew 4:13)

[And He came to Nazareth, where He had been brought up: and as His custom was, He went into the synagogue on the sabbath day, and stood up for to read. There was delivered unto Him the book of the prophet Esaias. And when He had opened the book, He found the place where it was written, The Spirit of the Lord *is* upon Me. because He hath anointed Me to preach the gospel to the poor; He hath sent Me to heal the brokenhearted, to preach deliverance to the captives, and recovering of sight to the blind, to set at liberty them that are bruised, to preach the acceptable year of the Lord. And He closed the book, and He gave *it* again to the minister, and sat down. And the eyes of all them that were in the synagogue were fastened on Him. He began to say unto them, This day is this scripture fulfilled in your ears And all bare Him witness, and wondered at the gracious words which proceeded out of His mouth. And they said, Is not this Joseph's son? He said unto them, Ye will surely say unto Me this proverb. Physician, heal Thyself: whatsoever we have heard done in Capernaum, do also here in Thy country. And He said, Verily I say unto you, no prophet is accepted in his own country. But I tell you of a truth, many widows were in Israel in the days of Elias, when the heaven was shut up three years, and six months, when great famine was throughout all the land; But unto none of them was Elias sent, save unto Sarepta, a *city* of Sidon, unto a woman *that was* a widow. And many lepers were in Israel in the time of Eliseus the prophet; and none of them was cleansed, saving Naaman the Syrian. And all they in the synagogue, when they heard these things, were filled with wrath, and rose up, and thrust Him out of the city, and led Him unto the brow of the hill whereon their city was built, that they might cast Him down headlong. But He passing through the midst of them went His way (leaving Nazareth)]

(20) (13) **<John 4:46–54>**

<So Jesus came into Cana of Galilee, where He made the water wine. And there was a certain nobleman, whose son was sick at Capernaum. When he heard that Jesus was come out of Judaea into Galilee, he went unto Him, and besought Him that He would come down, and heal his son: for he was at the point of death. Then said Jesus unto him, Except ye see signs and wonders, ye will not believe. The nobleman saith unto Him, Sir, come down ere my child die. Jesus saith unto him, Go thy way; thy son liveth. And the man believed the word that Jesus had spoken unto him, and he went his way. And as he was going down, his servants met him, and told *him*, saying, Thy son liveth. Then enquired he of them the hour when he began to amend. And they said unto him, Yesterday at the seventh hour the fever left him. So the father knew that *it was* at the same hour, in the which Jesus said unto him, Thy son liveth: and himself believed, and his whole house. This *is* again the second miracle *that* Jesus did, when he was come out of Judaea into Galilee.>

(21) (8) **{Mark 1:16–20}** (Mathew 4:17–22)

{Now as He walked by the sea of Galilee, He saw Simon (called Peter) and Andrew his brother casting a net into the sea: for they were fishers. And Jesus said unto them, Come ye after Me, and I will make you to become fishers of men. And straightway they forsook their nets, and followed Him. And when He had gone a little further thence, He saw (other two brethren) James the son of Zebedee, and John his brother, who also were in the ship mending their nets. And straightway He called them: and they (immediately) left their father Zebedee in the ship with the hired servants, and went after Him.}

(22) (9) **{Mark 1:21–39}** (Mathew 4:12–16, 23–25, 8:14–17) [Luke 4:31–44]

(Now when Jesus had heard that John was cast into prison, He departed into (all) Galilee: And leaving Nazareth, He came) And they went [down] (and dwelt) into Capernaum; (which is upon the sea coast, in the borders of Zebulon and Naphthalim: That it might be fulfilled which was spoken by Esaias the prophet, saying, The land of Zebulon, and the land of Naphthalim, *by* the way of the sea, beyond Jordan, Galilee of the gentiles; The people which sat in darkness saw great light; and to them which sat in the region and shadow of death light is sprung up.) and straightway on the sabbath day [s] He entered into the [their] synagogue [s], and taught (teaching and preaching the gospel of the kingdom). And they were astonished at His doctrine; [for His word was with power] for He taught them as one that had authority, and not as the scribes. And there was in their synagogue a man with an unclean spirit; and he cried out [with a loud voice,] saying, Let *us* alone; what have we to do with Thee, Thou Jesus of Nazareth? Art Thou come to destroy us? I Know Thee who Thou art, the Holy One of God. And Jesus rebuked him, saying, Hold thy peace, and come out of him. And when the [devil] unclean spirit had *tom* [thrown] him [in the midst], and cried with a loud voice, he came out of him [and hurt him not]. And they were all amazed, insomuch that they [spake] questioned among themselves, saying, What thing *is* this [a word *is* this]? What new doctrine *is* this? For with authority [and power] commandeth He even the unclean spirits, and they do obey Him [come out]. And immediately [The] His fame spread abroad (went throughout all Syria) throughout all the region [into every place of the country round about] Galilee.

And forthwith, when they [He arose] (Jesus was) were come out of the synagogue, they entered into the house of Simon (Peter's) house and Andrew, with James and John: But (He saw) Simon's wife's mother lay (laid) sick of a [was taken] [with] a [great] fever, and anon they tell [besought] Him of [for] her. And He came [and stood over her,] and took her by the hand (touched her), [and rebuked the fever] and lifted her up; and immediately the fever [it] left her, and (she arose) she ministered unto them. And [now] at even, when (was come) the sun did set [was setting] [All] they brought [them] unto Him all (many) that [they] were diseased (with divers diseases and torments), and them that were possessed with devils (and those which were lunatick, and those that had the palsy). And all the city was gathered together at the door. And [laid His hands on everyone of them and] He healed (them) many (all manner) that were sick of divers (all manner of) diseases (among the people), and cast out many devils (the spirits with *His* word.), [crying out and saying, Thou art Christ the Son of God. (And healed all that were sick) and suffered not the devils [them] to speak, because they knew Him [that He was Christ]. (That it might be fulfilled which was spoken by Esaias the prophet, saying, Himself took our infirmities, and bare *our* sicknesses.)

And in the morning, rising up a great while before day, [when it was day] he went out, and departed into a solitary [desert] place, and there prayed. And Simon and they that were with him followed after Him. And when they had found Him, they said unto Him, All *men* seek for Thee. And He said unto them, Let us go into the next towns, that I any preach there also: for therefore came I forth. And He preached in their synagogues throughout all Galilee, and cast out devils. (And there followed Him great multitudes of the people [sought him], [and came unto Him, and stayed Him, that He should not, depart from them. And He said unto them, I must preach the kingdom of God to other cities also: for therefore am I sent.] from Galilee, and *from* Decapolis, and *from* Jerusalem, and *from* Judaea, and *from* beyond Jordan.)

(23) (10) **[Luke 5:1–6:5]** (Matthew 8:2–4, 9:1–17, 12:1–8){Mark 1:40–2:28}

[And it came to pass, that, as the people pressed upon Him to hear the Word of God, He stood by the lake Gennesaret, and saw two ships standing by the lake: but the fishermen were gone out of them, and were washing *their* nets. And He entered into one of the ships, which was Simon's and prayed him that he would thrust out a little from the land. And He sat down, and taught the people out of the ship. Now when he had left speaking, He said unto Simon, launch out into the deep, and let down your nets for a draught. And Simon answering said unto him, Master, we have toiled all night, and have taken nothing: nevertheless at Thy word I will let down the net. And when they had this done, they inclosed a great multitude of fishes: and their net brake. And the beckoned unto *their* partners, which were in the other ship, that they should come and help them. And they came and filled both the ships, so that they began to sink.

When Simon Peter saw *it*, he fell down at Jesus' knees, saying, depart from me; for I am a sinful man, O Lord. For he was astonished, and all that were with him, at the draught of the fishes which they had taken: And so *was* also James, and John, the sons of Zebedee, which were partners with Simon. And Jesus said unto Simon, Fear not; from henceforth thou shalt catch men. And when they had brought their ships to land, they forsook all, and followed Him. And it came to pass, when He was in a certain city behold (there came a leper)

{to Him} a man full of leprosy: who seeing Jesus fell on *his* face (and worshipped Him) and besought Him, saying, Lord, if Thou wilt Thou canst make me clean. And He (Jesus) put forth *His* hand, and touched him, saying, I will: be thou clean. And {as soon as He had spoken} immediately the leprosy (was cleansed) and departed from him. And He (Jesus) {straightly} charged him (See thou) tell no man: but go, and shew thyself to the priest. And offer for thy cleaning (the gift) according as Moses commanded, for a testimony unto them, {and forthwith sent him away}. But {he went out} so much the more {and began to publish it much and to blaze abroad the matter} then went there a fame abroad of Him: {insomuch that Jesus could no more openly enter into the city, but was without in desert places} and great multitudes came together {from every quarter} to hear, and to be healed by Him, of their infirmities. And He withdrew Himself into the wilderness, and prayed.

And it came to pass on a certain day (He entered into a ship, and passed over, and came into His own city.) {many were gathered together} as He was teaching, {He preached the word unto them} that there were Pharisees and doctors of the law sitting by, which were come out of every town of Galilee, and Judaea, and Jerusalem: and the power of the Lord was *present* to heal them.

And, behold, men brought in a bed with a man which was taken (sick) with a palsy {which was borne of four}: and they sought *means* to bring him in, and to lay *him* before Him. And when they could not find by what *way* they might bring him in because of the multitude, they went upon the house top, {they uncovered the roof where he was: and when they had broken it up.}, and let him down through the tiling with *his* couch into the midst before Jesus. And when He

{Jesus} saw their faith, He said unto him (sick of the palsy), Man {Son}, (be of good cheer;) thy sins are forgiven thee **And (behold)** (certain of) the scribes and Pharisees {sitting there} began to reason {in their hearts}, saying, who is this which speaketh blasphemies? Who can forgive sins, but God alone {only}? But {immediately} when Jesus perceived {in His Spirit} their thoughts {that they rea-soned within themselves}, He answering said unto them (wherefore think ye evil) What reason ye {these things} in your hearts? Whether is easier, to say, {to the sick of palsy}, Thy sins be forgiven thee; or to say, Rise {take thy bed} up and walk? But that ye may know that the Son of Man hath power upon earth to forgive sins **(He said unto the sick of the palsy)** I say unto thee, Arise, and take up thy couch, and go into thine house. **And immediately he rose up before them {all},** and took up that whereon he lay, and departed to his own house, glo-rifying God. And they (the multitudes) were all amazed (marvelled), and they glorified God (which had given such power unto men.) and were filled with fear, saying, we have seen {never saw it on this fash-ion} strange things to day.

And after these things **He went forth** {again by the sea side: and all the multitude resorted unto Him, and He taught them}, and {as He passed by} saw a publican (a man), named Levi (Matthew), {the son of Alphaeus} sitting at the receipt of custom; **and He said unto Him, Follow me. And he left all, rose up, and followed Him. And** Levi made Him a great feast in his own house: **and there was a great company of publicans and of others {sinners} that sat down with them (Him and His disciples.) But their scribes and Pharisees** (saw it) **murmured against His disciples, saying, Why do ye eat and drink with publicans and sinners? (But) Jesus {heard it} answering said unto them,** they that are whole need not a physician; but they that are sick. (But go ye and learn what that meaneth, I will have mercy, and not sacrifice: for) I came not to call the righteous, but sinners to repentance.

(Then came to Him the disciples of John) and they said unto Him, why do (we) the disciples of John fast often (but thy disciples fast not?) and make prayers, and likewise *the disciples* **of the Pharisees; but thine eat and drink? And He said unto them,** can ye make the children of the bridechamber fast (mourn), while the bridegroom is with them? {as long as they have the bridegroom with them, they cannot fast} But the days will come, when the bridegroom shall be taken away from them, and then shall they fast in those days.

And He spake also a parable unto them; No man putteth a piece of a new garment (cloth) upon an old (garment) if otherwise, then both the new (that which is put in to fill it up taketh from the garment) maketh a (worse) rent, and the piece that was *taken* out of the new agreeth not with the old. And no man putteth new wine into old bottles; else the new wine will burst the bottles, and {the wine} be spilled, and the bottles shall perish. But new wine must be put into new bottles; and both are preserved. No man also having drunk old *wine* straightway desireth new: for he saith, the old is better.

(At that time) it came to pass on the second sabbath **after the first, that He (Jesus) went through the com fields; and His disciples (were an hungred and) plucked the ears of corn, and did eat, rubbing** *them* in *their* **hands. And certain of the Pharisees (when they saw it) said unto them (Him), (behold) why do ye (Thy disciples) that which is not lawful to do on the sabbath days? And Jesus answering them said,** Have ye not read so much as this, what David did, when himself {had need and} was an hungred, {he} and they which were with him; How he went into the house of God {in the days of Abiathar the high priest,} and did take and eat the shew bread, and gave also to them that were with him; which is not lawful (for them) to eat but (only) for the priests alone? (Or have ye not read in the law that on the sabbath days the priests in the temple profane the sabbath, and are blameless? But I say unto you, That in this place is one greater than the temple. But if ye had known what this meaneth, I will have mercy, and not sacrifice, ye would not have condemned the guiltless.) **And He said unto them (**The sabbath was made for man, and not man for the sabbath;) That the Son of Man is Lord (even) also of the sabbath (day).]

(24) (14) **<John 5:1–47>**

<After this there was a feast of the Jews, and Jesus went up to Jerusalem. Now there is at Jerusalem by the sheep *market* a pool,

which is called in the Hebrew tongue Bethesda, having five porches. In these lay a great multitude of impotent folk, of blind, halt, withered, waiting for the moving of the water. For an angel went down at a certain season into the pool, and troubled the water; whosoever then first after the troubling of the water stepped in was made whole of whatsoever disease he had. And a certain man was there, which had an infirmity thirty and eight years. When Jesus saw him lie, and knew that he had been now a long time *in that case*, He saith unto him, Wilt Thou be made whole? The Impotent man answered Him, Sir, I have no man, when the water is troubled, to put me into the pool; but while I am coming, another steppeth down before me. Jesus saith unto him, Rise, take up thy bed, and walk. And immediately the man was made whole, and took up his bed, and walked: and on the same day was the sabbath.

The Jews therefore said unto him that was cured, It is the sabbath day: it is not lawful for thee to carry *thy* bed. He answered them, He that made me whole, the same said unto me, Take up thy bed, and walk. Then asked they him, What man is that which said unto thee, Take up thy bed, and walk? And he that was healed wist not who it was: for Jesus had conveyed Himself away, a multitude being in *that* place. Afterward Jesus findeth him in the temple, and said unto him, Behold, thou art made whole: sin no more, lest a worse thing come unto thee. The man departed, and told the Jews that it was Jesus, which had made him whole. And therefore did the Jews persecute Jesus, and sought to slay Him, because He had done these things on the sabbath day.

But Jesus answered them, My Father worketh hitherto, and I work. Therefore the Jews sought the more to kill Him, because He not only had broken the sabbath, but said also that God was His Father, making Himself equal with God. Then answered Jesus and said unto them, Verily verily I say unto you, The Son can do nothing of Himself, but what He seeth the Father do: for what things soever He doeth, these also doeth the Son likewise. For the Father loveth the Son, and sheweth Him all things that Himself doeth: and He will shew Him greater works than these, that ye may marvel. For as the Father raiseth up the dead, and quickeneth *them*; even so the Son quickeneth whom He will. For the Father judgeth no man, but hath committed all judgement unto the Son: That all *men* should honour the Son, even as they honour the Father. He that honoureth not the Son, honoureth not the Father which has sent Him. Verily, verily, I say unto you, He that heareth My word, and believeth on Him that sent Me, hath everlasting life, and shall not come into condemnation; but is passed from death unto life. Verily, verily, I say unto you, The hour is coming, and now is, when the dead shall hear the voice of the Son of God: and they that hear shall live For as the Father hath life in Himself; so hath He given to the Son to have life in Himself; And has given Him authority to execute judgement also, because He-is the Son of man. Marvel not at this: for the hour is coming, in the which all that are in the graves shall hear His voice, and shall come forth; they that have done good, unto the resurrection of life; and they that have done evil, unto the resurrection of damnation. I can of my ownself do nothing: as I hear, I judge: and My judgement is just; because I seek not Mine own will, but the will of the Father which has sent Me. If I bear witness of Myself, My witness is not true.

There is another that beareth witness of *me*: and I know that the witness which He witnesseth of Me is true. Ye sent unto John, and he bare witness unto the truth. But I receive not testimony from man: but these things I say, that ye might be saved. He was a burning and shining light: and ye were willing for a season to rejoice in his light.

But I have greater witness than *that* of John: for the works which the Father hath given *me* to finish, the same works that I do, bear witness of Me, that the Father hath sent Me. And the Father Himself, which hath sent me, hath borne witness of Me. Ye have neither heard His voice at any time, nor seen His shape. And ye have not His word abiding in you: for whom He hath sent, Him ye believe not.

Search the scriptures: for in them ye think ye have eternal life: and they are they which testify of *me*. And ye will not come to me, that ye might have life. I receive not honour from men. But I know you, that ye have not the love of God in you. I am come in My Father's name, and ye receive me not: if another shall come in his own name, him ye will receive. How can ye believe, which receive honour one of another, and seek not the honour that cometh, from

God only? Do not think that I will accuse you to the Father: there is one that accuseth you, even Moses, in whom ye trust. For had ye believed Moses, ye would have believed Me: for he wrote of Me. But if ye believe not his writings, how shall ye believe My words?>

(25) (11) **[Luke 6:6–11]** (Matthew 12:9–13) {Mark 3:1–5}

[(And when He was departed thence) it came to pass also on another sabbath, **That** He (went) entered {again} into the (their) synagogue and taught: and (behold) there was a man whose right hand was withered And the scribes and Pharisees (they asked Him saying Is it lawful to heal on the sabbath days?) watched Him, whether He would heal on the sabbath day; that they might find an accusation against Him. But He knew their thoughts, and said to the man which had the withered hand, Rise up, and stand forth in the midst. And he arose and stood forth. Then said {He} Jesus unto them, I will ask you one thing; Is it lawful on the sabbath days to do good, or to do evil? To save life, or to {kill} destroy *it*? And He said unto them (What man shall there be among you, that shall have one sheep, and if it fall into a pit on the sabbath day, will he not lay hold on it, and lift *it* out? How much then is a man better than a sheep? Wherefore it is lawful to do well on the sabbath days.) {But they held their peace} And looking {when He had look} round about upon {on} them all, {with anger, being grieved for the hardness of their hearts.} (Then) He said unto the man, stretch forth thy hand. And he did so (stretched *it* forth) {out}: and his hand was (it) restored whole (like) as the other. And they were filled with madness; and communed one with another what they might do to Jesus.]

(26) (12) **(Matthew 12:14–21)** {Mark 3:6–12}

(Then the Pharisees went out {forth}, and {straightway} held {took} a council {with the Herodians} against Him, how they might destroy Him. But when Jesus knew *it*, He withdrew Himself {with His disciples} from thence: {to the sea} and great multitudes followed Him, {from Galilee, and from Judaea, and from Jerusalem, and from Idumaea, and *from* beyond Jordan; and they about Tyre and Sidon, when they had heard what great things He did, came to Him. And

He spake to His disciples, that a small ship should wait on Him because of the multitude, lest they should throng Him.} and He healed them all: {many} {insomuch that they pressed upon Him, for to touch Him, as many as had plagues. And unclean spirits, when they saw Him, fell down before Him, and cried, saying, Thou art the Son of God,} and {He straitly} charged them that they should not make Him known: That it might be fulfilled which was spoken by Esaias the prophet, saying, behold My servant, whom I have chosen; My beloved, in whom My soul is well pleased: I will put My Spirit upon Him, and He shall shew judgement to the Gentiles. He shall not strive, nor cry; neither shall any man hear His voice in the streets. A bruised reed shall He not break, and a smoking flax shall He not quench, till He send forth judgement unto victory. And in His name shall the Gentiles trust.)

(27) (13) **(Matthew 5:1–8:4)** {Mark 3:13–19} [Luke 6:12–38]

(And [it came to pass in those days] seeing the multitudes, [that] He went up into a mountain [to pray and continued all night in prayer to God, and when it was day, He called {whom He would}

[*unto Him,* His disciples:] and when He was set, His disciples came unto Him: [and of them He chose {and He ordained} [twelve,] {that they should be with Him, and that He might send them forth to preach, and to have power to heal sicknesses, and to cast out devils:} [whom also He named apostles; Simon,] (whom) He also {surnamed} Peter) [and Andrew his brother, James] {the *son* of Zebedee} [and John] {*his* brother, He surnamed them Boanerges which is the sons of thunder,} [Philip and Bartholomew, Matthew and Thomas, James the *son* of Alphaeus, and Simon called Zelotes, {the Canaanite}, [and Judas] {Thaddaeus} [the brother of James, and Judas Iscariot, which also was the traitor,] {*who* betrayed Him}. [And He came down with them, and stood in the plain, and the company of His disciples, and a great multitude of people out of all Judaea and Jerusalem, and from the sea coast of Tyre and Sidon, which came to hear Him, and to be healed of their diseases; and they that were vexed with unclean spirits: and they were healed. And the whole multitude sought to touch Him: for there went virtue out of

Him, and healed them all. And He lifted up His eyes on His disciples] And He opened His mouth and taught them, saying, Blessed *are* the poor in spirit: for theirs is the kingdom of [God] heaven. Blessed *are* they that mourn: for they shall be comforted. [Blessed are ye that weep now: for ye shall laugh.] Blessed *are* the meek: for they shall inherit the earth. Blessed *are* they which do hunger [now] and thirst after righteousness: for they shall be filled. Blessed *are* the merciful: for they shall obtain mercy. Blessed *are* the pure in heart; for they shall see God. Blessed *are* the peacemakers; for they shall be called the children of God. Blessed *are* they which are persecuted for righteousness' sake: for theirs is the kingdom of heaven. Blessed are ye, when *men* shall revile [hate] you, and persecute [and reproach] you,[and shall separate you *from their company*] and shall say all manner of evil against you falsely [and cast out your name as evil], for My [the son of man's] sake. Rejoice [ye in that day], and [leap for joy] be exceeding glad: [Behold] for great *is* your reward in heaven: for [in like manner did their fathers] so persecuted they the prophets which were before you. [But woe unto you that are rich! For ye have received your consulation. Woe unto you that are full! For ye shall hunger. Woe unto you that laugh now! For ye shall mourn and weep. Woe unto you, when all men shall speak well of you! For so did their fathers to the false prophets.]

Ye are the salt of the earth: but if the salt have lost his savour, wherewith shall it be salted? It is henceforth good for nothing, but to be cast out, and be trodden under foot of men. Ye are the light of the world, a city that is set on a hill cannot be hid. Neither do men light a candle, and put it under a bushel, but on a candle stick: and it giveth light unto all that are in the house. Let your light so shine before men, that they may see your good works, and glorify your Father which is in heaven.

Think not that I am come to destroy the law, or the prophets; I am not come to destroy, but to fulfil. For verily I say unto you, Till heaven and earth pass, one jot or one tittle shall in no wise pass from the law, till all be fulfilled. Whosoever therefore shall break one of these least commandments and shall teach men so, he shall be called the least in the kingdom of heaven: but whosoever shall do and *teach them*, the same shall be called great in the kingdom of heaven. For I say unto you, That except your righteousness shall exceed the *righteousness* of the scribes and Pharisees, ye shall in no case enter into the kingdom of heaven.

Ye have heard that it was said by them of old time, thou shalt not kill: and whosoever shall kill shall be in danger of the judgement: But I say unto you, that whosoever is angry with his brother without a cause shall be in danger of the judgement: and whosoever shall say to his brother, Raca, shall be in danger of the council: but whosoever shall say, thou fool, shall be in danger of hell fire. Therefore if thou bring thy gift to the altar, and there rememberest that thy brother hath ought against thee; leave there thy gift before the altar, and go thy way; first be reconciled to thy brother, and then come and offer thy gift. Agree with thine adversary quickly, whiles thou art in the way with him; lest at any time the adversary deliver thee to the judge, and the judge deliver thee to the officer, and thou be cast into prison. Verily I say unto thee, thou shalt by no means come out thence, till thou hast paid the uttermost farthing.

Ye have heard that it was said by them of old time, thou shalt not commit adultery: But I say unto you, That whosoever looketh on a woman to lust after her hath committed adultery already in his heart. And if thy right eye offend thee, pluck it out, and cast *it* from thee: for it is profitable for thee that one of thy members should perish, and not *that* thy whole body should be cast into hell. And if thy right hand offend thee, cut it off, and cast it: for it is profitable for thee that one of thy members should perish, and not that thy whole body should be cast into hell. It hath been said, whosoever shall put away his wife, let him give her a writing of divorcement: But I say unto you, that whosoever shall put away his wife, saving for the cause of fornication, causeth her to commit adultery: and whosoever shall marry her that is divorced commiteth adultery.

Again, ye have heard that it hath been said by them of old time, thou shalt not forswear thyself, but shalt perform unto the Lord thine oaths: But I say unto you, Swear not at all; neither by heaven; for it is God's throne: nor by the earth: for it is His footstool: neither by Jerusalem; for it is the city of the great King. Neither shalt thou swear by thy head, because thou canst not make one hair white or black. But let your communication be, Yea, yea; Nay, nay; for whatsoever is more than these cometh of evil.

Ye have heard that it hath been said, An eye for an eye, and a tooth for a tooth: But I say unto you, That ye resist not evil: but whosoever shall smite thee on thy right cheek, turn to him [and offer] the other also. And if any man will sue thee at the law, and take away thy coat, let him have *thy* cloke also. And whosoever shall compel thee to go a mile, go with him twain. [As ye would that men should do to you, do ye also to them likewise.] Give to him [every man] that asketh thee, [give, and it shall be given unto you; good measure, press down, and shaken together, and running over, shall men give into your bosom. For with the same measure that ye mete withal it shall be measured to you again.] And from him that would borrow of thee turn not away. [If you lend to *them* of whom ye hope to receive what thank have ye? For sinners also lend to sinners, to receive as much again. But love ye your enemies, and do good, and lend hoping for nothing again; and your reward shall be great, and ye shall be the children of the Highest: for He is kind unto the unthankful and *to* the evil. Be ye therefore merciful, as your Father also is merciful.]

Ye have heard that it hath been said, Thou shalt Love thy neighbour, and hate thine enemy.

But I say unto you, [you which hear] Love your enemies, bless them that curse you; do good to them that [which] hate you, and pray for them which despitefully use you, and persecute you; That ye may be the children of your Father which is in heaven: for He makes His sun to rise on the evil and on the good, and sendeth rain on the just and on the unjust. For if ye love them which love you, what reward [thank] have ye? Do not even the publicans [sinners] [also do] the same? [And if ye do good to them which do good to you, what thank have ye? For sinners also do even the same] And if ye salute your brethren only, what do ye more *than others*? Do not even the publicans so? Be ye therefore perfect, even as your Father which is in heaven is perfect.

Take heed that ye do not your alms before men, to be seen of them; otherwise ye have no reward of your Father which is in heaven.

Therefore when thou doest *thine* alms, do not sound a trumpet before thee, as the hypocrites do in the synagogues and in the streets, that they may have glory of men. Verily I say unto you, they have their reward. But when thou doest alms, let not thy left hand know what thy right hand doeth: That thine alms may be in secret: and thy Father which seeth in secret Himself shall reward thee openly. And when thou prayest, thou shalt not be as the hypocitres *are*: for they love to pray standing in the synagogues and in the corners of the streets, that they may be seen of men. Verily I say unto you, they have their reward. But thou, when thou prayest, enter into thy closet, and when thou hast shut thy door, pray to thy Father which is in secret: and thy Father which seeth in secret shall reward thee openly. But when ye pray, use not vain repetitions, as the heathen *do*; for they think that they shall be heard for their much speaking. Be not ye therefore like unto them: for your Father knoweth what things ye have need of, before ye ask Him. After this manner therefore pray ye: Our Father which art in heaven, Hallowed be Thy name. Thy kingdom come. Thy will be done in earth, as *it is* in heaven. Give us this day our dailey bread. And forgive us our debts as we forgive our debtors. And lead us not into temptation, but deliver us from evil: For Thine is the kingdom, and the power, and the glory, forever, Amen. For if ye forgive men their trespasses your heavenly Father will also forgive you: But if ye forgive not men their trespasses, neither will your Father forgive your trespasses.

Moreover when ye fast, be not, as the hypocrites, of a sad countenance: for they disfigure their faces, that they may appear unto men to fast. Verily I say unto you, They have their reward. But thou, when thou fastest, anoint thine head, and wash thy face; That thou appear not unto men to fast, but unto thy Father, which seeth in secret, shall reward thee openly.

Lay not up for yourselves treasures upon earth, where moth and rust doeth corrupt: and where thieves break through and steal: but lay up for yourselves treasures in heaven, where neither moth nor rust doeth corrupt, and where thieves do not break through nor steal: For where your treasure is, there will your heart be also. The light of the body is the eye: if therefore thine eye be single, thy whole body shall be full of light. But if thine eye be evil, thy whole body shall be full of darkness. If therefore the light that is in thee be darkness, how great *is* that darkness!

No man can serve two masters: for either he will hate the one. and love the other; or else he will hold to the one, and despise the other. Ye cannot serve God and mammon. Therefore I say unto you, Take no thought for your life, what ye shall eat, or what ye shall drink; nor yet for your body, what ye shall put on. Is not the life more than meat, and the body than raiment? Behold the fowls of the air: for they sow not, neither do they reap, nor gather into barns; yet your heavenly Father feedeth them, Are ye not much better than they? Which of you by taking thought can add one cubit unto his stature? And why take ye thought for raiment? Consider the lilies of the field, how they grow; they toil not, neither do they spin: and yet I say unto you, that even Solomon in all his glory was not arrayed like one of these. Wherefore if God so clothe the grass of the field, which today is, and tomorrow is cast into the oven, *shall He* not much more *clothe* you, O ye of little faith? Therefore take no thought, saying, what shall we eat? Or what shall we drink? Or, wherewithal shall we be clothed? (For after all these things do the Gentiles seek:) for your heavenly Father knoweth that ye have need of all these things. But seek ye first the kingdom of God, and His righteousness: and all these things shall be added unto you. Take therefore no thought for the morrow: for the morrow shall take thought for the things of itself. Sufficient unto the day *is* the evil thereof.

Judge not, that ye be not judged, For with what judgement ye judge, ye shall be judged: [condemn not, and ye shall not be condemned: forgive, and ye shall be forgiven:] and with what measure ye mete, it shall be measured to you again. And why beholdest thou the mote that is in thy brothers eye, but considerest not the beam that *is* in thine own eye? Or how wilt thou say to thy brother, Let me pull out the mote out of thine eye; and behold, a beam is in thine own eye? Thou hypocrite, first cast out the beam out of thine own eye; and then shalt thou see clearly to cast out the mote out of thy brother's eye.

Give not that which is holy unto the dogs, neither cast ye your pearls before swine, lest they trample them under their feet, and turn again and rend you.

Ask, and it shall be given you; seek, and ye shall find; knock, and it shall be opened unto you: For everyone that asketh receiveth; and he that seeketh findeth; and to him that knocketh it shall be opened. Or what man is there of you, whom if his son ask bread, will he give him a stone? Or if he ask a fish, will he give him a serpent? If ye then, being evil, know how to give good gifts unto your children, how much more shall your Father which is in heaven give good things to them that ask Him? Therefore all things whatsoever ye would that men should do to you, do ye even so to them: for this is the law and the prophets.

Enter ye in at the strait gate: for wide *is* the gate, and broad *is* the way, that leadeth to destruction, and many there be which go in thereat: Because strait *is* the gate, and narrow *is* the way, which leadeth unto life, and few there be that find it.

Beware of false prophets, which come to you in sheep's clothing, but inwardly they are ravening wolves. Ye shall know them by their fruits. Do men gather grapes of thorns, or figs of thistles? Even so every good tree bringeth forth good fruit; but a corrupt tree bringeth forth evil fruit. A good tree cannot bring forth evil fruit, neither *can* a corrupt tree bring forth good fruit. Every tree the bringeth not forth good fruit is hewn down, and cast into the fire Wherefore by their fruits ye shall know them.

Not every one that saith unto me, Lord, Lord, shall enter into the kingdom of heaven; but he that doeth the will of my Father which is in heaven. Many will say to Me in that day, Lord, Lord, have we not prophesied in thy name? And in thy name have cast out devils? And in thy name done many wonderful works? And then will I profess unto them, I never knew you: depart from Me, ye that work iniquity.

Therefore whosoever heareth these sayings of Mine, and doeth them, I will liken him unto a wise man, which built his house upon a rock: And the rain descended, and the floods came, and the winds blew, and beat upon that house; and it fell not: for it was founded upon a rock. And every one that heareth these sayings of mine, and doeth them not, shall be likened unto a foolish man, which built his house upon the sand: And the rain descended, and the floods came, and the winds blew, and beat upon that house; and it fell: and great was the fall of it.

And it came to pass, when Jesus had ended these sayings, the people were astonished at His doctrine: For He taught them as one having authority, and not as the scribes.

When He was come down from the mountain, great multitudes followed Him. And behold, there came a leper and worshipped Him, saying, Lord, if Thou wilt, Thou canst make me clean. And Jesus put forth *His* hand, and touched him saying, I will; be thou clean. And immediately his leprosy was cleansed. And Jesus saith unto him, See thou tell no man; but go thy way, shew thyself to the priest and offer the gift that Moses commanded, for a testimony unto them.)

(28) (14) **(Matthew 12:22–45)** {Mark 3:22–30} [Luke 11:14–26]

(Then was brought unto Him *one* possessed with a devil, blind, and dumb: and He healed him, insomuch that the blind and dumb both spake and saw. And all the people were amazed, and said, is not this the son of David? But when the Pharisees {and the scribes which came down from Jerusalem} heard *it*, they said, {He hath Beelzebub} this *fellow* doth not cast out devils, but by Beelzebub the prince [chief] of the devils. [And others, tempting *Him*, sought of Him a sign from heaven] and Jesus knew their thoughts, {He called them *unto Him*,} and said unto them, {in parables}, Every kingdom divided against itself is brought to desolation; and every city or house divided against itself shall not stand: And if Satan cast out Satan, he is divided against himself; how shall then his kingdom stand? {If a house be divided against itself, that house can not stand.} {but he hath an end}. And if I by Beelzebub cast out devils, by whom do your children cast *them* out? Therefore they shall be your judges. But if I cast out devils by the Spirit of God, [with the finger of God], then the kingdom of God is come unto [upon] you. Or else how can one enter into an [Armed] strong man's house, and spoil his goods, except [when a stronger than he shall come upon him] he first bind the strong man [by overcoming him he taketh from him all his armour wherein he trusted]? And then he will spoil his house. He that is not with me is against me: and he that gathereth not with me scattereth abroad. [When the unclean spirit is gone out of a man, he walketh through dry places, seeking rest; and finding none, he saith I will return unto my house whence I came out. And when he cometh he findeth it swept and garnished then goeth he, and taketh to him seven other spirits more wicked than himself: and they enter in and dwell there: and the last state of that man is worst than the first.] Even so shall it be also unto this wicked generation.

Wherefore {verily} I say unto you, All manner of sin and blasphemy shall be forgiven unto {the sons of} men: but the blasphemy *against* the *Holy* Ghost shall not be forgiven unto men {but is in danger of eternal damnation:}. And whosoever speaketh a word against the Son of man, it shall be forgiven him: but whosoever speaketh against the Holy Ghost, it shall not be forgiven him, neither in this world, neither in the *world* to come. Either make the tree good, and his fruit good: or else make the tree corrupt, and his fruit corrupt: for the tree is known by *his* fruit. O generation of vipers, how can ye, being evil, speak good things? For out of the abundance of the heart the mouth speaketh. A good man out of the good treasure of the heart bringeth forth good things: and an evil man out of the evil treasure bringeth forth evil things. But I say unto you, that every idle word that men shall speak, they shall give account thereof in the day of judgement For by thy words thou shalt be justified, and by thy words thou shalt be condemned. {Because they said, He hath an unclean spirit.}

Then certain of the scribes and of the Pharisees answered, saying, Master, we would see a sign from thee. But He answered and said unto them, An evil and adulterous generation seeketh after a sign; and there shall no sign be given to it, but the sign of the prophet Jonas: For as Jonas was three days and three nights in the whale's belly; so shall the Son of man be three days and three nights in the heart of the earth. The men of Ninevah shall rise in judgement with this generation, and shall condemn it: because they repented at the preaching of Jonas; and, behold, a greater than Jonas is here The queen of the south shall rise up in judgement with this generation, and shall condemn it: for she came from the uttermost parts of the earth to hear the wisdom of Solomon; and, behold, a greater than Solomon *is* here. When the unclean spirit is gone out of a man, he walketh through dry places, seeking rest, and findeth none. Then he saith, I will return into my house from whence I came out; and when he is come, he findeth *it* empty, swept, and garnished. Then goeth he, and taketh with himself seven other spirits more wicked than himself, and they enter in and dwell there: and the last *state* of that man is worse than the first. Even so shall it be also unto this wicked generation.)

(29) (15) **[Luke 7:1–10]** (Matthew 8:5–13)

[Now when He had ended all His sayings in the audience of the people, He entered into Capernaum And a certain centurion's servant, who was dear unto him, was sick, and ready to die. And when he had heard of Jesus, he sent unto Him the elders of the Jews, beseeching Him that He would come and heal his servant. And when they came to Jesus, they besought Him instantly, saying, that he was worthy for whom he should do this: For he loveth our nation, and he hath built us a synagogue. Then Jesus went with them. And when He was now not far from the house the centurion sent friends to Him (and came unto Him a centurion beseeching Him) saying unto Him Lord (my servant lieth at home sick of the palsy, grievously tormented) trouble not Thyself: for I am not worthy that thou shouldest enter (come) under my roof: Wherefore neither thought I myself worthy to come unto thee: but say in a (speak the) word (only), and my servant shall be healed, For I also am a man set under authority, having under me soldiers, and I say unto one, Go, and he goeth; and to another come and he cometh; and to my servant, Do this, and he doeth *it*. When Jesus heard these things, He marvelled at him, and turned Him about, and said unto the people that followed Him (Verily) I say unto you, I have not found so great faith, no not in Israel. (And I say unto you, That many shall come from the east and west, and shall sit down with Abraham, and Isaac, and Jacob, in the Kingdom of heaven. But the children of the kingdom shall be cast out into outer darkness: there shall be weeping and gnashing of teeth. And Jesus said unto the centurion, Go thy way; and as thou hast believed, so be it done unto thee.) And they that were sent, returning to the house, found the servant (was healed) whole that had been sick (in the selfsame hour).]

(30) (15) **[Luke 7:11–17]**

[And it came to pass the day after, that He went into a city called Nain; and many of His disciples went with Him, and much people. Now when He came nigh to the gate of the city, behold, there was a dead man carried out, the only son of his mother, and she was a widow: and much people of the city was with her. And when the Lord saw her, He had compassion on her, and said unto her, Weep not. And He came and touched the bier; and they that bare *him* stood still. And He said, Young man, I say unto thee, Arise And he that was dead sat up, and began to speak. And He delivered him to his mother. And there came a fear on all: and they glorified God, saying, That a great prophet is risen up among us; and, That God hath visited His people. And this rumour of Him went forth throughout all Judaea, and throughout all the region round about.]

(31) (16) **(Matthew 11:2–15)** [Luke 7:18–30]

([And the disciples of John shewed him of all these things] Now when John had heard in the prison the works of Christ, he [called *and*] sent two of his, disciples [to Jesus], and said unto Him, Art thou He that should come, or do we look for another?

[And in the same hour He cured many of *their* infirmities and plaques, and of evil spirits; and unto many that were blind He gave sight.] Jesus answered and said unto them, Go [your way] and shew John again those things which ye do hear and see: the blind receive their sight, and the lame walk, the lepers are cleansed, and the deaf hear, the dead are raised up, the poor have the gospel preached to them. And blessed is *he*, whosoever shall not be offended in Me. And as they [the messengers of John were] depart, Jesus began to say unto the multitudes concerning John, what went ye out into the wilderness to see? A reed shaken in the wind? But what went ye out for to see? A man clothed in soft raiment? Behold, they that wear soft [gorgeous] *clothing* [and live delicately] are in kings' houses. But what went ye out for to see? A prophet? Yea, I say unto you, and [much] more than a prophet. For this is *he*, of whom it is written, Behold, I send My messenger before Thy face, which shall prepare Thy way before Thee. Verily I say unto you, among them that are born, of women there hath not risen a greater than John the Baptist: Notwithstanding he that is least in the kingdom of heaven [God] is greater than he. And from the days of John the Baptist until now the kingdom of heaven suffereth violence, and the violent take it by force. For all the prophets and the law prophesied until John. And if ye will receive *it*, this is Elias, which was for to come. He that hath ears to hear, let them hear. [And all the people that heard *Him*, and the publicans, justified God, being baptized with the baptism of John. But the Pharisees and lawyers rejected the counsel of God against themselves, being not baptized of him.])

(32) (17) **(Matthew 11:16–19)** [Luke 7:31–35]

([And The Lord said,] But whereunto [then] shall I liken [the men of] this generation [and to what are they like]? It is like unto children sitting in the market [place], and calling unto their fellows, and saying, we have piped unto you, and ye have not danced; we have mourned unto you, and ye have not lamented [wept]. For John [the Baptist] came neither eating [bread] nor drinking [wine]; and they say, he hath a devil. The Son of man came eating and drinking, and they say, Behold a man gluttonous, and a winebibber, a friend of publicans and sinners. But wisdom is justifed of [all] her children.)

(33) (16) **(Matthew 11:20–30)**

(Then began He to upbraid the cities wherein most of His mighty works were done, because they repented not: Woe unto thee, Chorazin! Woe unto thee, Bethsaida! For if the mighty works, which were done in you, had been done in Tyre and Sidon, they would have repented long ago in sackcloth and ashes. But I say unto you, it shall be more tolerable for Tyre and Sidon at the day of judgement, than for you. And thou Capernaum, which art exalted unto heaven, shalt be brought down to hell: for if the mighty works, which have been done in thee, had been done in Sodom, it would have remained until this day, But I say unto you, That it shall be more tolerable for the land of Sodom in the day of judgement, than for thee.

At that time Jesus answered and said, I thank thee, O Father, Lord of heaven and earth, because Thou hast hid these things from the wise and prudent, and hast revealed them unto babes. Even so, Father: for so it seemed good in Thy sight. All things are delivered unto me of my Father: and no man knoweth the Son but the Father; neither knoweth any man the Father, save the Son, and *he* to whomsoever the Son will reveal *Him.*

Come unto Me, all ye that labour and are heavy laden, and I will give you rest. Take My yoke upon you, and learn of Me; for I am meek and lowly in heart: and ye shall find rest unto your souls. For My yoke *is* easy, and My burden is light.)

(34) (17) [**Luke 7:36–8:3**]

[And one of the Pharisees desired Him that He would eat with him. And He went into the Pharisee's house, and sat down to meat. And, behold, a woman in the city, which was a sinner, when she knew that *Jesus* sat at meat in the Pharisee's house brought an alabaster box of ointment, And stood at His feet behind *Him* weeping, and began to wash His feet with tears, and did wipe *them* with the hairs of her head, and kissed His feet, and anointed *them* with the ointment. Now when the Pharisee which had bidden Him saw *it*, he spake within himself, saying. This man, if He were a prophet, would have known who and what manner of woman *this is* that toucheth Him: for she is a sinner. And Jesus answering said unto him, Simon, I have somewhat to say unto thee. And he saith Master, say on. There was a certain creditor which had two debtors: the one owed five hundred pence, and the other fifty. And when they had nothing to pay, he frankly forgave them both. Tell me therefore, which of them will love him most? Simon answered and said, I suppose that he, to whom he forgave most. And He said unto him, Thou hast rightly judged. And He turned to the woman, and said unto Simon, Seest thou this woman? I entered into thine house, thou gavest Me no water for My feet: but she hath washed

My feet with tears, and wiped *them* with the hairs of her head. Thou gavest Me no kiss: but this woman since the time I came in hath not ceased to kiss my feet. My head with oil thou didst not anoint: but this woman hath anointed My feet with ointment. Wherefore I say unto thee, Her sins, which are many, are forgiven; for she loveth much: but to whom little is forgiven, *the same* loveth little. And He said unto her, Thy sins are forgiven. And they that sat at meat with Him began to say within themselves, Who is this that forgiveth sins also? And He said to the woman, Thy faith hath saved thee; go in peace.

And it came to pass afterward, that He went throughout every city and village, preaching and shewing the glad tidings of the kingdom of God: and the twelve *were* with Him, and certain women, which had been healed of evil spirits and infirmities, Mary called Magdalene, out of whom went seven devils, and Joanna the wife of Chuza Herod's steward, and Susanna, and many others, which ministered unto Him of their substance.]

(35) (18) **(Matthew 12:46–13:52)** {Mark 3:30–4:34) [Luke 6:39–49, 8:5–21]

(While He yet talked to the people, behold, {there came then} *His* mother and His brethren [and could not come at Him for the press] stood without, {sent unto Him, calling Him} desiring to speak with Him. {The multitudes sat about Him,} Then [by] one [certain which] said unto Him. [Behold Thy mother, and Thy brethren stand without {and seek for thee} desiring to see thee.] But He said unto him that told Him, {saying} Who is My mother? And who are My brethren? {And He looked round about on them which sat about Him,} and He stretched forth His hand toward His disciples, and said, Behold My mother and My brethren! For whosoever shall [hear the word of God, and] do the will of {God} My Father which is in heaven, the same is My brother, and sister, and mother.

The same day went Jesus out of the house, {He began again to teach,} and sat by the sea side And great multitudes were gathered together unto Him, so that He went into a ship, and sat {in the sea}; and the whole multitude stood {by} on the {land} shore. And He spake {and taught them} many things unto them in parables, saying,

{Harken} behold, a sower went forth to sow; [his seed] And {it came to pass} when He sowed, some *seeds* fell by the way side, [and it was trodden down,] and the fowls {of the air}came and devoured them up: {And} some fell upon stony places, where they had not much earth: and forthwith {immediately} they sprang up, because they had no deepness of earth: And when the sun was up, they were scorched: and because they had no root, they withered away [because it lacked moisture]. And some fell among thorns; and the thorns sprung up, and choked them {and it yielded no fruit}: But other fell into good ground, and brought forth fruit, {that sprang up and increased} some an hundredfold, some sixtyfold, some thirtyfold. {And He said [these things, He cried,] unto them} Who has ears to hear, let him hear.

{When He was alone, they that were about Him,} the disciples came, and said unto Him, Why speakest thou unto them in parables? [What might this parable be] He answered and said unto them, Because it is given unto you to know the mysteries of the kingdom of heaven {God}, but unto them {that are without, all *these* things are done in parables:} it is not given. For whosoever hath, to him shall be given, and he shall have more abundance: but whosoever hath not, from him shall be taken away even that he hath. Therefore speak I to them in parables: because they seeing see not {and not perceive}; and hearing they hear not, neither do they understand. And in them is fulfilled the prophecy of Esaias, which saith, By hearing ye shall hear, and shall not understand; and seeing ye shall see, and shall not perceive: For this peoples heart is waxed gross, and *their* ears are dull of hearing, and their eyes they have closed; lest at anytime they should see with *their* eyes, and hear with *their* ears, and should understand with *their* heart, and should be converted, {and *their* sins should be forgiven them,} and I should heal them.

{And He said unto them, Know ye not this parable'? And how then will ye know all parables'?} But blessed *are* your eyes, for they see: and your ears, for they hear. For verily I say unto you, that many prophets and righteous *men* have desired to see *those things* which ye see, and have not seen *them;* and to hear *those things* which ye hear, and have not heard *them.*

Hear ye therefore the parable of the sower. {The sower soweth the word,} [the seed is the word of God] when anyone heareth the word of the kingdom and understandeth *it* not, then cometh the wicked *one* {Satan}[the devil], and catcheth away {the word} that which was sown in his {their} heart. This is he which received seed by the way side. But he that received seed into stony places, the same is he {they} that heareth the word, and anon with {Immediate gladness} joy receiveth it; Yet hath he not root in himself, but dureth {endure but} for a while {time}: for when {affliction} tribulation or persecution ariseth because of the word {sake} by and by {Immediately they} he is offended [and fall away]. He also that received seed among the thorns is he that heareth the word; and the cares of this world, and the deceitfulness of riches, {and the lust of other things entering in,} [the pleasures of this life,] choke the word, and becometh unfruitful. But he that received seed into the good ground is he [which in an honest and good heart,] that heareth the word, {and receive it,} and understandeth *it*; [and keep it] which also beareth fruit,[with patience] and bringeth forth, some an hundredfold, some sixty, some thirty.

Another parable put He forth unto them saying, The kingdom of heaven is likened unto a man which sowed good seed in his field: But while men slept, his enemy came and sowed tares among the wheat, and went his way. But when the blade was sprung up, and brought forth fruit, then appeared the tares also. So the servant of the householder came and said unto him, Sir, didst not thou sow good seed in thy field? From whence then hath it tares? He said unto them, an enemy hath done this. The servants said unto him, wilt thou then that we go and gather them up? But he said, Nay; lest while ye gather up the tares, ye root up also the wheat with them. Let both grow together until the harvest: and in the time of harvest I will say to the reapers, gather ye together first the tares, and bind them in bundles to burn them: but gather the wheat into my barn.

Another parable put He forth unto them saying, {Whereunto shall we liken} the kingdom of heaven {God}? ((Or with what comparison shall we compare it?)) is like to a grain of mustard seed, which a man took, and sowed in his field: which indeed is the least of all seeds {that be in the earth}: but when {it is sown} it is grown, {up and becometh} it is the greatest among {all} herbs, and {shooteth out great branches;} and becometh a tree, so that the birds {fowls} of the air come and lodge {under the shadow of it} in the branches thereof.

{And He said unto them, Is a candle brought to be put under a bushel, or under a bed? And not to be set on a candlestick? [that they which enter in may see the light?] For there is nothing hid, [secret] which shall not be manifested; neither was any thing kept secret, but that it should [be known and] come abroad. If any man have ears to hear, let him hear. **And He said unto them,** Take heed what [how] ye hear: with what measure ye mete, it shall be measure to you: and unto you that hear shall more be given. For he that hath, to him shall be given: and he that hath not, from him shall be taken even that which he hath.

And He said, So is the kingdom of God, as if a man should cast seed into the ground; and should sleep, and rise night and day, and the seed should spring and grow up, he knoweth not how. For the earth bringeth forth fruit of herself; first the blade, then the ear, after that the full corn in the ear.

But when the fruit is brought forth, immediately he putteth in the sickle, because the harvest is come.}

[**And He spake a parable unto them,** Can the blind lead the blind? Shall they not both fall into a ditch? The disciple is not above his master. And why beholdest thou the mote that is in thy brother's eye, but perceivest not the beam that is in thine own eye? Either now canst thou say to thy brother Brother, let me pull out the mote that is in thine eye, when thou thyself beholdest not the beam that is in thine own eye? Thou hypocrite, cast out first the beam out of thine own eye, and then shall thou see clearly to pull out the mote that is in thy brother's eye. For a good tree bringeth not forth corrupt fruit; neither doeth a corrupt tree bring forth good fruit. For every tree is known by his own fruit. For of thorns men do not gather figs, nor of a bramble bush gather they grapes. A good man out of the good treasure of his heart bringeth forth that which is good; and an evil man out of the evil treasure of his heart bringeth forth that which is evil: for of the abundance of the heart his mouth speaketh.

And why call ye Me, Lord, Lord, and do not the things which I say? Whosoever cometh to Me, and heareth My sayings, and doeth them, I will shew you to whom he is like: He is like a man which built an house, and digged deep, and laid the foundation on a rock: and when the flood arose, the stream beat vehemently upon that house, and could not shake it: for it was founded upon a rock. But he that heareth, and doeth not, is like a man that without a foundation built an house upon the earth; against which the stream did beat vehemently, and immediately it fell; and the ruin of that house was great.]

Another parable spake He unto them: The kingdom of heaven is like unto leaven, which a woman took, and hid in three measures of meal, till the whole was leavened. All these things spake Jesus unto the multitude in parables; and without a parable spake He not unto them: That it might be fulfilled which was spoken by the prophet, saying, I will open my mouth in parables; I will utter things which have been kept secret from the foundation of the world.

Then Jesus sent the multitude away, and went into the house and His disciples came unto Him, saying, Declare unto us the parable of the tares of the field. He answered and said unto them, He that soweth the good seed is the Son of man; the field is the world; the good seed are the children of the kingdom; but the tares are the children of the wicked one; the enemy that sowed them is the devil; the harvest is the end of the world; and the reapers are the angels. As therefore the tares are gathered and burned in the fire; so shall it be in the end of this world. The Son of man shall send forth His angels, and they shall gather out of His kingdom all things that offend, and them which do iniquity; And shall cast them into a furnace of fire: there shall be wailing and gnashing of teeth. Then shall the righteous shine forth as the sun in the kingdom of their Father. Who hath ears to hear, let him hear.

Again the kingdom of heaven is like unto treasure hid in a field; the which when a man hath found, he hideth, and for joy thereof goeth and selleth all that he hath, and buyeth that field.

Again, the kingdom of heaven is like unto a merchant man seeking goodly pearls; Who when he had found one pearl of great price, went and sold all that he had, and bought it.

Again, the kingdom of heaven is like unto a net, that was cast into the sea, and gathered of every kind: which, when it was full, they drew to shore, and sat down, and gathered the good into vessels, but cast the bad away. So shall it be at the end of the world: the angels shall come forth, and sever the wicked from among the just, and shall cast them into the furnace of fire: there shall be wailing and gnashing of teeth. Jesus said unto them, Have ye understood all these things?

They say unto Him, Yea, Lord. Then said He unto them, Therefore every scribe *which is* instructed unto the kingdom of heaven is like unto a man *that is* an householder, which bringeth forth out of his treasure *things* new and old.

{And with many such parables spake He the word unto them, as they were able to hear *it*. But without a parable spake He not unto them: and when they were alone, He expounded all things to His disciples.})

(36) (19) **(Matthew 8:18–27)** {Mark 4:35–41} [Luke 8:22–25]

(Now [it came to pass on a certain day,] when Jesus saw great multitudes about Him, {And when they had sent away the multitude} {the same day, when even was come,} He gave commandment to depart, {He saith unto them, Let us pass over unto the other side [of the lake]} And a certain scribe came, and said unto Him, Master, I will follow Thee withersoever Thou goest. And Jesus saith unto him, The foxes have holes, and the birds of the air *have* nests; but the Son of man hath no where to lay *His* head. And another of His disciples said unto Him, Lord, suffer me first to go and bury my father. But Jesus said unto him, Follow Me: and let the dead bury their dead.

And when He was entered into a ship, {they took Him even as He was in the ship. And there were also with Him other little ships,} His disciples followed Him [and they launched forth,] And behold, there arose a great tempest {storm of wind} {and the waves beat into the ship} in the sea, insomuch that the ship was covered with the waves: {so that it was now full} [and were in jeopardy] {And He was in the hinder part of the ship} but He was asleep. {on a pillow}. And His disciples came unto Him, and awoke Him, saying, Lord, {[Master,]} save us: {carest Thou not that} we perish. [Then] {He arose, and rebuked the wind, and said unto the sea [the raging of the water] Peace, be still. And the wind ceased, and there was a great calm.} And He said unto them, Why are ye fearful, O ye of little faith? [Where is your faith?] But the men {they feared exceedingly, and} marvelled saying, What manner of man is this, that even the winds and the sea obey Him!)

(37) (20) **{Mark 5:1–20}** (Matthew 8:28–34) [Luke 8:26–39]

{And they came over unto the other side of the sea, [they arrived at] into the country of the Gadarenes, [which is over against Galilee.] And when He was come out of the ship, [He went forth to land,] immediately there met Him (two possessed with devils) out of the tombs [out of the city] (exceeding fierce, so that no man might pass by that way.) a [certain] man with an unclean spirit [along time] who had *his* dwelling among the tombs; [and ware no clothes, neither abode in any house,] and no man could bind him, no, not with chains: Because that he had been often bound with fetters and chains, and the chains had been plucked asunder by him, and the fetters broken in pieces: neither could any *man* tame him. And always, night and day, he was in the mountains, and in the tombs, crying, and cutting himself with stones. But when he saw Jesus afar off, he ran and worshipped Him, and cried with a loud voice [and fell down before Him], and said, What have I (we) to do with thee, Jesus *thou* Son of the most high God? (Art thou come hither to torment us before the time?) I adjure [beseech] thee by God, that Thou torment me not. For He said unto him, Come out of the man, Thou unclean spirit. [For oftentimes it had caught him: and he was driven by the devil into the wilderness] And He asked him, What *is* thy name? And he answered, saying, My name *is* Legion: for we are many [devils]. And he besought Him much that He would not send them away out of the country [into the deep]. Now there was there nigh (a good way off from them) unto the mountians a great herd of (many) swine feeding. And all the devils besought Him, saying (if thou cast us out) Send us into the (herd of) swine, that we may enter into them. And forthwith Jesus gave them leave. (And He said unto them, Go) And the unclean spirits went out [of the man] and entered into them. (herd of) swine: and (behold) the (whole) herd (of swine) ran violently down a steep place into the sea (they were about two thousand;) and were choked (and perished) in the sea (waters). And they that fed (and kept) the swine fled, and told it in the city, and in the country (everything, and what was befallen to the possessed of the devil). And (behold the whole city came out to meet Jesus:) to see what it was that was done. And they came to Jesus (and when they [found the man] saw him) that was possessed with the devil, and had the legion, sitting, [at the feet of Jesus] and clothed, and in his right mind: they were afraid. And they that saw *it* told them how it befell to him that was possessed with the devil, [was healed], and *also* concerning the swine. And they began to pray Him (they besought *Him*) to depart [from them] out of their coasts. [for they were taken with great fear:]

And when He was come into the ship, he that had been possessed with the devil, prayed [besought] Him that he might be with Him. Howbeit Jesus suffered him not, but saith unto him, Go [return to thine own] home to thy friends, and tell them how great things the Lord [God] hath done for thee, and hath had compassion on thee. And he departed, and began to publish [throughout the whole city and] in Decapolis how great things Jesus had done for him: and all *men* did marvel.

(38) (21) {**Mark 5:21–43**} (Matthew. 9:18–26) [Luke 8:40–56]

{And when Jesus was passed over again by ship unto the other side [and was returned], much people [gladly received Him, and] gathered unto Him: [for they were all waiting for Him]. He was nigh unto the sea and, behold, there cameth (a man) one of the ruler's of the synagogue, Jairus by name; and when he saw Him, he fell at His [Jesus] feet. (and worshipped Him.) And besought Him greatly [that He would come into His house], saying, my one only little daughter lieth at the point of death: (is even now dead) (But come) *I pray thee,* come and lay thy hands on her, that she may be healed; and she shall live. And *Jesus* (arose, and) went with him; and much people followed Him (so *did* His disciples), and thronged Him, And (behold) a certain woman, which (was diseased with) an issue of blood twelve years, and had suffered many things of many physicians, and had spent all [her living] that she had, and was nothing bettered, [neither could be healed of any] but rather grew worse, When she had heard of Jesus, came in the press behind (Him) and touched (the hem [border] of) His garment. For she said (within herself), if I may touch but His clothes (garment), I shall be whole. And (immediately) straightway the fountain of her blood was dried up; and she felt in *her* body that she was healed of that plague.

But Jesus, immediately knowing in Himself that virtue had gone out of Him, turned Him about in the press, and said, Who touched [Me], My clothes? [Peter] and His disciples said unto Him [Master] Thou seest the multitude thronging Thee, [and the press] and sayest Thou, Who touched Me? [And Jesus said, Somebody touched Me for I perceive that virtue is gone out of Me.] [When all denied] and He looked round about to see her that had done this thing. But the woman [saw that she was not hid] fearing and trembling, knowing what was done in her, came and fell down before Him, and told Him [Before] all [the people] the truth [for what cause she had touched Him and how she was healed immediately.] And He said unto her, Daughter (be of good comfort:), thy faith hath made thee whole; go in peace, and be whole of thy plague.

While He yet spake, there came from the ruler of the synagogue's *house certain* [one] which said, Thy daughter is dead: why troublest thou the Master any further? [But] as soon as Jesus heard the word that was spoken, He saith unto the ruler of the synagogue, be not afraid, only believe [and she shall be made whole.] And He suffered no man to follow Him, save Peter, and James, and John, the brother of James. And He cometh to the house of the ruler of the synagogue, and seeth the tumult, and them that wept and wailed greatly. And when He (Jesus) was come in (and saw the minstrels and the people making a noise) He saith unto them (Give place: Why make ye this ado, and weep? The (maid) damsel is not dead, but sleepeth. And they laughed Him to scorn. But when He had put them all out, He taketh the father and the mother of the damsel, and them that were with Him, and entereth in where the damsel was lying. And He took the damsel by the hand, and said unto her, Talitha cumi; which is, being interpreted, Damsel [maid], I say unto thee, arise. And straightway [her spirit came again and she] the damsel arose, and walked: for she was *of the age* of twelve years. And they were astonished with a great astonishment. And He charged them straitly that no man should know it; and commanded that something should be given her to eat. (And the fame hereof went abroad into all that land.)}

(39) (18) **(Matthew 9:27–34)**

(When Jesus departed thence, two blind men followed Him, crying, and saying, *Thou* Son of David, have mercy on us. And when he was come into the house, the blind men came to Him: and Jesus saith unto them, Believe ye that I am able to do this? They said unto Him, Yea, Lord. Then touched He their eyes, saying, According to your faith be it unto you. And their eyes were opened; and Jesus straitly charged them, saying, See *that* no man know *it*. But they, when they were departed, spread abroad His fame in all that country.

As they went out, behold, they brought to Him a dumb man possessed with a devil. And when the devil was cast out, the dumb spake: and the multitudes marvelled, saying. It was never so seen in Israel. But the Pharisees said, He casteth out devils through the prince of the devils.)

(40) (22) **{Mark 6:1–6}** (Matthew 13:54–58, 9:35–38)

{And He went out from thence, and came into His own country; and His disciples follow Him. When the sabbath day was come, He began to teach (them) in (their) synagogue: and many (insomuch) hearing *Him* were astonished, saying, From whence hath this *man* these things? What wisdom *is* this which *is* given unto Him, that even such mighty works are wrought by His hands? Is not this the carpenter (is not this the carpenter's son), the son of Mary (is not His mother called Mary?) the brother of James, and Joses, and of Juda

(Judas), and Simon? Are not (all) His sisters here with us? And they were offended at (in) Him. But Jesus said unto them, A prophet in not without honour, but (save) in His own country, and among His own kin, and in His own house. And He could there do no mighty work, save that He laid His hands upon a few sick folk, and healed *them*. And He marvelled because of their unbelief. And He (Jesus) went round about (all the cities and) the villages, teaching (in their synagogues, and preaching the gospel of the kingdom, and healing every sickness and every disease among the people.)

(But when He saw the multitudes, He was moved with compassion on them, because they fainted, and were scattered abroad, as sheep having no shepherd. Then saith He unto His disciples, The harvest truly *is* plenteous, *but* the labourers *are* few; Pray ye therefore the Lord Of the harvest, that He will send forth labourers into His harvest.)}

(41) (19) **(Matthew 10:1–4)**

(And when He had called unto *Him* His twelve disciples, He gave them power *against* unclean spirits, to cast them out, and to heal all manner of sickness and all manner of disease. Now the names of the twelve apostles are these; The first, Simon, who is called Peter, and Andrew his brother; James *the son* of Zebedee, and John his brother; Philip, and Bartholomew; Thomas, and Matthew the publican; James *the son* of Alphaeus, and Lebbaeus, whose surname was Thaddaeus; Simon the Canaanite, and Judas Iscariot, who also betrayed Him.)

(42) (23) **(Matthew 10:5–42)** {Mark 6:7–13} [Luke 9:1–6]

These twelve Jesus sent forth [to preach the kingdom of God, and heal the sick], and commanded them, saying, Go not into the way of the Gentiles, and into *any* city of the Samaritans enter ye not: But go rather to the lost sheep of the house of Israel. And as ye go, preach, saying the kingdom of heaven is at hand. Heal the sick, cleanse the lepers, raise the dead, cast out devils: freely ye have received freely give {take nothing for *their* journey save a staff only, no bread}. Provide neither gold, nor silver {no money}, nor brass, in your purses, nor script for *your* journey, neither two coats [apiece], neither shoes, nor yet staves: for the workmen is worthy of his meat. And into whatsoever city or town ye shall enter, enquire who in it is worthy: and there abide till ye go thence. And when ye come into an house, salute it. And if the house be worthy, let your peace come upon it; but if it be not worthy, let your peace return to you, and whosoever shall not receive you, nor hear your words, when ye depart out of that house or city, shake off the dust [under] of your feet {for a testimony against them}. Verily I say unto you, It shall be more tolerable for the land of Sodom and Gomorrha in the day of judgment, than for that city.

Behold, I send you forth as sheep in the midst of wolves: be ye therefore wise as serpents, and harmless as doves. But beware of men: for they will deliver you up to the councils, and they will scourge you in their synagogues; and ye shall be brought before governors and kings for my sake, for a testimony against them and the Gentiles. But when they deliver you up, take no thought how or what ye shall speak: for it shall be given you in that same hour what ye shall speak. For it is not ye that speak, but the Spirit of your Father which speaketh in you. And brother shall deliver up the brother to death, and the father the child: and the children shall rise up against *their* parents, and cause them to be put to death. And ye shall be hated of all *men* for my names sake: but he that endureth to the end shall be saved. But when they persecute you in this city, flee ye into another: for verily I say unto you, Ye shall not have gone over the cities of Israel, till the son of Man be come. The disciple is not above *His* master, nor the servant above his Lord It is enough for the disciple that he be as His Master, and the servant as His Lord. If they have called the master of the house Beelzebub, how much more *shall they call* them of His household? Fear them not therefore: for there is nothing covered, that shall not be revealed; and hid, that shall not be known. What I tell you in darkness, *that* speak ye in light: and what ye hear in the ear, *that* preach ye upon the housetops, And fear not them which kill the body, but are not able to kill the soul: but rather fear Him which is able to destroy both soul and body in hell.

Are not two sparrows sold for a farthing? And one of them shall not fall on the ground without your Father. But the very hairs of your head are all numbered. Fear ye not therefore, ye are of more value than many sparrows. Whosoever therefore shall confess Me before men, him will I confess also before My Father which is in heaven. But whosoever shall deny Me before men, him will I also deny before My Father which is in heaven. Think not that I am come to send peace on earth: I came not to send peace; but a sword. For I am come to set a man at varience against his father, and the daughter against her mother, and the daughter in law against her mother in law. And a man's foes *shall* be they of his own household. He that loveth father or mother more than me is not worthy of Me: and he that loveth son or daughter more than Me is not worthy of Me. And he that taketh not his cross, and followeth after Me, is not worthy of Me. He that findeth his life shall lose it: and he that loseth his life for My sake shall find it.

He that receiveth you receiveth Me, and he that receiveth Me receiveth Him that sent Me. He that receveth a prophet in the name of a prophet shall receive a prophet's reward; and he that receiveth a righteous man in the name of a righteous man shall receive a righteous man's reward.

And whosoever shall give to drink unto one of these little ones a cup of cold *water* only in the name of a disciple, verily I say unto you, he shall in no wise lose his reward.

{And they went out [departed and went through the towns], and preached [the gospel] that men should repent and they cast out many devils, and anointed many with oil many that were sick, and healed *them*} [everywhere].)

(43) (20) (Matthew 11:1)

(And it came to pass, when Jesus had made an end of commanding His twelve disciples, He departed thence to teach and to preach in their cities.)

(44) (24) **{Mark 6:14–29}** (Matthew 14:1–12) [Luke 9:7–9]

{(At that time) king Herod (the tetrarch) heard *of* [all that was done by Him: and he was perplexed.] (heard of the fame of Jesus;) for His name was spread abroad: and he said (unto his servant That (this is) John the Baptist (he) was risen from the dead, and therefore mighty works do shew forth themselves in him. Others, said, That it is Elias. And others said, that it is a prophet, or as one of the prophets. But when Herod heard *thereof,* he said It is John, whom I beheaded: he is risen [again] from the dead. For Herod himself had sent forth and laid hold upon John, and bound him in prison for Herodias' sake, his brother Philip's wife: for he had married her. For John had said unto Herod, it is not lawful for thee to have thy brother's wife (and when he would have put him to death, he feared the multitude, because they counted him as a prophet.) Therefore Herodias had a quarrel against him; but she could not: For Herod feared John, Knowing that he was a just man and an holy, and observed him; and when he heard him, he did many things, and heard him gladly. And when a convenient day was come, that Herod on his birthday made a supper to his lords, high captains, and chief *estates* of Galilee: And when the daughter of the said Herodias came in, and danced (before them), and pleased Herod, and them that sat with him, the king said unto the damsel (whereupon he promised with an oath to give her whatsoever she would ask.) Ask of me whatsoever thou wilt, and I will give *it* thee. And he sware unto her, Whatsoever thou shalt ask of me, I will give *it* thee, unto the half of my kingdom. And she went forth, and said unto her mother, what shall I ask? And she said, the head of John the Baptist. And she came in straightway with haste unto the king (being before instructed of her mother) and asked, say-ing, I will that thou give me (here) by and by in a charger the head of John the Baptist. And the king was exceeding sorry; *yet* (nevertheless) for his oath's sake, and for their sakes which sat with him (at meat), he would not reject her. And immediately the king (commanded *it* to be given *her*) sent an executioner, and commanded his head to be brought: and he went and beheaded him in the prison. And brought his head in a charger, and gave it to the damsel: and the damsel gave it to her mother. [And Herod said, John have I beheaded: but who is this, of whom I hear such things? And he desired to see Him.] And when John disciples heard of *it*, they came and took up his corpse, and laid it in a tomb. (and went and told Jesus.)}

(45) (25) **{Mark 6:30–44}** (Matthew 14:13–21) [Luke 9:10–17] <John 6:1–14>

{(When Jesus heard of *it*, He departed thence) And the apostles [when they were returned] gathered themselves together unto Jesus, and told Him all things, both what they had done, and what they had taught. And He said unto them, Come ye yourselves apart into a desert place, and rest a while: for there were many coming and going, and they had no leisure so much as to eat. <After these things Jesus went over the sea of Galilee which is the sea of Tiberias> And they departed into a desert place [belonging to the city of Bethsaida] by ship privately (apart). And the people saw (and heard) them departing, and many knew Him (they followed Him) and ran afoot (on foot) thither out of all cities, and out went them, and came together unto Him. And Jesus, when He came out <then lifted up *His* eyes, and>, saw (a great multitude *of*) Much people, <He saith unto Philip, Whence shall we buy bread, that these may eat? And this He said to prove him: for He himself knew what He would do,> and was moved with compassion toward them [and He received them, and spoke unto them, of the kingdom of God] (and He healed their sick) [that had need of healing], because they were as sheep not having a shepherd: and He began to teach them many things. <And a great multitude followed Him, far because they saw His miracles which He did on them that were diseased> And when the day was now far spent (when it was evening) <Jesus went up into a mountain, and>,His disciples came unto Him [the twelve] <there He sat with His disciples and the passover of the Jews was nigh.> And they said This is a desert place, and now the time is far passed: Send them (the Multitudes) away, that they may go into the country round about, and into villages, and buy themselves bread: for they have nothing to eat. (But Jesus) He answered and said unto them (they need not depart:) Give ye them to eat. <And Philip answered Him,> they say unto Him, Shall we go and buy two hundred pennyworth of bread, [and lodge] (and get vituals) <is not sufficient for them, that every

one of them may take a little.> and give them to eat? He saith unto them, How many loaves have ye? Go and see. And when they knew, <one of the disciples, Andrew, Simon Peter's brother, saith unto Him,> they say [we have no more but] <there is a lad here, which hath> five <barley loaves>, and two <small> fishes. <But what are they among so many?> (He said, Bring them hither to Me.) And He commanded them to make all sit down, upon the grass, by companies <Now there was much> green grass <in the place>. And they <the men> sat down in ranks, by hundreds and by fifties. <about five thousand.> And when He <Jesus> had taken the five loaves and the two fishes, He looked up to heaven, <gave thanks> and blessed, and brake the loaves, and gave <distributed> them to His disciples to set before them; and the two fishes divided He among them all <as much as they would>. And they did all eat, and were filled. <He said unto His disciples, Gather up the fragments that remain that nothing be lost.> And <therefore> they <gathered *them* together, and> took up twelve baskets full (that remained) <over and above unto them that had eaten,> of the fragments, <of the five barley loaves,> and of the fishes. And they that did eat of the loaves were about five thousand men. (Beside women and children.) <Then those men, when they had seen the miracles that Jesus did, said, This is of a truth that Prophet that should come into the world.}

(46) (26) **(Matthew 14:22–33)** {Mark 6:45–52} <John 6:15–21>

(And straightway Jesus constrained His disciples to get into a ship, <unto the sea, and entered into a ship, and went over the sea toward Capernaum.> to go before Him unto the other side {over against Bethsaida}, while He sent the {people} multitudes away. And when He had sent {them} the multitudes away, <When Jesus therefore perceived that they would come and take Him by force, to make Him a king,> He {departed} <again> went up into a mountain apart to pray: and when the evening was come, He was there alone {on the land}. <And it was now dark, and Jesus was not come to them. And the sea arose by reason of a great wind that blew. So when they had rowed about five and twenty or thirty furlongs,> the ship was now in the midst of the sea, and tossed with the waves: {and He saw them toiling in rowing:} for the wind was contrary. {unto them}. And in {about} the forth watch of the night Jesus went unto them, walking on {upon} the sea <and drawing nigh unto the ship> {and would have passed them}. And when {they} the disciples saw Him walking on the sea, they were troubled <and afraid>, saying, {they supposed} It is a spirit; and they cried out for fear. But straightway {immediately} Jesus spake unto them, saying, Be of good cheer; it is I; be not afraid. And Peter answered Him and said, Lord if it be Thou, bid me come unto Thee on the water. And He said, Come. And when Peter was come down out of the ship, he walked on the water, to go to Jesus. But when he saw the wind boisterous, he was afraid; and beginning to sink, he cried, saying, Lord, save me. And immediately Jesus stretched forth *His* hand, and caught him, and said unto him, O thou of little faith, wherefore didst thou dought? And when they were come into the ship, <then they willingly received Him,> the wind ceased. <and immediately the ship was at the land whither they went.> {they were sore amazed in themselves beyond measure, and wondered. For they considered not *the miracle* of the loaves: for their heart was hardened.} Then they that were in the ship came and worshipped Him, saying, of a truth thou art the Son of God.)

(47) (27) **{Mark 6:53–56}** (Matthew 14:34–36)

{And when they had passed (gone) over, they came into the land of Gennesaret, and drew to the shore. And when they (the men of that place) were come out of the ship, straightway they knew (and had knowledge of) Him (they sent out into all that country) and ran through the region round about, and began to carry about in beds (all) those that were sick (and diseased;) where they heard He was. And whithersoever He entered, into villages, or cities, or country, they laid the sick in the streets, and besought Him that they might (only) touch if it were but the border (hem) of His garment: and as many as touched Him were made (perfectly) whole.}

(48) (21) **<John 6:22–71>**

<The day following, when the people which stood on the other side of the sea saw that there was none other boat there, save that one whereinto His disciples were entered, And that Jesus went not with His disciples into the boat, But *that* His disciples were gone away alone; Howbeit there came other boats from Tiberias nigh unto the place where they did eat bread, after that the Lord had given thanks: When the people therefore saw that Jesus was not there, neither His disciples, they also took shipping, and came to Capernaum, seeking for Jesus. And when they had found Him on the other side of the sea, they said unto Him, Rabbi, when camest Thou hither? Jesus answered them and said, Verily, verily, I say unto you, Ye seek Me, not because ye saw the miracles, but because ye did eat of the loaves, and were filled. Labour not for the meat which perisheth, but for that meat which endureth unto everlasting life, which the Son of man shall give unto you: for Him hath God the Father sealed. Then said they unto Him, What shall we do, that we might work the works of God? Jesus answered and said unto them, This is the work of God, that ye believe on Him whom He has sent. They said therefore unto Him, What sign shewest Thou then, that we may see, and believe thee? What dost Thou work? Our fathers did eat manna in the desert; as it is written, He gave them bread from heaven to eat. Then Jesus said unto them, Verily, verily, I say unto you, Moses gave you not that Bread from heaven; but My Father giveth you the true Bread from heaven. For the bread of God is He which cometh down from heaven, and giveth life unto the world. Then said they unto Him, Lord, evermore give us this bread. And Jesus said unto them, I am the Bread of life; he that cometh to Me shall never hunger; and he that believeth on Me shall never thirst. But I said unto you, That ye also have seen Me, and believe not. All that the Father giveth Me shall come to Me; and him that cometh to Me I will in no wise cast out. For I came down from heaven, not to do Mine own will, but the will of Him that sent Me. And this is the Father's will which hath sent Me, that of all which He hath given Me I should lose nothing, but should raise it up again at the last day. And this is the will of Him that sent Me, that every one which seeth the Son, and believeth on Him, may have everlasting life: and I will raise him up at the last day.

The Jews then murmured at Him, because He said, I am the bread which came down from heaven. And they said, Is not this Jesus, the son of Joseph, whose father and mother we know? How is it then that He saith, I came down from heaven? Jesus therefore answered and said unto them, Murmur not among yourselves No man can come to Me, except the Father which hath sent Me draw him: and I will raise him up at the last day. It is written in the prophets, And they shall all be taught of God. Every man therefore that hath heard, and hath learned of the Father, cometh unto Me. Not that any man hath seen the Father, save He which is of God, He hath seen the Father. Verily, verily, I say unto you, He that believeth on Me hath everlasting life. I am that Bread of life. Your Fathers did eat manna in the wilderness, and are dead. This is the Bread which cometh down from heaven, that a man may eat thereof, and not die. I am the living Bread which came down from heaven: if any man eat of this Bread, he shall live for ever; and the Bread that I will give is My flesh, which I will give for the life of the world. The Jews therefore strove among themselves, saying, How can this man give us *his* flesh to eat? Then Jesus said unto them, Verily, verily, I say unto you, Except ye eat the flesh of the Son of man, and drink His blood, ye have no life in you. Whoso eateth My flesh, and drinketh My blood, hath eternal life; and I will raise him up at the last day. For My flesh is meat indeed, and My blood is drink indeed. He that eateth My flesh, and drinketh My blood, dwelleth in Me, and I in him. As the living Father has sent Me, and I live by the Father: so he that eateth Me, even he shall live by Me. This is that bread which came down from heaven: not as your fathers did eat manna, and are dead: he that eateth of this bread shall live for ever. These things said He in the synagogue, as He taught in Capernaum. Many therefore of His disciples, when they had heard *this*, said, This is an hard saying; who can hear it? When Jesus knew in Himself that His disciples murmured at it, He said unto them, Doth this offend you? *What* and if ye shall see the Son of man ascend up where He was before? It is the Spirit that quickeneth; the flesh profiteth nothing: the words that I speak unto you, *they* are Spirit, and *they* are life But there are some of you that believe not. For Jesus knew from the beginning who they were that believed not, and who should betray Him. And He said, Therefore said I unto you that no man can come unto Me, except it were given unto him of My Father.

From that *time* many of His disciples went back, and walked no more with Him. Then Jesus said unto the twelve, Will ye also go away? Then Simon Peter answered Him, Lord, to whom shall we go? Thou hast the words of eternal life. And we believed and are sure that Thou art the Christ the Son of the living God. Jesus answered them, Have not I chosen you twelve, and one of you is a devil? He spake of Judas Iscariot *the son* of Simon: for he it was that should betray Him, being one of the twelve.>

(49) (28) **{Mark 7:1–9:1}** (Matthew 15:1–16:28) [Luke 9:18–28a]

{Then came together unto Him (Jesus). The Pharisees, and certain of the scribes, which came from Jerusalem. And when they saw some of His disciples eat bread with defiled, that is to say, with unwashen, hands, they found fault. For the Pharisees, and all the Jews, except they wash *their* hands oft, eat not, holding the tradition of the elders. And *when they come* from the market, except they wash, they eat not. And many other things there be, which they have received to hold, *as* the washing of cups, and pots, brasen vessels, and of tables. Then the Pharisees and scribes asked Him (saying) why walk not thy disciples according to the tradition of the elders, but (transgress) eat bread with unwashen hand? (But) He answered and said unto them, Well hath Esaias prophesied of you hypocrites, as it is written, This people honoureth (draws nigh unto) Me with *their* lips (mouth), but their heart is far from Me Howbeit in vain do they worship Me, teaching *for* doctrines the commandments of men. For laying aside the commandment of God ye hold the tradition of men, *as* the washing of pots and cups: and many other such like things ye do. And He said unto them, Full well ye reject the commandment of God, that ye may keep your own tradition. For Moses said, Honour thy father and thy mother; and, whoso (he) curseth father or mother, let him die the death: But ye say, If a man (whosoever) shall say to his father or mother *It is* Corban, that is to say, a gift, by whatsoever thou mightest be profited by me; (And honour not his Father and his Mother) *he shall be free.* And ye suffer him no more to do ought for his father or his mother; Making the word of God of none effect through your traditions, which ye have delivered: and many such like things do ye.

And when He had called all the people (multitude) *unto Him*, He said unto them, Harken unto Me every one of you, and understand: There is nothing from without a man, that entering into him can defile him: but the things which come out of (the mouth of) him, those are they that defile the man. If any man have ears to hear, let him hear.

(Then came His disciples, and said unto Him, Knoweth thou that the Pharisees were offended, after they heard this saying? But He answered and said, Every plant, which my heavenly Father hath not planted, shall be rooted up, Let them alone: they be blind leaders of the blind. And if the blind lead the blind, both shall fall into the ditch.)

And when He was entered into the house from the people. (Then answered Peter and) His disciples asked Him concerning the parable (and said unto Him Declare unto us this parable.) And He (Jesus) saith unto them, Are ye so (yet) without understanding also? Do ye not (yet) perceive (understand), that whatsoever thing from without entereth into the man, *it* cannot defile him; Because it entereth not into his heart, but into the (mouth and goeth into the) belly, and goeth out (cast) into the draught, purging all meats? And He said (But those things) that which cometh (proceed) out of the (mouth come forth from the heart of) man, that (they) defileth the man. For from within, out of the heart of men, proceed evil thoughts, adulteries, fornications, murders, thefts (false witness) coveteousness, wickedness, deceit, lasciviousness, an evil eye, blasphem(ies) pride, foolishness: All these (are) evil things (which) come from within, and defile the man. (But to eat with unwashen hands defileth not a man.)

And from thence He (Jesus) arose (departed) and went into the borders (coasts) of Tyre and Sidon, and entered into an house, and would have no man know *it*: but He could not be hid. For (behold) a *certain* woman (of Canaan), whose young daughter had an unclean spirit, heard of Him, and came and fell at His feet: The woman was a Greek, a Syro-Phoenician by nation; and she besought Him (cried unto Him). (Saying have mercy on me O Lord thou Son of David; my daughter is grievously vexed) that He would cast forth the devil out of her daughter. (But He answered her not a word. And His disciples came and besought Him, saying, Send her away; for she cries after us. But He answered and said, I am not sent but unto the lost sheep of the house of Israel. Then came she and worshipped Him, saying Lord, help me.) But (He) Jesus (answered and) said unto her, Let the children first be filled: for it is not meet to take the children's bread, and to cast *it*, unto the dogs. And she answered and said unto Him, yes (Truth) Lord: yet the dogs under the table eat (which fall from their masters' table.) of the children's crumbs. And (then) He (Jesus answered and) said unto her (O woman great is thy faith be it unto thee even as thou wilt.) For this saying go thy way; the devil is gone out of thy daughter. And When she was come to her house, she found the devil gone out, and daughter (was made whole from that very hour.) laid upon the bed.

And again (Jesus), departing from (thence) the coasts of Tyre and Sidon, He came unto the sea of Galilee, through the midst of the coasts of Decapolis. (And went up into a mountain, and sat down there. And great multitudes came unto Him, having with them *those that were* lame, blind, dumb, maimed, and many others, and cast them down at Jesus' feet; and He healed them: Insomuch that the multitude wondered, when they saw the dumb to speak, the maimed to be whole, the lame to walk, the blind to see: and they glorified the God of Israel.) And they bring unto Him one that was deaf, and had an impediment in his speech; and they beseech Him to put His hand upon him. And He took him aside from the multitude, and put his finger into his ears, and He spit, and touched his tongue; And looking up to heaven, He sighed, and saith unto him, Ephphatha, that is, Be opened. And straightway his ears were opened, and the string of his tongue was loosed, and he spake plain. And He charged them that they should tell no man: but the more He charged them so much the more a great deal they published *it*; And were beyond measure astonished, saying, He hath done all things well: He maketh both the deaf to hear, and the dumb to speak.

In those days the multitude being very great, and having nothing to eat (Then) Jesus called His disciples *unto Him*, and saith unto them, I have compassion on the multitude, because they (continue and) have now been with Me three days, and have nothing to eat: And if I send them away fasting (which I will not) to their own houses (lest) they will faint (in) by the way: for divers of them came from far. And His disciples answered Him, From whence can a man (or should we) satisfy these men with (so much) bread here in the wilderness (as to fill so great a multitude?) And He (Jesus) asked them, How many loaves have ye? And they said, Seven. And He commanded the (multitude of) the people to sit down on the ground: and He took the seven loaves and gave thanks, and brake, and gave to His disciples to set before *them;* and they did set *them* before the people. And they had a few small fishes: and He blessed, and commanded to set them also before them. (them). So they did eat, and were filled: and they took up of the broken *meat* that was left seven baskets (full). And they that had eaten were about four thousand (men, beside women and children): and He sent them (the Multitude) away.

And straightway He entered into a ship with His disciples, and came into the parts of (the coasts of) Dalmanutha (Magdala). And the Pharisees (also with the Saducees) came forth, and began to question with Him, seeking of Him a sign from heaven, tempting Him. And He sighed deeply in His spirit (and answered) and saith (unto them) Why doth this generation seek after a sign? Verily I say unto you, There shall no sign be given unto this generation. And He left them, and entering into the ship again departed to the other side.

(He answered and said unto them, When it is evening, ye say, It will be fair weather: for the sky is red. And in the mourning, *It will* befoul weather to day: for the sky is red and lowring. O *ye* hypocrites, ye can discern the face of the sky; but ye can not *discern* the signs of the times?) Verily I say unto you (a wicked and adulterous generation seeketh after a sign: and) there shall no sign be given unto (it) this generation (but the sign of the prophet Jonas. And He left them, and entering into the ship again departed to the other side). (And when His disciples were come to the other side) Now (they) *the disciples* had forgotten to take bread, neither had they in the ship with them more than one loaf. And (then) He (Jesus) charged (and said unto) them, Take heed, beware of the leaven of the Pharisees (and of the Sadducees), and of the leaven of Herod. And they reasoned among themselves, saying, it is because we have (taken) no bread. And when Jesus knew it, He saith unto them, why reason ye, because ye have (brought) no bread? Perceive ye not yet, neither (ye) understand? Have ye your heart yet hardened? Having eyes, see ye not? And having ears, hear ye not? And do ye not remember? When I brake the five loaves among five thousand, how many baskets full of fragments took ye up? They say unto Him, Twelve. And when the seven (loaves) among four thousand, how many baskets full of fragments took ye up? And They said, Seven. And He said unto them, How is it that ye do not understand? (That I spake it not to you concerning bread, that ye should beware of the leaven of the Pharisees and of the Sadducees) (Then understood they how that He bade them not beware of the leaven of bread, but of the doctrine of the Pharisees and of the Sadducees.)

And He cometh to Bethsaida; and they bring a blind man unto Him, and besought Him to touch him. And He took the blind man by the hand, and led him out of the town; and when He had spit on his eyes, and put His hands upon him, He asked him if he saw ought. And he looked up, and said, I see men as trees, walking. After that He put His hands again upon his eyes, and made him look up: and he was restored, and saw every man clearly. And He sent him away to his house, saying, Neither go into the town, nor tell it to any in the town.

And (when) Jesus went out, and His disciples, into the (coasts and) towns of Caesarea Phillippi: [it came to pass, as He was alone praying, His disciples were with Him:] and by the way He asked [them] His disciples, saying unto them, Whom do men say that (the Son of man) I am? And they answered (and said some say that thou art) John the Baptist: but some say Elias; and others (Jeremias or) one of the [old] prophets [is risen again.] And He saith unto them, But whom say ye that I am? And (Simon) Peter answereth and saith unto Him, Thou art the Christ [of God] (the Son of the living God). (And Jesus answered and said unto Him. Blessed art thou, Simon Barjona:

for flesh and blood hath not revealed it unto thee, but My Father which is in heaven. And I say unto thee, That thou art Peter, and upon this rock I will build My church; and the gates of hell shall not prevail against it. And I will give unto thee the keys of the kingdom of heaven: and whatsoever thou shalt bind on earth shall be bound in heaven: and whatsoever thou shalt loose on earth shall be loosed in heaven.) And (then) He [straightly] charged them (His disciples), that they should tell no man [that thing] of Him (that He was Jesus the Christ)

(From that time forth began Jesus to shew unto His disciples, how that He must go unto Jerusalem) And He [saying] began to teach them, that the Son of man must suffer many things and be rejected of the elders, and *of* the chief priests, and scribes, and be killed [slain], and after three days rise again. And He spake that saying openly. And (then) Peter took Him, and began to rebuke Him (saying, be it far from thee, Lord: This shall not be unto thee). But when He had turned about and looked on His disciples, He rebuked Peter, saying, Get thee behind Me Satan: for thou; savourest not the things that be of God, but the things that be of men.

And when He (Jesus) had called the people *unto Him* with His disciples also, He said unto them [all], Whosoever (if any man) will come after Me, let deny himself, and take up his cross [dailey], and follow Me. For whosoever will save his life shall lose it; but whosoever shall (will) lose his life for my sake and the gospel's, the same shall save (find) it. For what shall it prophet [advantaged] a man. if he shall gain the whole world, and lose [himself] his own soul [or be cast away]? Or what shall a man give in exchange for his soul? [For] Whosoever therefore shall be ashamed of Me and of My words in this adulterous and sinful generation; of him also shall the Son of man be ashamed, when He (shall) cometh in [His own glory] the glory of His Father with (His) the holy angel's (and then He shall reward every man according to his works.) And He said unto them, [But] Verily I say [tell] unto you [of a truth], that there be some of them that stand here, which shall not taste death, till they have seen (the Son of man coming in His) the kingdom of God come with power.

[And it came to pass about an eight days after these sayings,]

(50) (29) **(Matthew 17:1–13)** {Mark 9:2–13} [Luke 9:28–36]

(And after six days Jesus taketh {*with Him*} Peter, James, and John his brother, and bringeth {leadeth} them up into an high mountain apart {by themselves} [to pray] [But Peter and they that were with him were heavy with sleep; and when they were awake, they saw His glory,] and [as He prayed, the fashion of His countenance] was transfigured [altered] before them: and His face did shine as the sun, and His raiment was {became} white {as snow, shining} [glistering] as the light {so as no fuller on earth can white them.} And, behold, there appeared unto them [two men that stood with Him] Moses and Elias {they were} talking with Him {Jesus} [Who appeared in glory, and spake of His decease which He should accomplish at Jerusalem.] [And it came to pass, as they departed from Him] Then answered Peter, and said unto Jesus, Lord, {Master}, it is good for us to be here; if Thou wilt, let us make here three tabernacles; one for Thee, one for Moses, and one for Elias {for he wist not what to say; for they were sore afraid.} While he yet spake, behold, {there} [came] a bright cloud {that} overshadowed them [and they feared as they entered into the cloud,] and behold [there] a voice {came} out of the cloud, which said, This is My Beloved Son, in whom I am well pleased; hear ye Him. And when the disciples heard *it*, they fell on their face, and were sore afraid. And Jesus came and touched them, and said, Arise, and be not afraid. And when they had lifted up their eyes {suddenly} {when they looked round about} they saw no man {any more}, save Jesus only {with themselves}. And as they came down from the mountain. Jesus {He} charged them, saying, {that they should} Tell the vision to no man {what things they had seen}, until the Son of man {were} be risen again from the dead. {And they kept [*it* close] that saying with themselves, [and told no man in those days any of those things which they had seen.] questioning one with another what the rising from the dead should mean.} And {they} His disciples asked Him, saying, Why then say the scribes that Elias must first come? And {He} Jesus answered and said {told} unto them, Elias truly {verily} shall first come, and restore all things, {and how it is written of the Son of man, that He must suffer many things, and be set at nought,} But I say unto you, that Elias is [indeed] come already, and they knew him not, but have done unto him whatsoever they listed, {as it is written of him.} Likewise shall also the Son of man suffer of them. Then the disciples understood that He spake unto them of John the Baptist.)

(51) (30) **{Mark 9:14–29}** (Matthew 17:14–21) [Luke 9:37–42]

{[And it came to pass on the next day, when they were come down from the hill,] and when He came to *His* disciples, He saw a great multitude about them (when they were come to the multitude) [much people met Him.] and the scribes questioning with them. And straightway all the people, when they beheld Him, were greatly amazed, and running to *Him* saluted Him. And He asked the scribes, What question ye with them? And [behold] (there came to Him a *certain* man) one of the multitude [company] (kneeling down to Him) answered and said [cryed out] (Lord) Master, [I beseech thee] I have brought unto Thee my son, which hath a dumb spirit (he is lunatick and sore vexed); and wheresoever he taketh him: [he suddenly crieth out;] he [it] teareth him: and he foameth [again], [and bruising him hardly] and gnasheth with his teeth, and pineth away; [departeth from him.] and (I brought him to Thy disciples) and I spake [besought] Thy disciples that they should cast him out; and they could not (they could not cure him.) He (Jesus) answereth him and saith, O faithless (and perverse) generation, how long shall I be with you? How long shall I suffer you? Bring him [thy son hither] to Me. And they brought him [and as he was yet coming] unto him: and when He saw him, straightway the spirit [devil threw him down and] tare him; and he fell on the ground, and wallowed foaming. And He asked the father, How long is it ago since this came unto him? And he said, of a child, and ofttimes it hath cast him into the fire, and into the waters, to destroy him: but if Thou canst do any thing, [look upon and] have compassion (mercy) on us (my son) and help us. [For he is mine only child.] Jesus said unto him, If thou canst believe, all things are possible to him that believeth. And straightway the father of the child cried out, and said with tears, Lord, I believe; help Thou mine unbelief. When Jesus saw that the people came running together, He rebuked the foul [unclean] spirit (devil), saying unto him, *Thou* dumb and deaf spirit, I charge thee, come out of him, and enter no more into him. And *the spirit* cried, and rent him sore, and came (departed) out of him: and he was as one dead; insomuch that many said, he is dead. But Jesus took him by the hand, and lifted him up; (and the child was cured [healed] from that very hour.) and he arose. [And delivered him again to his father.] [And they were all amazed at the mighty power of God.] And when He was come into the house (then came) His disciples (to Jesus apart and) asked Him privately, Why could not we cast him out? And (Jesus) He said unto them (Because of your unbelief: for verily I say unto you, If ye have faith as a grain of mustard seed, ye shall say unto this mountain, Remove hence to yonder place, and it shall remove; and nothing shall be impossible unto you.) (Howbeit) this kind can come forth *by* nothing (goeth not out) but by prayer and fasting.}

(52) (31) **(Matthew 17:22–18:35)** {Mark 9:30–50} [Luke 9:44–50]

({And they departed from thence} [But while they wondered every one at all things which Jesus did,] And while they abode in {and passed through} Galilee {and He would not that any man should know *it*} {For He} Jesus {taught His disciples and} said unto them, [Let these sayings sink down into you ears: for] the Son of man shall {is} be betrayed {delivered} into the hands of men: And they shall kill Him, {and after that He is killed} the third day He shall be raised again. And they were exceeding sorry. {But they understood not that [this] saying, [and it was hid from them that they perceived it not:] and [they] were afraid [feared] to ask Him [of that saying.]

And when they {and He} were come to Capernaum, they that received tribute *money* came to Peter, and said, Doth not your master pay tribute? He saith, Yes. And when He was come into the house, {being in the house}, Jesus {He} prevented {asked them} him saying, What thinkest thou, Simon? Of whom do the kings of the earth take custom or tribute? Of their own children, or of strangers? Peter saith unto Him, of strangers. Jesus saith unto him, Then are the children free. Notwithstanding, lest we should offend them, go thou to the sea, and cast an hook, and take up the fish that first cometh up; and when thou hast opened his mouth, thou shalt find a piece of money: that take, and give unto them for Me and thee.

[Then there arose a reasoning among them, which of them should be greatest. And Jesus, perceiving the thought of their heart, took a child, and set him by Him, and said unto them,] {What was it that ye disputed among yourselves by the way. But they held their peace: for by the way they had disputed among themselves, who *should be* the greatest.} At the same time came His disciples unto Jesus, saying, Who is the greatest in the kingdom of heaven? {And He sat down and called the twelve, and said unto them, If any man desire to be first, *the same* shall be last of all, and servant of all.} [Whosoever shall receive, this child in My name recieveth Me: and whosoever shall receive Me receiveth Him that sent Me: for he that is least among you all, the same shall be great.] And Jesus {He took and} called a little child unto Him, and set him in the midst of them, {and when He had taken him in His arms,} and {He} said, unto them, Verily I say unto you, Except ye be converted, and become as little children, ye shall not enter into the kingdom of heaven. Whosoever therefore shall humble himself as this little child, the same is great-est in the kingdom of heaven. And whoso [ever] shall receive one such [this] little child in My name receiveth Me {and whosoever shall receive Me, receiveth not Me, but Him that sent Me.}

{And John answered Him, saying, Master, we saw one casting out devils in thy name, and he followeth not us: and we forbad him, because he followeth not [with] us. But Jesus said [unto him], Forbid him not: for there is no man which shall do a miracle in My name, that can lightly speak evil of Me. For he that is not against us is on our part [for us]. For whosoever shall give you a cup of water to drink in My name, because ye belong to Christ, verily I say unto you, he shall not lose his reward.} [for he that is least among you all, the same shall be great]. But whoso {ever} shall offend one of these little ones which believe in Me, it {is} were better for him that a millstone were hanged about his neck, and *that* he were {cast} drowned in {to} the depth of the sea.

Woe unto the world because of offences! For it must needs be that offences come; but woe to that man by whom the offence com-eth! Wherefore if thy hand or thy foot offend thee, cut them off, and cast *them* from thee: it is better for thee to enter into life halt or maimed, rather than having two hands or two feet to be cast into {hell} everlasting fire {that never shall be quenched}. {Where their worm dieth not.} And if thine eye offend thee, pluck it out. And cast it from thee: it is better for thee to enter into life {the kingdom of God} with one eye, rather than having two eyes to be cast into hell fire. {For every one shall be salted with fire, and every sacrifice shall be salted with salt. Salt *is* good: but if the salt have lost his saltness, wherewith will ye season it? Have salt in yourselves, and have peace one with another.}

Take heed that ye despise not one of these little ones; for I say unto you, That in heaven their angels do always behold the face of My Father which is in heaven. For the Son of man is come to save that which was lost. How think ye? If a man have an hundred sheep, and one of them be gone astray, doth he not leave the ninety and nine, and goeth into the mountains, and seeketh that which is gone astray? And if so be that he find it, verily I say unto you, he rejoiceth more of that *sheep,* than of the ninety and nine which went not astray. Even so it is not the will of your Father which is in heaven, that one of these little ones should perish.

Moreover if thy brother shall trespass against thee, go and tell him his fault between thee and him alone: if he shall hear thee, thou hast gained thy brother. But if he will not hear *thee, then* take with thee one or two more, that in the mouth of two or three witnesses every word may be established. And if he shall neglect to hear them, tell *it* unto the church: but if he neglect to hear the church, let him be unto thee as an heathen man and a publican Verily I say unto you, Whatsoever ye shall bind on earth shall be bound in heaven: and whatsoever ye shall loose on earth shall be loosed in heaven. Again I say unto you, That if two of you shall agree on earth as touching any thing that they shall ask, it shall be done for them of my Father which is in heaven. For where two or three are gathered together in My name, there am I in the midst of them.

Then came Peter to Him, and said, Lord, how oft shall my brother sin against me, and I forgive him? Till seven times? Jesus saith

unto him. I say not unto thee, Until seven times: but, Until seventy times seven.

Therefore is the kingdom of heaven likened unto a certain king, which would take account of his servants. And when he had begun to reckon, one was brought unto him, which owed him ten thousand talents. But forasmuch as he had not to pay, his lord commanded him to be sold, and his wife, and children, and all that he had, and payment to be made. The servant therefore fell down, and worshipped him, saying, Lord, have patience with me, and I will pay thee all. Then the lord of that servant was moved with compassion, and loosed him, and forgave him the debt. But the same servant went out, and found one of his fellow servants, which owed him an hundred pence and he laid his hands on him. and took *him* by the throat, saying, Pay me that thou owest. And his fellow servant fell down at his feet, and besought him, saying, Have patience with me, and I will pay thee all. And he would not: but went and cast him into prison, till he should pay the debt. So when his fellow servants saw what was done, they were very sorry, and came and told unto their lord all that was done. Then his lord, after that he had called him, said unto him, O thou wicked servant, I forgave thee all that debt, because thou desiredst me: Shouldest not thou also have had compassion on thy fellow servant even as I had pity on thee? And his lord was wroth, and delivered him to the tormentors, till he should pay all that was due unto him. So likewise shall My heavenly Father do also unto you, if ye from your hearts forgive not every one his brother their trespasses.)

(53) (22) [Luke 9:51–10:42]

[And it came to pass, when the time was come that He should be received up, He stedfastly set His face to go to Jerusalem. And sent messengers before His face: and they went, and entered into a village of Samaritans, to make ready for Him. And they did not receive Him, because His face was as though He would go to Jerusalem. And when His disciples James and John saw *this,* they said, Lord, wilt thou that we command fire to come down from heaven, and consume them, even as Elias did? But He turned, and rebuked them, and said, Ye know not what manner of spirit ye are of. For the Son on man is not come to destroy men's lives, but to save them. And they went to another village.

And it came to pass, that, as they went in the way, a certain *man* said unto Him, Lord, I will follow thee whithersoever thou goest. And Jesus said unto him, Foxes *have* holes, and birds of the air have nests; But the Son of man hath not where to lay *His* head. And He said unto another, Follow Me. But he said, Lord, suffer me first to go and bury my father. Jesus said unto him, Let the dead bury their dead: but go thou and preach the kingdom of God. And another also said, Lord, I will follow thee; but let me first go bid them farewell, which are at home at my house. And Jesus said unto him, No man, having put his hand to the plough, and looking back, is fit for the kingdom of God.

After these things the Lord appointed other seventy also, and sent them two and two before His face into every city and place, whither He himself would come. Therefore said He unto them, The harvest truly *is* great, but the labourers *are* few: pray ye therefore the Lord of the harvest that He would send forth labourers into His harvest. Go your ways: behold, I send you forth as lambs among wolves. Carry neither purse, nor scrip, nor shoes: and salute no man by the way. And into whatsoever house ye enter, first say, Peace *be* to this house. And if the son of peace be there, your peace shall rest upon it: if not, it shall turn to you again. And in the same house remain, eating and drinking such things as they give: for the labourer is worthy of his hire Go not from house to house. And into whatsoever city ye enter, and they receive you, eat such things as are set before you: And heal the sick that are therein, and say unto them, The kingdom of God is come nigh unto you. But into whatsoever city ye enter, and they receive you not, go your ways out into the streets of the same, and say, even the very dust of your city, which cleaveth on us, we do wipe off against you: notwithstanding be ye sure of this, that the kingdom of God is come nigh unto you. But I say unto you, that it shall be more tolerable in that day for Sodom, than for that city. Woe unto thee, Chorazin! Woe unto thee, Bethsaida! For if the mighty works had been done in Tyre and Sidon, which have been done in you, they had a great while ago repented, sitting in sackcloth and ashes. But it shall be more tolerable for Tyre and Sidon at the judgement, than for you And thou Capernaum, which art exalted to heaven, shalt be thrust down to hell. He that heareth you heareth Me; and he that despiseth you, despiseth Me: and he that despieth Me despieth Him that sent Me.

And the seventy returned again with joy, saying, Lord even the devils are subject unto us through thy name. And He said unto them, I beheld Satan as lightning fall from heaven. Behold I give unto you power to tread on serpents and scorpions, and over all the power of the enemy: and nothing shall by any means hurt you. Notwithstanding in this rejoice not, that the spirits are subject unto you; but rather rejoice, because your names are written in heaven.

In that hour **Jesus rejoiced in spirit, and said,** I thank thee, O Father, Lord of heaven and earth, that thou hast hid these things from the wise and prudent, and hast revealed them unto babes: even so, Father: for so it seemed good in thy sight. All things are delivered to Me of My Father: and no man knoweth who the Son is, but the Father; and who the Father is, but the Son, and *he* to whom the Son will reveal *him.*

And He turned him unto His disciples, and said privately, Blessed *are* the eyes which see the things that ye see; For I tell you, that many prophets and kings have desired to see those things which ye see, and have not seen *them;* and to hear those things which ye hear, and have not heard *them.*

And, behold, a certain lawyer stood up, and tempted Him, saying, Master, what shall I do to inherit eternal life? He said unto him, What is written in the law how readest thou? **And he answering said, Thou shalt love the Lord thy God with all thy heart, and with all thy soul, and with all thy strength, and with all thy mind; and thy neighbour as thyself. And He said unto him,** Thou hast answered right: this do, and thou shalt live. **But he willing to justify himself, said unto Jesus And who is my neighbour? And Jesus answering said,** A certain man went down from Jerusalem to Jericho, and fell among thieves, which stripped him of his raiment, and wounded *him*, and departed leaving *him* half dead. And by chance there came down a certain priest that way: and when he saw him, he passed by on the other side. And likewise a Levite, when he was at the place, came and looked on *him*, and passed by on the other side But a certain Samaritan, as he journeyed, came where he was: and when he saw him, he had compassion on *him*. And went to *him*, and bound up his wounds, pouring in oil and wine, and set him on his own beast, and brought him to an inn, and took care of him. And on the morrow when he departed, he took out two pence, and gave *them* to the host, and said unto him, Take care of him; and whatsoever thou spendest more, when I come again, I will repay thee. Which now of these three, thinkest thou, was neighbour unto him that fell among the thieves? And he said, He that shewed mercy on him. Then said Jesus unto him Go, and do thou likewise.

Now it came to pass, as they went, that He entered into a certain village: and a certain woman named Martha received Him into her house. And she had a sister called Mary, which also sat at Jesus' feet, and heard His word. But Martha was cumbered about much serving, and came to Him, and said Lord, dost thou not care that my sister hath left me to serve alone? Bid her therefore that she help me. And Jesus answered and said unto her, Martha, Martha, thou art careful and troubled about many things: But one thing is needful: and Mary hath chosen that good part, which shall not be taken away from her.]

(54) (23) **<John 7:10–10:42>**

<But when His brethren were gone up, then went He also up unto the feast, not openly, but as it were in secret. Then the Jews sought Him at the feast, and said, Where is He? And there was much murmuring among the people concerning Him: for some said, He is a good man: others said, Nay; but he deceiveth the people. Howbeit no man spake openly of Him for fear of the Jews.

Now about the midst of the feast Jesus went up into the temple, and taught. And the Jews marvelled, saying, How knoweth this man letters, having never learned? Jesus answered them, and said, My doctrine is not Mine, but His that sent Me. If any man will do His will, he shall know of the doctrine, whether it be of God, or *whether* I speak of Myself. He that speaketh of himself seeketh his own glory: but He that seeketh His glory that sent Him, the same is true, and no unrighteousness is in Him. Did not Moses give you the law, and *yet* none of you keepeth the law? Why go ye about to kill Me? **The people answered and said, Thou hast a devil: who goeth about to kill thee? Jesus answered and said unto them,** I have done one work, and ye all marvel. Moses therefore gave unto you circumcision; (not because it is of Moses, but of the fathers;) and ye on the sabbath day circumcise a man. If a man on the sabbath day receive circumcision, that the law of Moses should not be broken; are ye angry at Me, because I have made a man every whit whole on the sabbath day? Judge not according to the appearance, but judge righteous judgement. **Then said some of them of Jerusalem, Is not this He, whom they seek to kill? But, lo, He speaketh boldy, and they say nothing unto Him. Do the rulers know indeed that this is the very Christ? Howbeit we know this man whence He is: but when Christ cometh, no man knoweth whence He is. Then cried Jesus in the temple as He taught, saying,** Ye both know Me, and ye know whence I am: and I am not come of Myself, but He that sent Me is true, whom Ye know not. But I know Him: for I am from Him, and He hath sent Me. **Then they sought to take Him: but no man laid hands on Him, because His hour was not yet come. And many of the people believed on Him, and said, When Christ cometh, will He do more miracles than these which this** *man* **hath done?**

The Pharisees heard that the people murmured such things concerning Him; and the Pharisees and the chief priests sent officers to take Him. **Then said Jesus unto them,** Yet a little while am I with you, and *then* I go unto Him that sent Me. Ye shall seek *Me.* and shall not find Me. And where I am, *thither* ye cannot come. **Then said the Jews among themselves, Whither will he go, that we shall not find him? Will he go unto the dispersed among the Gentiles, and teach the Gentiles? What manner of saying is this that he said, Ye shall seek me, and shall not find me: and where I am, thither ye cannot come?**

In the last *day*, that great day of the feast, **Jesus stood and cried, saying,** If any man thirst let him come unto Me, and drink. He that believeth on Me, as the scripture hath said, out of his belly shall flow rivers of living water. (But this spake He of the Spirit, which they that

178

believe on Him should receive: for the Holy Ghost was not yet *given*; because that Jesus was not yet glorified.)

Many of the people therefore, when they heard this saying, said Of a truth this is the Prophet. Others said, This is the Christ. But some said, Shall Christ come out of Galilee? Hath not the scripture said, That Christ cometh of the seed of David, and out of the town of Bethlehem, where David was? So there was a division among the people because of Him. And some of them would have taken Him; but no man laid hands on Him.

Then came the officers to the chief priests and Pharisees; and they said unto them, Why have ye not brought him? The officers answered, Never man spake like this man. Then answered them the Pharisees, Are ye also deceived? Have any of the rulers or of the Pharisees believed on Him? But this people who knoweth not the law are cursed. Nicodemus saith unto them (he that came to Jesus by night, being one of them) Doth our law judge *any* man, before it hear Him, and know what He doeth? They answered and said unto him, Art thou also of Galilee? Search, and look: for out of Galilee ariseth no prophet. And every man went unto his own house.

Jesus went unto the mount of Olives. And early in the morning He came again into the temple, and all the people came unto Him; and He sat down, and taught them. And the scribes and Pharisees brought unto Him a woman taken in adultery; and when they set her in the midst, They say unto Him, Master, this woman was taken in adultery, in the very act. Now Moses in the law commanded us, that such should be stoned: but what sayest thou? This they said, tempting Him, that they might have to accuse Him. But Jesus stooped down, and with *His* finger wrote on the ground, *as though He heard them not.* So when they continued asking Him, He lifted up Himself, and said unto them, He that is without sin among you, let him first cast a stone at her. And again He stoop down, and wrote on the ground. And they which heard *it*, being convicted by *their own* conscience, went out one by one, beginning at the eldest *even* unto the last: and Jesus was left alone, and the woman standing in the midst. When Jesus had lifted up Himself, and saw none but the woman, He said unto her, Woman, where are those thine accusers? Hath no man condemned thee? She said, no man, Lord. And Jesus said unto her, Neither do I condemn thee; Go, and sin no more.

Then spake Jesus again unto them, saying, I am the light of the world: he that followeth Me shall not walk in darkness, but shall have the light of life. The Pharisees therefore said unto Him, Thou bearest record of thyself; thy record is not true. Jesus answered and said unto them, Though I bear record of Myself, yet My record is true: for I know whence I came, and whither I go; but ye cannot tell whence I come, and whither I go. Ye judge after the flesh; I judge no man. And yet if I judge, My judgement is true: For I am not alone, but I and the Father that sent Me. It is also written in your law, that the testimony of two men is true. I am one that bear witness of Myself, and the Father that sent Me beareth witness of Me. Then said they unto Him, Where is thy Father? Jesus answered, Ye neither know Me, nor My Father: if ye had known Me, ye should have known My Father also. These words spake Jesus in the treasury, as He taught in the temple: and no man laid hands on Him; for His hour was not yet come. Then said Jesus again unto them, I go My way, and ye shall seek Me, and shall die in your sins, whither I go, ye cannot come. Then said the Jews, will He kill himself? Because He saith, Whither I go, ye cannot come. And He said unto them, Ye are from beneath; I am from above: ye are of this world; I am not of this world. I said therefore unto you, that ye shall die in your sins: for if ye believe not that I am *He*, ye shall die in your sins. Then said they unto Him, Who art thou? And Jesus saith unto them, Even *the same* that I said unto you from the beginning. I have many thing to say and to judge of you: but He that sent Me is true; and I speak to the world those things which I have heard of Him. They understood not that He spake to them of the Father. Then said Jesus unto Them, When ye have lifted up the Son of man, then shall ye know that I am *He*, and *that* I do nothing of Myself; but as My Father hath taught Me, I speak these things. And He that sent Me is with Me: the Father hath not left Me alone; for I do always those things that please Him. As He spake these words, many believed on Him.

Then said Jesus to those Jews which believed on Him, If ye continue in My word, *then* are ye my disciples indeed; and ye shall know the truth, and the truth shall make you free.

They answered Him, We be Abraham's seed, and were never in bondage to any man: how sayest thou, Ye shall be made free? Jesus answered them, Verily, verily, I say unto you, Whosoever committeth sin is the servant of sin. And the servant abideth not in the house for ever: *but* the Son abideth ever. If the Son therefore shall make you free, ye shall be free indeed. I know that ye are Abraham's seed: but ye seek to kill Me, because My word hath no place in you. I speak that which I have seen with My Father: and ye do that which ye have seen with your father.

They answered and said unto Him, Abraham is our father. Jesus saith unto them, If ye were Abraham's children, ye would do the works of Abraham. But now ye seek to kill Me, a man that hath told you the truth, which I have heard of God: this did not Abraham. Ye do the deeds of your father. Then said they to Him, We be not born of fornication; we have one Father, *even* God.

Jesus said unto them, If God were your Father, ye would love Me: for I proceeded forth and came from God; neither came I of Myself, but He sent Me. Why do ye not understand my speech? *Even* because ye cannot hear My word. Ye are of *your* father the devil, and the lusts of your father ye will do. He was a murderer from the beginning, and abode not in the truth, because there is no truth in him. When he speaketh a lie, he speaketh of his own: for he is a liar, and the father of it. And because I tell *you* the truth, ye believe Me not. Which of you convinceth Me of sin? And if I say the truth, why do ye not believe Me? He that is of God heareth God's words: ye therefore hear *them* not, because ye are not of God. Then answered the Jews, and said unto him, Say we not well that thou art a Samaritan, and hast a devil? Jesus answered, I have not a devil; but I honour My Father, and ye do dishonour Me. And I seek not Mine own glory: there is one that seeketh and judgeth. Verily, verily, I say unto you, If a man keep My saying, he shall never see death. Then said the Jews unto Him, now we know that thou hast a devil. Abraham is dead, and the prophets; and thou sayest, If a man keep my saying, he shall never taste of death. Art thou greater than our father Abraham, which is dead? And the prophets are dead: whom makest thou thyself? Jesus answered, If I honour Myself, My honour is nothing: it is My Father that honoureth Me; of whom ye say, that He is your God: Yet ye have not known Him; but I know Him: and if I should say, I know Him not, I shall be a liar like unto you: but I know Him, and keep His saying. Your father Abraham rejoiced to see My day: and he saw it, and was glad. Then said the Jews unto Him, Thou art not yet fifty years old, and hast thou seen Abraham? Jesus said unto them, Verily, verily, I say unto you, Before Abraham was, I Am. Then took they up stones to cast at him: but Jesus hid himself, and went out of the temple, going through the midst of them, and so passed by.

And as *Jesus* passed by, He saw a man which was blind from *his* birth. And his disciples asked him, saying, Master, who did sin, this man, or his parents, that he was born blind? Jesus answered, Neither hath this man sinned, nor his parents: but that the works of God should be made manifest in him. I must work the works of Him that sent Me, while it is day: the night cometh, when no man can work. As long as I am in the world, I am the light of the world. When He had thus spoken, He spat on the ground, and made clay of the spittle, and He anointed the eyes of the blind man with the clay. And said unto him, Go, wash in the pool of Siloam (which is by interpretation, Sent) He went his way therefore, and washed, and came seeing.

The neighbours therefore, and they which before had seen him that he was blind, said, Is not this he that sat and begged? Some said, This is he: others *said,* He is like him: *but* he said I am *he.* Therefore said they unto him, How were thine eyes opened? He answered and said, A man that is called Jesus made clay, and anointed mine eyes, and said unto me, Go to the pool of Siloam, and wash: and I went and washed, and I received sight. Then said they unto him, Where is He? He said, I know not.

They brought to the Pharisees him that aforetime was blind. And it was the sabbath day when Jesus made the clay, and opened his eyes. Then again the Pharisees also asked him how he had received his sight. He said unto them, He put clay upon mine eyes, and I washed, and do see. Therefore said some of the Pharisees, This man is not of God, because he keepeth not the sabbath day. Others said, How can a man that is a sinner do such miracles? And there was a division among them. They say unto the blind man again, What sayest thou of Him, that He hath opened thine eyes? He said, He is a prophet. But the Jews did not believe concerning him, that he had been blind, and received his sight, until they called the parents of him that had received his sight. And they asked them, saying, Is this your son, who ye say was born blind? How then doth he now see? His parents answered them and said, We know that this is our son, and that he was born blind: But by what means he now seeth, we know not; or who hath opened his eyes, we know not: he is of age; ask him: he will speak for himself. These *words* spake his parents, because they feared the Jews: for the Jews had agreed already, that if any man did confess that He was Christ, he should be put out of the synagogue. Therefore said his parents, He is of age; ask him. Then again they called the man that was blind, and said unto him, Give God the praise: we know that this man is a sinner. He answered and said, Whether He be a sinner *or no*, I know not: one thing I know, that, whereas I was blind, now I see. Then said they to him again, What did He to thee? How opened He thine eyes? He answered them, I have told you already, and ye did not hear: wherefore would ye hear *it* again? Will ye also be His disciples? Then they reviled him, and said, Thou art His disciple; but we are Moses disciples. We know that God spake unto Moses: *as for* this *fellow*, we know not from whence He is. The man answered and said unto them, Why herein is a marvellous thing, that ye know not from whence He is, and *yet* He hath opened mine eyes. Now we know that God heareth not sinners: but if any man be a worshipper of God, and doeth His will, Him He heareth. Since the world began was it not heard that any man opened the eyes of one that was born blind. If this man were not of God, He could do nothing. They answered and said unto him, Thou wast altogether born in sins, and dost thou teach us? And they cast him out. Jesus heard that they had cast him out; and when he had found him, He said unto him, Dost thou believe on the Son of God? He answered and said, Who is he, Lord, that I might believe on Him? And Jesus said unto him, Thou hast both seen Him, and it is He that talketh with thee. And he said, Lord, I believe. And he worshipped Him.

And Jesus said, For judgement I am come into this world, that they which see not might see; and that they which see might be made blind. And *some* of the Pharisees which were with him heard these words, and said unto Him, Are we blind also? Jesus said unto them, If ye were blind ye should have no sin: but now ye say, We see; therefore your sin remaineth.

Verily, verily, I say unto you, He that entereth not by the door into the sheepfold, but climbeth up some other way, the same is a thief and a robber. But He that entereth in by the door is the shepherd of the sheep. To Him the porter openeth; and the sheep hear His voice: and He calleth His own sheep by name, and leadeth them out. And when He putteth forth His own sheep, He goeth before them, and the sheep follow Him: for they know His voice. And a stranger will they not follow, but will flee from him: for they know not the voice of strangers. This parable spake Jesus unto them: but they understood not what things they were which He spake unto them. Then said Jesus unto them again, Verily, verily, I say unto you, I am the Door of the sheep. All that ever came before Me are thieves and robbers: but the sheep did not hear them. I am the Door: by Me if any man enter in he shall be saved, and shall go in and out, and find pasture. The thief cometh not, but for to steal, and to kill, and to destroy: I am come that they might have life, and that they might have *it* more abundantly. I am the Good Shepherd: the Good Shepherd giveth His life for the sheep. But he that is a hireling, and not the Shepherd, whose own the sheep are not, seeth the wolf coming, and leaveth the sheep, and fleeth: and the wolf catcheth them, and scattereth the sheep. The hireling fleeth, because he is a hireling, and careth not for the sheep. I am the Good Shepherd, and know My *sheep,* and am known of Mine. As the Father knoweth Me, even so know I the Father: and I lay down My life for the sheep. And other sheep I have, which are not of this fold; them also I must bring, and they shall hear My voice; and there shall be one fold, *and* one Shepherd. Therefore doth My Father love Me, because I lay down My life, that I might take it again, no man taketh it from Me, but I lay it down of Myself. I have power to lay it down, and I have power to take it again This commandment have I received of My Father.

There was a division therefore again among the Jews for these sayings. And many of them said, He hath a devil, and is mad; why hear ye him? Others said, These are not the words of Him that hath a Devil. Can a devil open the eyes of the blind?

And it was at Jerusalem the feast of dedication, and it was winter. And Jesus walked in the temple in Solomon's porch. Then came the Jews round about Him, And said unto Him, How long dost thou make us to doubt? If thou be the Christ, tell us plainly. Jesus answered them, I told you and ye believed not: the works that I do in My Father's name, they bear witness of Me. But ye believe not, because ye are not of My sheep, as I said unto you. My sheep hear My voice, and I know them, and they follow Me: and I give unto them eternal life; and they shall never perish neither shall any *man* pluck them out of My hand My Father, which gave *them* Me, is greater than all; and no *man* is able to pluck *them* out of My Father's hand. I and *My* Father are one. Then the Jews took up stones again to stone Him. Jesus answered them, Many good works have I shewed you from My Father for which of those works do ye stone Me? The Jews answered Him, saying, For a good work we stone Thee not; but for blasphemy; and because that Thou, being a man, makest Thyself God. Jesus answered them, Is it not written in your law, I said, Ye are gods? If He called them gods, unto whom the word of God came, and the scripture cannot be broken; Say ye of Him, whom the Father hath sanctified, and sent into the world, Thou blasphemest; because I said, I am the Son of God? If I do not the works of My Father believe Me not. But if I do, though ye believe not Me, believe the works: that ye may know, and believe, that the Father *is* in Me, and I in Him. Therefore they sought again to take Him: but He escaped out of their hand, and went away again beyond Jordan into the place where John at first baptized; and there He abode. And many resorted unto Him, and said, John did no miracle: but all things that John spake of this man were true. And many believed on Him there.

(55) (24) **[Luke 11:1–18:14]**

[And it came to pass, that, as He was praying in a certain place, when He ceased, one of His disciples said unto Him, Lord, teach us to pray, as John also taught his disciples. And He said unto them, When ye pray, say, Our Father which art in heaven, Hallowed be Thy Name. Thy kingdom come. Thy will be done, as in heaven, so in earth. Give us day by day our daily bread. And forgive us our sins; for we also forgive everyone who is indebted to us. And lead us not into temptation; but deliver us from evil. **And He said unto them,** Which of you shall have a friend, and shall go unto him at midnight, and say unto him, Friend, lend me three loaves; For a friend of mine in his journey is come to me, and I have nothing to set before him? And he from within shall answer and say, Trouble me not: the door is now shut, and my children are with me in bed: I cannot rise and give thee. I say unto you, Though he will not rise and give him, because he is his friend, yet because of his importunity he will rise and give him as many as he needeth. And I say unto you, Ask, and it shall be given you; seek, and ye shall find; knock, and it shall be opened unto you. For every one that asketh receiveth; and he that seeketh findeth; and to him that knocketh it shall be opened. If a son shall ask bread of any of you that is a father, will he give him a stone? Or if *he ask* a fish, will he for a fish give him a serpent? Or if he shall ask an egg, will he offer him a scorpion? If ye then, being evil, know how to give good gifts unto your children: how much more shall *your* heavenly Father give the Holy Spirit to them that ask Him?

And He was casting out a devil, and it was dumb. And it came to pass, when the devil was gone out, the dumb spake; and the people wondered. But some of them said, He casteth out devils through Beelzebub the chief of the devils. And others, tempting *Him,* sought of Him a sign from heaven. But He, knowing their thoughts, said unto them, Every kingdom divided against itself is brought to desolation; and a house *divided* against a house falleth. If Satan also be divided against himself, how shall his kingdom stand? Because ye say that I cast out devils through beelzebub. And if I by Beelzebub cast out devils, by whom do your sons cast *them* out? Therefore shall they be your judges. But if I with the finger of God cast out devils, no doubt the kingdom of God is come upon you. When a strong man armed keepeth his palace, his goods are in peace: But when a stronger than he shall come upon him. and overcome him, he taketh from him all his armour wherein he trusted, and divideth his spoils. He that is not with Me is against Me: and he that gathereth not with Me scattereth. When the unclean spirit is gone out of a man, he walketh through dry places, seeking rest; and finding none, he saith, I will return unto my house whence I came out. And when he cometh, he findeth *it* swept and garnished. Then goeth he, and taketh *to him* seven other spirits more wicked than himself; and they enter in, and dwell there: and the last *state* of that man is worse than the first.

And it came to pass, as He spake these things, a certain woman of the company lifted up her voice, and said unto Him, *Blessed* is the womb that bare thee, and the paps which thou hast sucked. But He said, Yea rather, blessed *are* they that hear the word of God, and keep it.

And when the people were gathered thick together, He began to say, This is an evil generation: they seek a sign; and there shall no sign be given it, but the sign of Jonas the prophet. For as Jonas was a sign unto the Ninevites, so shall also the Son of man be to this generation. The queen of the south shall rise up in the judgement with the men of this generation, and condemn them: for she came from the utmost parts of the earth to hear the wisdom of Solomon; and, behold, a greater than Solomon *is* here. The men of Nineve shall rise up in the judgement with this generation, and shall condemn it: for they repented at the preaching of Jonas; and, behold, a greater than Jonas *is* here. No man, when he *hath* lighted a candle, putteth *it* in a secret place, neither under a bushel, but on a candlestick, that they which come in may see the light. The light of the body is the eye: therefore when *thine* eye is single, thy whole body also is full of light; but when *thine eye* is evil, thy body also *is* full of darkness. Take heed therefore that the light which is in thee be not darkness. If thy whole body therefore *be* full of light, having no part dark, the whole shall *be* full of light, as when the bright shining of a candle doth give thee light.

And as He spake, a certain Pharisee besought Him to dine with him: and He went in and sat down to meat. And when the Pharisee saw *it*, he marvelled that He had not first washed before dinner. And the Lord said unto him, Now do ye Pharisees make clean the outside of the cup and the platter; but your inward part is full of ravening and wickedness. *Ye* fools, did not He that made that which is without make that which is within also? But rather give alms of such things as ye have; and, behold, all things are clean unto you. But woe unto you, Pharisees! For ye tithe mint and rue and all manner of herbs, and pass over judgement and the love of God: these ought ye to have done, and not leave the other undone. Woe unto, Pharisees! for ye love the uppermost seats in the synagogues, and greetings in the markets. Woe unto you, scribes and Pharisees, hypocrites! For ye are as graves which appear not, and the men that walk over *them* are not aware *of them.*

Then answered one of the lawyers, and said unto Him, Master, thus saying Thou reproachest us also. And he said, Woe unto you also, ye lawyers! For ye lade men with burdens grievous to be borne, and ye yourselves touch not the burdens with one of your fingers. Woe unto you! For ye build the sepulchres of the prophets, and your fathers killed them. Truly ye bear witness that ye allow the deeds of your fathers: for they indeed killed them, and ye build their sepulchres. Therefore also said the wisdom of God, I will send them prophets and apostles, and *some* of them they shall slay and persecute: That the blood of all the prophets, which was shed from the foundation of the world, may be required of this generation; From the blood of Abel unto the blood of Zacharias, which perished between the altar and the temple: verily I say unto you, It shall be required of this generation. Woe unto you, lawyers! For ye have taken away the key of knowledge: ye entered not in yourselves, and them that were entering in ye hindered. And as He said these things unto them, the scribes and the Pharisees began to urge *Him* vehemently, and to provoke Him to speak of many things: Laying wait for Him, and seeking to catch something out of His mouth, that they might accuse Him.

In the mean time, when there were gathered together an innumerable multitude of people, insomuch that they trode one upon another, He began to say unto His disciples first of all, Beware ye of the leaven of the Pharisees, which is hypocrisy. For there is nothing covered, that shall not be revealed; neither hid, that shall not be known. Therefore whatsoever ye have spoken in darkness shall be heard in the light; and that which ye have spoken in the ear in closets shall be proclaimed upon the housetops. And I say unto you My friends. Be not afraid of them that kill the body, and after that have no more that they can do. But I will forewarn you whom ye shall fear: Fear Him, which after He hath killed hath power to cast into hell; yea, I say unto you, Fear Him. Are not five sparrows sold for two farthings, and not one of them is forgotten before God? But even the every hairs of your head are all numbered. Fear not therefore: ye are of more value than many sparrows. Also I say unto you, who¬soever shall confess Me before men, him shall the Son of man also confess before the angels of God: But he that denieth Me before men shall be denied before the angels of God. And whosoever shall speak a word against the Son of man, it shall be forgiven him: but unto him that blasphemeth against the Holy Ghost it shall not be forgiven. And when they bring you unto the synagogues, and *unto* magistrates, and powers, take ye no thought how or what thing ye shall answer, or what ye shall say: For the Holy Ghost shall teach you in the same hour what ye ought to say.

And one of the company said unto Him, Master, speak to my brother, that he divide the inheritance with me. And He said unto him Man, who made Me a judge or a divider over you? And He said unto them, Take heed, and beware of covetousness: for a man's life consisteth not in the abundance of the things which he possesseth. And He spake a parable unto them, saying, The ground of a certain rich man brought forth plentifully: And he thought within himself, saying, What shall I do, because I have no room where to bestow my fruits? And he said, This will I do: I will pull down my barns, and build greater; and there will I bestow all my fruits and my goods. And I will say to my soul, Soul, thou hast much goods laid up for many years; take thine ease, eat, drink, *and* be merry. But God said unto him, *Thou* fool, this night thy soul shall be required of thee: then whose shall those things be, which thou hast provided? So *is* he that layeth up treasure for himself, and is not rich toward God.

And He said unto His disciples, Therefore I say unto you. Take no thought for your life, what ye shall eat; neither for the body, what ye shall put on. The life is more than meat, and the body *is more* than raiment. Consider the ravens: for they neither sow nor reap; which neither have storehouse nor barn; and God feedeth them: how much more are ye better than the fowls? And which of you with taking thought can add to his stature one cubit? If ye then be not able to do that thing which is least, why take ye thought for the rest? Consider the lilies how they grow: they toil not, they spin not; and yet I say unto you, that Solomon in all his glory was not arrayed like one of these. If then God so clothe the grass, which is to day in the field, and to morrow is cast into the oven; how much more *will He clothe* you, O ye of little faith? And seek not ye what ye shall eat, or what ye shall drink, neither be ye of doubtful mind. For all these things do the nations of the world seek after: and your Father knoweth that ye have need of these things.

But rather seek ye the kingdom of God; and all these things shall be added unto you. Fear not, little flock; for it is your Father's good pleasure to give you the kingdom. Sell that ye have, and give alms; provide yourselves bags which wax not old, a treasure in the heavens that faileth not, where no thief approacheth, neither moth corrupteth. For where your treasure is, there will your heart be also. Let your lions be girded about, and *your* lights burning; And ye yourselves like unto men that wait for their lord, when He will return from the wedding; that when He cometh and knocketh, they may open unto Him immediately. Blessed are those servants, whom the lord when He cometh shall find watching: verily I say unto you, that He shall gird Himself, and make them to sit down to meat, and will come forth and serve them. And if He will come in the second watch, or come in the third watch, and find *them* so, blessed are those servants. And this know, that if the goodman of the house had known what hour the thief would come, he would have watched, and not suffered his house to be broken through. Be ye therefore ready also: for the Son of man cometh at an hour when ye think not.

Then Peter said unto Him, Lord, speakest thou this parable unto us, or even to all? And the Lord said, Who then is that faithful and wise steward, whom *His* lord shall make ruler over *His* household, to give *them their* portion of meat in due season? Blessed *is* the servant, whom His lord when He cometh shall find so doing. Of a truth I say unto you, that He will make him ruler over all that He hath. But and if that servant say in his heart, my lord delayeth His coming; and shall begin to beat the menservants and maidservants, and to eat and drink, and to be drunken; The lord of that servant will come in a day when he looketh not for *Him,* and at an hour when he is not aware, and will cut him in sunder, and will appoint him his portion with the unbelievers. And that servant, which knew His lord's will, and prepared not *himself,* neither did according to His will, shall be beaten with many *stripes.* But he that knew not, and did commit things worthy of stripes, shall be beaten with few *stripes.* For unto whomsoever much is given, of him shall be much required: and to whom men have committed much, of him they will ask the more.

I am come to send fire on the earth; and what will I, if it be already kindled? But I have a baptism to be baptized with; and how am I straighten till it be accomplished! Suppose ye that I am come to give peace on earth? I tell you, Nay; but rather division: For from henceforth there shall be five in one house divided, three against two, and two against three. The father shall be divided against the son, and the son against the father; the mother against the daughter, and the daughter against the mother; the mother in law against the daughter in law, and the daughter in law against the mother in law.

And He said also to the people, When ye see a cloud rise out of the west, straightway ye say, There cometh a shower; and so it is. And when *ye see* the south wind blow, ye say, There will be heat; and it cometh to pass. *Ye* hypocrites, ye can discern the face of the sky and of the earth; but how is it that ye do not discern this time? Yea, and why even of yourselves judge ye not what is right?

When thou goest with thine adversary to the magistrate, as *thou art* in the way give diligence that thou mayest be delivered from him; lest he hale thee to the judge, and the judge deliver thee to the officer, and the officer cast thee into prison. I tell thee, thou shalt not depart thence, till thou hast paid·the very last mite.

There were present at that season some that told Him of the Galilaeans, whose blood Pilate had mingled with their sacrifices. And Jesus answering said unto them, Suppose ye that these Galilaeans were sinners above all Galilaeans, because they suffer such things? I tell you Nay: but, except ye repent, ye shall likewise perish. Or those eighteen upon whom the tower of Siloam fell, and slew them, think ye that they were sinners above all men that dwelt in Jerusalem? I tell you, Nay: but, except ye repent, ye shall all likewise perish.

He spake also this parable; A certain *man* had a fig tree planted in his vineyard; and he came and sought fruit thereon, and found none. Then said he unto the dresser of his vineyard, Behold, these three years I come seeking fruit on this fig tree, and find none: cut it down; why cumbereth it the ground? And he answering said unto him, Lord, let it alone this year also, till I shall dig about it, and dung *it:* And if it bear fruit, *well:* and if not, *then* after that thou shalt cut it down.

And He was teaching in one of the synagogues on the sabbath. And, behold, there was a woman which had a spirit of infirmity eighteen years, and was bowed together, and could in no wise lift up *herself.* And when Jesus saw her, He called *her* to *Him,* and said unto her, Woman, thou art loosed from thine infirmity. And He laid *His* hands on her: and immediately she was made straight, and glorified God. And the ruler of the synagogue answered with indignation, because that Jesus had healed on the sabbath day, and said unto the people, There are six days in which men ought to work: in them therefore come and be healed, and not on the sabbath day. The Lord then answered him, and said, *Thou* hypocrite, doth not each one of you on the sabbath loose his ox or *his* ass from the stall, and lead *him* away to watering? And ought not this woman, being a daughter of Abraham, whom Satan hath bound, lo, these eighteen years, be loosed from this bond on the sabbath day? And when He had said these things, all His adversaries were ashamed: and all the people rejoiced for all the glorious things that were done by Him.

Then said He, Unto what is the kingdom of God like? And whereunto shall I resemble it? It is like a grain of mustard seed, which a man took, and cast into his garden; and it grew, and waxed a great tree; and the fowls of the air lodged in the branches of it. And again He said, Wherefore shall I liken the kingdom of God? It is like leaven, which a woman took and hid in three measures of meal, till the whole was leavened.

And He went through the cities and villages, teaching and journeying toward Jerusalem. Then said one unto Him, Lord, are there few that be saved? And He said unto them, Strive to enter in at the straight gate: for many, I say unto you, will seek to enter in, and shall not be able. When once the master of the house is risen up, and hath shut the door, and ye begin to stand without, and to knock at the door, saying, Lord, Lord, open unto us; and He shall answer and say unto you, I know you not whence ye are: Then shall ye begin to say, We have eaten and drunk in Thy presence, and Thou hast taught in our streets. But He shall say, I tell you, I know you not whence ye are; depart from Me, all ye workers of iniquity. There shall be weeping and gnashing of teeth, when ye shall see Abraham, and Isaac, and Jacob, and all the prophets, in the kingdom of God, and you *yourselves* thrust out. And they shall come from the east, and *from* the west, and *from* the north, and *from* the south, and shall sit down in the kingdom of God. And, behold, there are last which shall be first, and there are first which shall be last.

The same day there came certain of the Pharisees, saying unto Him, Get thee out, and depart hence: for Herod will kill thee. And He said unto them, Go ye, and tell that fox, Behold, I cast out devils, and I do cures today and to morrow, and the third *day* I shall be perfected. Nevertheless I must walk today and tomorrow, and the *day* following: for it can not be that a prophet perish out of Jerusalem. O Jerusalem, Jerusalem, which killest the prophets, and stonest them that are sent unto thee: how often would I have gathered thy children together, as a hen *doth gather* her brood under *her* wings, and ye would not! Behold, your house is left unto you desolate: and verily I say unto you, Ye shall not see me, until *the time* come when ye shall say, Blessed is He that cometh in the name of the lord.

And it came to pass, as He went into the house of one of the chief Pharisees to eat bread on the sabbath day, that they watched him. And, behold, there was a certain man before Him which had the dropsy. And Jesus answering spake unto the lawyers and

Pharisees, saying, Is it lawful to heal on the sabbath day? And they held their peace. And He took *him*, and healed him, and let him go; And answered them, saying, Which of you shall have an ass or an ox fallen into a pit. and and will not straightway pull him out on the sabbath day? And they could not answer Him again to these things.

And He put forth a parable to those which were bidden, when He marked how they chose out the chief rooms; saying unto them. When you are bidden of any *Man* to a wedding, sit not down in the highest room; lest a more honourable man than thou be bidden of him; and he that bade thee and him come and say to thee, Give this man place; and thou begin with shame to take the lowest room. But when you are bidden, go and sit down in the lowest room; that when he that bade thee cometh, he may say unto to thee, Friend, go up higher: then shalt thou have worship in the presence of them that sit at meat with thee. For whosoever exalteth himself shall be abased; and he that humbleth himself shall be exalted

Then said He also to him that bade Him, When thou makest a dinner or a supper, call not thy friends, nor thy brethren, neither thy kinsmen, nor *thy* rich neighbours; lest they also bid thee again, and a recompence be made thee. But when you makest a feast, call the poor, the maimed, the lame, the blind: And thou shalt be blessed; for they cannot recompense thee: for thou shalt be recompensed at the resurrection of the just.

And when one of them that sat at meat with Him heard these things, he said unto Him, Blessed *is* he that shall eat bread in the kingdom of God. Then said He unto him, A certain man made a great supper, and bade many: And sent his servant at supper time to say to them that were bidden, Come; for all things are now ready. And they all with one *consent* began to make excuse, The first said unto him, I have bought a piece of ground, and I must needs go and see it: I pray thee have me excused. And another said. I have bought five yoke of oxen, and I go to prove them: I pray thee have me excused. And another said I have married a wife, and therefore I cannot come. So that servant came, and shewed His lord these things. Then the master of the house being angry said to His servant, Go out quickly into the streets and lanes of the city, and bring in hither the poor the maimed, and the halt, and the blind. And the servant said, Lord, it is done as thou hast commanded, and yet there is room And the Lord said unto the servant, Go out into the highways and hedges, and compel *them* to come in. that My house may be filled. For I say unto you, That none of those men which were bidden shall taste of My supper.

And there went great multitudes with Him: and He turned, and said unto them. If any *man* come to Me, and hate not his father, and mother, and wife, and children, and brethren, and sisters, yea, and his own life also, he cannot be My disciple. And whosoever doth not bear his cross, and come after Me, cannot be My disciple. For which of you, intending to build a tower, sitteth not down first, and counteth the cost, whether he have *sufficient* to finish it. Lest haply, after he hath laid the foundation, and *is* not able to finish *it*, all that behold *it* begin to mock him, saying, this man began to build, and was not able to finish. Or what king, going to make war against another king, sitteth not down first, and consulteth whether he be able with ten thousand to meet him that cometh against him with twenty thousand? Or else, while the other is yet a great way off, he sendeth an ambassage and desireth conditions of peace. So likewise, whosoever he be of you that forsaketh not all that he hath, he cannot be My disciple.

Salt *is* good: but if the salt have lost his savour, wherewith shall it be seasoned? It is neither fit for the land, nor yet for the dunghill; but men cast it out, He that hath ears to hear, let him hear.

Then drew near unto Him all the publicans and sinners for to hear Him. And the Pharisees and scribes murmured, saying, This man receiveth sinners, and eateth with them.

And He spake this parable unto them, saying, What man of you, having an hundred sheep if he lose one of them, doth not leave the ninety and nine in the wilderness, and go after that which is lost, until he find it? And when he hath found *it*, he layeth *it* on his shoulders, rejoicing. And when he cometh home, he calleth together *his* friends and neighbours, saying unto them, Rejoice with me; for I have found My sheep which was lost. I say unto you, that likewise joy shall be in heaven over one sinner that repenteth, more than over ninety and nine just persons, which need no repentance.

Either what woman having ten pieces of silver, if she lose one piece, doth not light a candle, and sweep the house, and seek diligently till she find *it*? And when she has found *it*, she calleth *her* friends and *her* neighbours together, saying Rejoice with me; for I have found the piece which I had lost. Likewise, I say unto you, there is joy in the presence of the angels of God over one sinner that repenteth.

And He said, A certain man had two sons: And the younger of them said to *his* father, Father, give me the portion of goods that falleth *to me*. And he divided unto them *his* living. And not many days after the younger son gathered all together, and took his journey into a far country, and there wasted his substance with riotous living. And when he had spent all there arose a mighty famine in that land; and he began to be in want. And he went and joined himself to a citizen of that country; and he sent him into his fields to feed swine. And he would fain have filled his belly with the husks that the swine did eat: and no man gave unto him. And when he came to himself, he said, How many hired servants of my father's have bread enough and to spare, and I perish with hunger! I will arise and go to my father, and will say unto him, Father, I have sinned against heaven, and before thee, and am no more worthy to be called thy son: make me as one of thy hired servants. And he arose, and came to his father. But when he was yet a great way off, his father saw him, and had compassion, and ran, and fell on his neck, and kissed him.

And the son said unto him, Father, I have sinned against heaven, and in thy sight, and am no more worthy to be called thy son. But the father said to his servants. Bring forth the best robe, and put *it* on him; and put a ring on his hand, and shoes on *his* feet, and bring hither the fatted calf, and kill *it*; and let us eat and be merry: For this my son was dead and is alive again; he was lost, and is found. And they began to be merry. Now his elder son was in the field: and as he came and drew nigh to the house, he heard musick and dancing. And he called one of the servants, and asked what these things meant. And he said unto him, Thy brother is come; and thy father hath killed the fatted calf, because he hath received him safe and sound. And he was angry, and would not go in: therefore came his father out, and intreated him. And he answering said to *his* father, Lo, these many years do I serve thee, neither transgressed I at any time thy commandments: and yet thou never gavest me a kid, that I might make merry with my friends: But as soon as this thy son was come, which hath devoured thy living with harlots, thou hast killed for him the fatted calf. And he said unto him, Son, thou art ever with me, and all that I have is thine. It was meet that we should make merry, and be glad: for this thy brother was dead, and is alive again; and was lost, and is found.

And He said also unto His disciples, There was a certain rich man, which had a steward: and the same was accused unto him that he had wasted his goods. And he called him, and said unto him, How is it that I hear this of thee? Give an account of thy steward-ship; for thou mayest be no longer steward. Then the steward said within himself, What shall I do? For my lord taketh away from me the stewardship: I cannot dig; to beg I am ashamed. I am resolved what to do, that, when I am put out of the stewardship, they may receive me into their houses. So he called every one of his lord's debt-ors *unto him,* and said unto the first, How much owest thou unto my lord? And he said, An hundred measures of oil. And he said unto him, Take thy bill, and sit down quickly, and write fifty. Then said he to another, And how much owest thou? And he said, An hundred measures of wheat. And he said unto him, Take thy bill, and write fourscore. And the lord commended the unjust steward, because he had done wisely: for the children of this world are in their generation wiser than the children of light. And I say unto you, Make to your-selves friends of the mammon of unrighteousness; that, when ye fail, they may receive you into everlasting habitations. He that is faithful in that which is least is faithful also in much: and he that is unjust in the least is unjust also in much. If therefore ye have not been faithful in the unrighteous mammon, who will commit to your trust, the true *riches?* And if ye have not been faithful in that which is another man's, who shall give you that which is your own?

No servant can serve two masters: for either he will hate the one, and love the other: or else he will hold to the one, and despise the other. Ye cannot serve God and mammon.

And the Pharisees also, who were covetous, heard all these things: and they derided Him. And He said unto them. Ye are they which justify yourselves before men; God knoweth your hearts: for that which is highly esteemed among men is abomination in the sight of God. The law and the prophets *were* until John: since that time the kingdom of God is preached, and every man presseth into it. And it is easier for heaven and earth to pass, than one tittle of the law to fail. Whosoever putteth away his wife, and marrieth another, committeth adultery: and whosoever marrieth her that is put away from *her* husband committeth adultery.

There was a certain rich man, which was clothed in purple and fine linen, and fared sumptuously every day: And there was a certain beggar named Lazarus, which was laid at his gate, full of sores, and desiring to be fed with the crumbs which fell from the rich man's table: moreover the dogs came and licked his sores. And it came to pass, that the beggar died, and was carried by the angels into Abraham's bosom: the rich man also died, and was buried; And in hell he lift up his eyes, being in torments, and seeth Abraham afar off, and Lazarus in his bosom. And he cried and said, Father Abraham, have mercy on me, and send Lazarus, that he may dip the tip of his finger in water, and cool my tongue; for I am tormented in this flame. But Abraham said, Son, remember that thou in thy lifetime receivedst thy good things, and likewise Lazarus evil things: but now he is comforted, and thou art tormented. And beside all this, between us and you there is a great gulf fixed: so that they which would pass from hence to you cannot; neither can they pass to us, that *would come* from thence. Then he said, I pray thee therefore, father, that thou wouldest send him to my father's house: For I have five brethren; that he may testify unto them, lest they also come into this place of torment Abraham saith unto him, They have Moses and the prophets; let them hear them. And he said, Nay, father Abraham: but if one went unto them from the dead they will repent. And he said unto him, If they hear not Moses and the prophets, neither will they be persuaded, though one rose from the dead.

Then said He unto His disciples, It is impossible but that offences will come but woe *unto him,* through whom they come!

It were better for him that a millstone were hanged about his neck, and he cast into the sea, than that he should offend one of these little ones.

Take heed to yourselves: if thy brother trespass against thee, rebuke him; and if he repent, forgive him. And if he trespass against thee seven times in a day, and seven times in a day turn again to thee, saying, repent; thou shalt forgive him. **And the apostles said unto the Lord, Increase our faith. And the Lord said,** If ye had faith as a grain of mustard seed, ye might say unto this sycamine tree, Be thou plucked up by the root, and be thou planted in the sea; and it should obey you. But which of you, having a servant plowing of feeding cattle, will say unto him by and by, when he is come from the field, Go and sit down to meat? And will not rather say unto him, Make ready wherewith I may sup, and gird thyself, and serve me, till I have eaten and drunken; and afterward thou shalt eat and drink? Doth he thank that servant because he did the things that were commanded him? I trow not. So likewise ye, when ye shall have done all those things which are commanded you, say We are unprofitable servants: we have done that which was our duty to do.

And it came to pass, as He went to Jerusalem, that He passed through the midst of Samaria and Galilee And as He entered into a certain village, **there met Him ten men the were lepers, which stood afar off: And they lifted up their voices, and said, Jesus, Master, have mercy on us. And when He saw** *them,* **He said unto them,** Go shew yourselves unto the priests. **And it came to pass, that, as they went, they were cleansed. And one of them, when he saw that he was healed turned back, and with a loud voice glorified God, And fell down on** *his* **face at His feet, giving thanks: and he was a Samaritan. And Jesus answering said,** Were there not ten cleansed? But where *are* the nine? There are not found that returned to give glory to God, save this stranger. And He said unto him, Arise, go thy way: thy faith hath made thee whole.

And when He was demanded of the Pharisees, when the kingdom of God should come, He answered them and said, The kingdom of God cometh not with observation: Neither shall they say, Lo here! Or, lo there! For, behold, the kingdom of God is within you.

And He said unto His disciples, The days will come, when ye shall desire to see one of the days of the Son of man, and ye shall not see *it*. And they shall say to you, See here; or, see there: go not after *them*, nor follow *them*. For as the lightning, that lighteneth out of the one part under heaven, shineth unto the other part under heaven; so shall also the Son of man be in His day. But first must He suffer many things, and be rejected of this generation. And as it was in the days of Noe so shall it be also in the days of the Son of man. They did eat, they drank, they married wives, they were given in marriage, until the day Noe entered into the ark, and the flood came, and destroyed them all. Likewise also as it was in the days of Lot; they did eat, they drank, they bought, they sold, they planted, they builded; But the same day that Lot went out of Sodom it rained fire and brimstone from heaven, and destroyed *them* all. Even thus shall it be in the day when the Son of man is revealed. In that day, he which shall be upon the housetop, and his stuff in the house, let him not come down to take it away: and he that is in the field, let him likewise not return back. Remember Lot's wife. Whosoever shall seek to save his life shall lose it; and whosoever shall lose his life shall preserve it. I tell you, in that night there shall be two men in one bed; the one shall be taken, and the other shall be left. Two *wome*n shall be grinding together; the one shall be taken, and the other left. Two *men* shall be in the field; the one shall be taken, and the other left. **And they answered and said unto Him, Where, Lord? And He said unto them,** Wheresoever the body *is,* thither will the eagles be gathered together.

And He spake a parable unto them *to this end*, that men ought always to pray, and not to faint; Saying, There was in a city a judge, which feared not God, neither regarded man: and there was a widow in that city; and she came unto him, saying, Avenge me of mine adversary.

And he would not for a while: but afterward he said within himself, Though I fear not God, nor regard man; Yet because this widow troubleth me, I will avenge her, lest by her continual coming she weary me. **And the Lord said,** Hear what the unjust judge saith. And shall not God, avenge His own elect, which cry day and night unto Him, though He bear long with them? I tell you that He will avenge them speedily. Nevertheless when the Son of man cometh, shall He find faith on the earth? **And He spake this parable unto certain which trusted in themselves that they were righteous, and despised others:** Two men went up into the temple to pray; the one a Pharisee, and the other a publican. The Pharisee stood and prayed thus within himself. God I thank thee, that I am not as other men *are*, extortioners, unjust, adulterers, or even as this publican. I fast twice in the week, I give tithes of all that I possess. And the publican, standing afar off, would not lift up so much as *his* eyes unto heaven, but smote upon his breast, saying, God be merciful to me a sinner. I tell you, this man went down to his house justified *rather* than the other: for everyone that exalteth himself shall be abased; and he that humbleth himself shall be exalted.]

(56) (25) **<John 7:1–9>**

<After these things Jesus walked in Galilee: for He would not walk in Jewry, because the Jews sought to kill Him. Now the Jews feast of tabernacles was at hand. **His brethren said unto Him, Depart hence, and go into Judaea, that thy disciples also may see the works that Thou doest. For *there is* no man *that* doeth any thing secret, and he himself seeketh to be known openly. If thou do these things, shew thyself to the world. For neither did His brethren believe in Him. Then Jesus said unto them,** My time is not yet come: But your time is always ready. The world cannot hate you; but me it hateth, because I testify of it, that the works thereof are evil. Go ye up unto this feast: I go not up yet unto this feast; for my time is not yet full come. **When He had said these words unto them, He abode *still* in Galilee>**

(57) (32) **(Matthew 19:1–20:16)** {Mark 10:1–31}

(And it came to pass, *that* when Jesus had finished these sayings, He {arose from thence, and} departed from Galilee, **and came** into the coasts of Judaea, {by the farther side} **beyond Jordan; And** {the people} great multitudes {resort} **followed Him** {again}; {and, as He was wont, He taught them again} **and He healed them there.**

The Pharisees also came unto Him, {and asked Him} tempting Him, and saying unto Him, Is It lawful for a man to put away his wife for every cause? And He answered and said unto them, {What did Moses command you? And they said, Moses suffered to write a bill of divorcement, and to put *her* away.} Have ye not read, that he which made *them* at the beginning made them male and female, and said. For this cause shall a man leave, father and mother, and shall cleave to his wife: and they twain shall be one flesh? Wherefore they are no more twain, but one flesh. What therefore God hath joined together, let not man put asunder. They say unto Him, Why did Moses then command to give a writing of divorcement, and to put her away? He {Jesus answered and} saith unto them, Moses because of {for} the hardness of your hearts {he wrote you this precept,} suffered you to put away your wives: but from the beginning {of creation} it was not so. And I say unto you, Whosoever shall put away his wife, except *it be* for fornication, and shall marry another, committeth adultery {Against her}: and whoso marrieth her which is put away doth commit adultery. {And if a woman shall put away her husband, and be married to another, she committeth adultery.}

{And in the house} His disciples {asked} say unto Him {again of the same *matter.*}, If the case of the man be so with *his* wife, it is not good to marry. But he said unto them, All *men* cannot receive this saying, save *they* to whom it is given. For there are some eunuchs, which were so born from *their* mother's womb: and there are some eunuchs, which were made eunuchs of men: and there be eunuchs, which have made themselves eunuchs for the kingdom of heaven's sake. He that is able to receive *it,* let him receive *it.*

Then were there {they} brought unto Him little {young} children, that He should {touch them} put *His* hands on them, and pray: and the disciples rebuked them {those that brought *them.*} {But when} Jesus {saw *it,* He was much displeased, and} said {unto them}, Suffer little children, and forbid them not, to come unto Me: for of such is the kingdom of heaven {God}.

{Verily I say unto you, Whosoever shall not receive the kingdom of God as a little child, he shall not enter therein.} And He {took them up in His arms,} laid {put} *His* hands on {upon} them {and blessed them.} and departed thence.

And {when He was gone forth into the way,} behold, {there} one came {running, and kneeled} and said {asked} unto Him, Good Master, what good thing shall I do, that I may have {inherit} eternal life? And He {Jesus} said unto him, Why callest thou me good? There is none good but one, that is God: but if thou wilt enter into life, {thou knowest the commandments} keep the commandments. He saith unto Him, which? Jesus said, Thou shalt do no murder, Thou shalt not commit adultery, Thou shalt not steal, Thou shalt not bear false witness, {defraud not}, Honour thy father and thy mother: and, Thou shalt love thy neighbour as thyself. The young man {answered and} saith unto Him, {Master} all these things have I kept {observed} from my youth up: what lack I yet? {Then} Jesus {beholding him loved him and} said unto him, {One thing thou lackest:} If thou wilt be perfect, go and sell that {whatsoever} thou hast, and give to the poor, and thou shalt have treasure in heaven: and come {take up the cross,} and follow me But when the young man heard that saying, he {was sad at that saying and} went away sorrowful {grieved}: for he had great possessions.

Then said Jesus {and looked round about,} unto His disciples, {Children} Verily I say unto you, That a rich man {them that trust in riches} shall hardly enter into the kingdom of heaven {God}. And again I say unto you, It is easier for a camel to go through the eye of a needle, than for a rich man to enter into the kingdom of God. When His disciples heard it, they were {astonished out of measure,} exceedingly amazed {at His words}, saying, who then can be saved? But Jesus beheld them {looking upon them}, and {answereth again} said unto them With men this is impossible; but {not} with God {for with God} all things are possible.

Then answered Peter and said unto Him, behold {lo} we have forsaken {left} all, and {have} followed thee; what shall we have therefore? And Jesus {answered and} said unto them, Verily I say unto you, That ye which have followed Me, in the regeneration when the Son of man shall sit in the throne of His Glory, ye also shall sit upon twelve thrones, judging the twelve tribes of Israel. And everyone that has forsaken houses, or brethren, or sisters, of father, or mother, or wife, or children, or lands for My name's sake {and the gospel's}, {But he} shall receive an hundredfold, {Now in this time houses, and brethren,

and sisters, and mothers, and children, and lands, with persecutions;}
and shall {in the world to come} inherit everlasting {eternal} life. But
many *that are* first shall be last; and the last *shall be* first.

For the kingdom of heaven is like unto a man *that is* an householder, which went out early in the morning to hire labourers into his
vineyard. And when he had agreed with the labourers for a penny a
day, he sent them into his vineyard. And he went out about the third
hour, and saw others standing idle in the marketplace And said unto
them; Go ye also into the vineyard, and whatsoever is right I will give
you. And they went their way. Again he went out about the sixth
hour and ninth hour, and did likewise. And about the eleveneth hour
he went out, and found others standing idle, and said unto them,
Why stand ye here all the day idle? They say unto him, because no
man hath hired us. He saith unto them, go ye also into the vineyard;
and whatsoever is right, *that* shall ye receive. So when even was come,
the lord of the vineyard saith unto his steward, call the labourers, and
give them *their* hire, beginning from the last unto the first. And when
they came that *were hired* about the eleveneth hour, they received
every man a penny. But when the first came, they supposed that they
should have received more: and they likewise received every man a
penny. And when they had received *it*. They murmured against the
goodman of the house Saying, these last that have wrought but one
hour, and thou hast made them equal unto us, which have borne the
burden and heat of the day. But he answered one of them, and said,
Friend I do thee no wrong: didst not thou agree with me for a penny?
Take *that* thine is, and go thy way: I will give unto this last, even as
unto thee. Is it not lawful for me to do what I will with mine own? Is
thine eye evil, because I am good? So the last shall be first, and first
last: for many be called, but few chosen.)

(58) (26) **(Matthew 20:17–28)**

(And Jesus going up to Jerusalem **took the twelve disciples apart
in the way, and said unto them,** Behold, we go up to Jerusalem; and
the Son of man shall be betrayed unto the chief priests and unto the
scribes, and they shall condemn Him to death. And shall deliver Him

to the Gentiles to mock, and to scourge, and to crucify *Him:* and the third day He shall rise again.

Then came to Him the mother of Zebedee's children with her sons, worshipping *Him,* and desiring a certain thing of Him. And He said unto her, What wilt thou? She said unto Him, Grant that these my two sons may sit, the one on thy right hand, and the other on the left, in thy kingdom. But Jesus answered and said, Ye know not what ye ask. Are ye able to drink of the cup that I shall drink of, and to be baptized with the baptism that I am baptized with? They say unto Him, we are able. And He saith unto them, Ye shall drink indeed of My cup. and be baptized with the baptism that I am baptized with; but to sit on My right hand, and on My left, is not mine to give but *it shall be given to them* for whom it is prepared of My Father. And when the ten heard *it,* they were moved with indignation against the two brethren. But Jesus called them *unto Him,* and said, Ye know that the princes of the Gentiles exercise dominion over them, and they that are great exercise authority upon them. But it shall not be so among you; but whosoever will be great among you, let him be your minister; And whosoever will be chief among you. let him be your servant: Even as the Son of man came not to be ministered unto, but to minister, and to give His life a ransom for many.)

(59) (27) **[Luke 18:15–34]**

[And they brought unto Him also infants, that He would touch them: but when *His* disciples saw *it,* they rebuked them. But Jesus called them *unto Him,* and said, Suffer little children to come unto me, and forbid them not: for of such is the kingdom of God. Verily I say unto you, Whosoever shall not receive the kingdom of God as a little child shall in no wise enter therein. And a certain ruler asked Him, saying, Good Master, what shall I do to inherit eternal life? And Jesus said unto him, Why callest thou Me good? None is good, save one, *that is,* God. Thou Knowest the commandments, Do not commit adultery, Do not kill, Do not steal, Do not bear false witness, Honour thy father and thy mother. And he said, All these have I kept from my youth up. Now when Jesus heard these things, He said unto him, Yet lackest thou one thing: sell all that thou hast, and distribute unto the poor, and thou shalt have treasure in heaven: and come, follow Me. And when he heard this, he was very sorrowful: for he was very rich.]

And when Jesus saw that he Was very sorrowful, he said, How hardly shall they that have riches enter into the kingdom of God! For it is easier for a camel to go through a needle's eye, than for a rich man to enter into the kingdom of God. And they that heard *it* said, Who then can be saved? And he said, The things which are impossible with Men are possible with God. Then Peter said, Lo, we have left all, and Followed thee. And he said unto them, Verily I say unto you, There is no man that hath left house, or parents, or brethren, or wife, or children, for the kingdom of God's sake, Who shall not receive manifold more in this present time, and in the World to come life everlasting.

Then He took *unto Him* the twelve, and said unto them, Behold we go up to Jerusalem, and all things that are written by the prophets concerning the Son of man shall be accomplished. For He shall be delivered unto the Gentiles, And shall be mocked, and spitefully entreated, and spitted on: And they shall scourge *Him*, and put Him to Death: and the third day He shall rise again. And they understood none of these things: and this saying was hid from them, neither knew they the things which were spoken.

(60) (28) {Mark 10:32–45}

{And they were in the way going up to Jerusalem; and Jesus went before them: and they were amazed; and as they followed, they were afraid. And He took again the twelve, and began to tell them what things should happen unto Him. *Saying* Behold, we go up to Jerusalem; and the Son of man shall be delivered unto the chief priests, and unto the scribes; and they shall condemn Him to death, and shall deliver Him to the Gentiles: and they shall mock Him, and shall scourge Him, and shall spit upon Him, and shall kill Him: and the third day He shall rise again.

And James and John, the sons of Zebedee, come unto Him, saying, Master, we would that Thou shouldest do for us whatsoever we shall desire. And He said unto them, What would ye that I should do for you? They said unto Him, Grant unto us that we may sit, one on Thy right hand, and the other on Thy left hand, in Thy glory. But Jesus said unto them, Ye know not what ye ask: can ye drink of the cup that I drink of? And be baptized with the baptism that I am baptized with? And they said unto Him, we can. And Jesus said unto them, Ye shall indeed drink of the cup that I drink of; and with the baptism that I am baptized withal shall ye be baptized: But to sit on My right hand and on My left hand is not Mine to give; but *it shall be given to them* for whom it is prepared. And when the ten heard *it,* they began to be much displeased with James and John. But Jesus called them to *Him,* and saith unto them, Ye know that they which are accounted to rule over the Gentiles exercise lordship over them; and their great ones exercise authority upon them. But so shall it not be among you; but whosoever will be great among you, shall be your minister: And whosoever of you will be the chiefest, shall be servant of all. For even the Son of man came not to be ministered unto, but to minister, and to give His life a ransom for many.}

(61) (33) **[Luke 18:35–19:10]** (Matthew 20:29–34) {Mark 10:46–52}

[And it came to pass, that as (they) {came to} He was come nigh unto Jericho, {and as He went out of} (they departed from) Jericho, {with His disciples and} (a great multitude {number of people} followed Him.)

(And behold, two men) a certain blind man {Bartimaeus, the son of Timaeus, sat (sitting) by the way {highway} side begging: And (when {he} they heard) hearing the multitude pass by, he asked what it meant. And they told him, that {that it was} Jesus of Nazareth passeth (passed) by. And he (they) {began to cry} cried (out), {and say} saying, Jesus (O Lord) *Thou* Son of David, have mercy on me (us). And {many} they which went before rebuked {charged} him, that he should hold his peace: but he cried so much the more {a great deal} *Thou* Son of David, have mercy on me. And Jesus stood (still), and commanded (called them) him to be brought {called} unto Him: {And they call the blind man, saying unto him, Be of good comfort, rise; He calleth thee. And he, casting away; his garment, rose, and came to Jesus.} and when he was come near, {And Jesus} He ask {answered him, saying (and said) What wilt thou (will ye) that I shall do unto thee (you)? And he {the blind man said (they say {unto} Him) Lord, that I (our eyes) may {might} (be opened) receive my sight. And (so) Jesus (had compassion on *them,* and touched their eyes: {and Jesus} said unto him, {Go thy way;} Receive thy sight: thy faith hath saved {made thee whole.} And immediately (their eyes) he received his sight, and (they) followed Him, {Jesus in the way} glorifying God: and all the people, when they saw it, gave praise unto God.

And Jesus entered and passed through Jericho, and, behold, *there was* a man named Zacchaeus, which was the chief among the publicans, and he was rich. And he sought to see Jesus who He was; and could not for the press, because he was little of stature. And he ran before and climbed up into a sycamore tree to see him: for He was to pass that *way.* And when Jesus came to the place, He looked up, and saw him, and said unto him, Zacchaeus, make haste, and come down; for to day I must abide at thy house. And he made haste, and came down, and received him joyfully. And when they saw *it,* they all murmured, saying, That he was gone to be guest with a man that is a sinner. And Zacchaeus stood, and said unto the Lord; Behold, Lord, the half of my goods I give to the poor; and if I have taken any thing from any man by false accusation, I restore *him* fourfold. And Jesus said unto him, This day is salvation come to this house, for so much as he also is a son of Abraham. For the Son of man is come to seek and to save that which was lost.]

(62) (29) <John 11:18–12:11>

<Now Bethany was nigh unto Jerusalem, about fifteen furlongs off; and many of the Jews came to Martha and Mary, to comfort them concerning their brother. Then Martha, as soon as she heard that Jesus was coming, went and met Him: but Mary sat *still* in the house. Then said Martha unto Jesus, Lord, if thou hadst been here, my brother had not died. But I know, that even now, what soever Thou wilt ask of God, God will give *it* Thee. Jesus saith unto her, Thy brother shall rise again. Martha saith unto Him, I know that he shall rise again in the resurrection at the last day. Jesus said unto her,

I AM the resurrection, and the life: he that believeth in Me. Though he were dead, yet shall he live: And whosoever liveth and believeth in Me shall never die, Believest thou this? She saith unto Him, Yea, Lord: I believe that Thou art the Christ, the Son of God, which should come into the world. And when she had so said, she went her way, and called Mary her sister secretly, saying, The Master is come, and calleth for thee. As soon as she heard *that*, she arose quickly, and came unto Him, Now Jesus was not yet come into the town, but was in the place where Martha met Him. The Jews then which were with her in the house, and comforted her, when they saw Mary, that she rose up hastily and went out, followed her, saying, She goeth unto the grave to weep there. Then when Mary was come where Jesus was, and saw Him, she fell down at His feet, saying unto Him, Lord, if Thou hadst been here, my brother had not died. When Jesus therefore saw her weeping, and the Jews also weeping which came with her, He groaned in the spirit, and was troubled, and said, Where have ye laid him? They said unto Him, Lord, come and see. Jesus Wept. Then said the Jews, Behold how He loved him! And some of them said, Could not this man, which opened the eyes of the blind, have caused that even this man should not have died? Jesus therefore again groaning in Himself cometh to the grave. It was a cave, and a stone lay upon it. Jesus said, Take ye away the stone. Martha, the sister of him that was dead, saith unto Him, Lord, by this time he stinketh: for he hath been dead four days. Jesus saith unto her, Said I not unto thee, that, if thou wouldest believe, thou shouldest see the glory of God? Then they took away the stone *from the place* where the dead was laid. And Jesus lifted up His eyes, and said, Father, I thank Thee that Thou hast heard Me. And I knew that Thou hearest Me always: but because of the people which stand by I said *it*, That they may believe that Thou hast sent Me. And when He thus had spoken, He cried with a loud voice, Lazarus, come forth. And he that was dead came forth, bound hand and foot with grave clothes: and his face was bound about with a napkin. Jesus saith unto them, Loose him, and let him go. Then many of the Jews which came to Mary, and had seen the things which Jesus did, believed on Him. But some of them went their ways to the Pharisees, and told them what things Jesus had done.

Then gathered the chief priests and the Pharisees a council, and said, What do we? For this man doeth many miracles. If we let Him thus alone, all *men* will believe on Him: and the Romans shall come and take away both our place and nation. And one of them, *named* Caiphas being the high priest that same year, said unto them, Ye know nothing at all, nor consider that it is expedient for us, that one man should die for the people, and that the whole nation parish not. And this spake he not of himself: but being high priest that year, he prophesied that Jesus should die for that nation; And not for that nation only, but that also He should gather together in one the children of God that were scattered abroad. Then from that day forth they took counsel together for to put Him to death. Jesus therefore walked no more openly among the Jews; but went thence unto a country near to the wilderness, into a city called Ephraim, **and there** continued with His disciples.

And the Jews passover was nigh at hand: and many went out of the country up to Jerusalem before the passover, to purify themselves. Then sought they for Jesus, and spake among themselves, as they stood in the temple, What think ye, that He will not come to the feast? Now both the chief priests and the Pharisees had given a commandment, that, if any man knew where He were, he should shew *it,* that they might take Him.

Then Jesus six days before the passover came to Bethany, where Lazarus was **which had been dead, whom He raised from the dead. There they made a supper; and Martha served: but Lazarus was one of them that sat at the table with Him. Then took Mary a pound of ointment of spikenard, very costly, and anointed the feet of Jesus, and wiped His feet with her hair: and the house was filled with the odour of the ointment. Then said one of His disciples, Judas Iscariot, Simon's *son,* which should betray Him, why was not this ointment sold for three hundred pence, and given to the poor? This he said, not that he cared for the poor; but because he was a thief, and had the bag and bare what was put therein. Then said Jesus,** Let her alone: against the day of My burying hath she kept this. For the poor always ye have with you; but Me ye have not always. Much people of the Jews therefore knew that He was there: and they came not for Jesus sake only, but that they might see Lazarus also, whom He had raised from the dead.

But the chief priests consulted that they might put Lazarus also to death; Because that by reason of him many of the Jews went away, and believed on Jesus.>

(63) (30) **[Luke 19:11–28]**

[And as they heard these things, He added and spake a parable, because He was nigh to Jerusalem, and because they thought that the kingdom of God should immediately appear. He said therefore, A certain nobleman went into a far country to receive for Himself a kingdom, and to return. And He called His ten servants, and delivered then ten pounds, and said unto them occupy till I come. But His citizens hated Him, and sent a message after Him, saying, We will not have this *man* to reign over us. And it came to pass, that when He was returned, having received the kingdom, then He commanded these servants to be called unto Him, to whom He had given the money, that He might know how much every man had gained by trading. Then came the first, saying, Lord, thy pound hath gained ten pounds. And He said unto him, Well, thou good servant: because thou hast been faithful in a very little, have thou authority over ten cities. And the second came, saying, Lord, thy pound hath gained five pounds. And He said likewise to him, Be thou also over five cities. And another came, saying, Lord, *here is* thy pound, which I have kept laid up in a napkin: For I feared thee, because thou art an austere man: thou takest up that thou layedst not down, and reapest that thou didst not sow. And He said unto him, Out of thine own mouth will I judge thee, *thou* wicked servant. Thou knewest that I was an austere man, taking up that I laid not down, and reaping that I did not sow: Wherefore then gavest not thou my money into the bank, that at My coming I might have required Mine own with usury? And He said unto them that stood by, Take from him the pound, and give *it* to him that hath ten pounds. (And they said unto Him, Lord, he hath ten pounds.) For I say unto you, That unto everyone which hath shall be given; and from him that hath not, even that he hath shall be taken away from him. But those mine enemies, which would not that I should reign over them, bring hither, and slay *them* before Me.

And when He had thus spoken, He went before, ascending up to Jerusalem]

(64) **(34)** **[Luke 19:29–44]** (Matthew 21:1–9) {Mark 11:1–10} <John 12:12–19>

[<On the next day much people that were come to the feast, when they heard that Jesus was coming to Jerusalem> And it came to pass, when He (they drew nigh unto Jerusalem and were) was come nigh to Bethphage and Bethany, at (unto) the mount called *the mount* of Olives, He (Jesus) sent {forth} two of His disciples. Saying (unto them) Go ye {your way} into the village over against *you;* in the which (straightway) at your entering ye shall a (and ass tied, and) a colt tied (with her), whereon yet never man sat: loose him (*them*) and bring *him* (*them*) *hither* (unto Me). And if any man ask (say ought unto) you, Why do ye loose *him?* Thus shall ye say unto him, Because the Lord hath need of him. (them; and straightway he will send them.) And they (the disciples) that were sent went their way and found even as He (Jesus) had (commanded) said unto them. (All this was done, that it might be fulfilled which was spoken by the prophet, <as it is written, fear not,>saying, Tell ye the daughter of Sion, Behold, thy King cometh unto thee, meek, and sitting upon an ass, <'s colt>, and a colt the foal of an ass.)

And as they were loosing the colt, the owners thereof said unto them, Why loose ye the colt? And they said, the lord hath need of him. And they brought him (the ass and the colt) to Jesus: and they cast (put) their garments upon {on him} the colt, and they set Jesus <when He had found a young ass, sat> thereon. And as He went, [many] (a very great multitude) <went forth to meet Him, and> they spread their clothes {garments} (others cut down branches, from the trees, and strawed *them*) in the way. And when He was come nigh, even now at the descent of the mount of Olives, the whole multitude of the disciples [they that went before, and they that followed] began to rejoice and praise God with a loud voice for all the mighty works that they had seen; [cried] saying, [Hosanna] (to the Son of David) Blessed *be* [He] the king that cometh in the name of the Lord: [Blessed be the kingdom of our father David that cometh, in the name of the Lord: Hosanna in the highest.] peace in heaven, and glory in the highest. And some of the Pharisees from among the multitude said unto Him, Master, rebuke thy disciples. And He answered and said unto them, I tell you that if, these should hold their peace, the stones would immediately cry out.

And when He was come near, He beheld the city, and wept over it. Saying, If thou hadst known, even thou, at least in this thy day. the things *which belong* unto thy peace! But now they are hid from thine eyes. For the days shall come upon thee, that thine enemies shall cast a trench about thee, and compass thee round, and keep thee in on every side, and shall lay thee even with the ground, and thy children within thee; and they shall not leave in thee one stone upon another; because thou knewest not the time of thy visitation.

<These things understood not His disciples at the first: but when Jesus was glorified, then remembered they that these things were written of Him, and *that* they had done these things unto Him. The people therefore that was with Him when he called Lazarus out of his grave, and raised him from the dead, bare record. For this cause the people also met Him, for that they heard that He had done this miracle. The Pharisees therefore said among themselves, Perceive ye how ye prevail nothing? Behold, the world is gone after Him.>]

(65) **(35)** **(Matthew 21:10–16)** {Mark 11:11, 14–19} [Luke 19:45–48]

(And when He [Jesus] was come [went] {entered} into Jerusalem,(into the temple of God) all the city was moved, saying Who is this? And the multitude said, This is Jesus the prophet of Nazareth of Galilee. {and when He had looked round about upon all things} and [began to] cast out all them that sold and bought [therein] in the temple, and overthrew the tables of the money changers, and the seats of them that sold doves, {and would not suffer that any man should carry *any* vessel through the temple} and {He taught} said unto them, It is written, My house shall be called [is] the house of prayer; but ye have made it a den of thieves. And the blind and the lame came to Him in the temple; and He healed them. And when the chief priests and scribes saw {heard it and sought how they might destroy Him: for they feared Him, because all the people was astonished at His doctrine.} the wonderful things that He did, and the children crying in the temple, saying, Hosanna to the Son of David they, were sore displeased. And said unto Him, hearest thou what these say? And Jesus saith unto them, Yea; have ye never read, Out of the mouth of babes and sucklings thou hast perfected praise? [And He taught dailey in the temple. But the chief priest and the scribes and the chief of the people sought to destroy Him,] And could not find what they might do: for all the people were very attentive to hear Him.} [[and now {when} eventide was come, {He went out of the city} unto Bethany with the twelve.}])

(66) **(36) {Mark 11:12–26}** (Matthew 21:17–22)

{(And He left them, and went out of the city into Bethany: and He lodged there.) And (Now in the morning) on the morrow, when they were come from Bethany (As He returned into the city) He was hungry: And (when) seeing (He saw) a fig tree (in the way) afar off having leaves, He came, if haply He might find any thing thereon: and when He came to it (And) He found nothing (thereon), but leaves (only); for the time of figs was not *yet*. And Jesus answered and said unto it. (Let no fruit grow on) No man eat fruit of thee hereafter (henceforward) for ever. And His disciples heard it. (And presently the fig tree withered away.)

And they come to Jerusalem: and Jesus went into the temple, and began to cast out them that sold and bought in the temple, and overthrew the tables of the moneychangers, and the seats of them that sold doves; and would not suffer that any man should carry *any* vessel through the temple. And He taught, saying unto them, Is it not written, My house shall be called of all nations the house of prayer? But ye have made it a den of thieves. And the scribes and chief priests heard *it,* and sought how they might destroy Him: for they feared Him, because all the people was astonished at His doctrine. And when even was come He went out of the city.

And in the morning, as they passed by (And when) they (the disciples) saw (it) the fig tree dried up from the roots. (they marvelled, saying How soon is the fig tree withered away!) And Peter calling to remembrance saith unto Him, Master, behold, the fig tree which thou cursedst is withered away. And Jesus answering saith unto them, Have faith in God. For verily I say unto you. (If ye have faith and doubt not, ye shall not only do that *which is done* to the fig tree, but also) that (if ye) whosoever shall say unto this mountain, Be thou removed, and be thou cast into the sea; and shall not doubt in his heart, but shall believe those things which he saith shall come to pass; he shall have whatsoever he saith. (it shall be done) Therefore I say unto you, What things soever ye desire, when ye pray, believe that ye receive *them,* and ye shall have *them.* And when ye stand praying, forgive, if ye have ought against any; that your Father also which is in heaven may forgive you your trespasses. But if do not forgive, neither will your Father which is in heaven forgive your trespasses (And all things, whatsoever ye shall ask in prayer, believing, ye shall receive.)}

(67) **(37)** **(Matthew 21:23–22:14)** {Mark 11:27–12:12} [Luke 20:1–18]

([And it came to pass, *that* on one of those days,] {they came again to Jerusalem:} And when He {as He} was {walking} come into the temple, the chief priests {and the scribes,} and [with] the elders of the people came unto [upon] Him as He [taught the people and preached the gospel] was teaching, and [spoke] said, {say unto Him} [saying] By what authority doest thou these things? And who [is he that] gave thee this authority? {To do these things?} And [He] Jesus answered and said unto them, I also will ask {of} you one thing {question}, which if ye tell {and answer} Me, I in like wise will tell you by what authority I do these things. The baptism of John, whence was it? From heaven, or of men {answer Me.} And they reasoned with themselves, saying, If we say, from heaven; He will say unto us, Why did ye not then believe [ye] him? But [and] if we shall say, of men; we {they} fear [all] the people [will stone us]; for [they] all {men counted} [be persuaded] hold John as {that he was} a prophet {indeed}. And they answered Jesus, and said [that they], we can not [could not] tell. [Whence it was] And He {Jesus answering} said unto them, Neither tell I you by what authority I do these things.

But what think ye? A *certain* man had two sons; and he came to the first, and said, Son, go work to day in my vineyard. He answered and said, I will not: but afterward he repented, and went. And he came to the second, and said likewise. And he answered, I *go*, sir: and went not. Whether of them twain did the will of *his* father? **They say unto him, The first. Jesus saith unto them,** Verily I say unto you, That the publicans and harlots go into the kingdom of God before you. For John came unto you in the way of righteousness, and ye believed him not: but the publicans and the harlots believed him: and ye, when ye had seen *it*, repented not afterward, that ye might believe him. {And [Then] {He began to speak unto them} [the people] by [this] parables.} Hear another parable: There was a certain {man} householder, which planted a vineyard, and hedged it round about, {*it*) and digged a {*place for* the winefat.} wine press in it, and built a tower, and let it out to husbandmen, and went into, a far country [for a long time]: and when the time of the fruit drew near, [{at the season}], He sent [{a servant}] His servants to the husbandmen, that they {He} might receive [should give Him of] the fruits of [the vineyard] it. {from the husbandmen}. And [but] the husbandmen {they} {caught him} took his servants, and beat one, [{*him,* and sent him away empty}], and {again he sent unto them} killed another. [a third; and they wounded him also, and cast him out.] and [{again he sent] unto them [another servant,] And at him they cast stones} stoned another {and wounded him in the head, and sent him away shamefully handled,} [and empty] {many} other servants more than the first: and they did unto them likewise {beating some, and killing some.}. But [then] last of all {having yet therefore one son,}, [Then said the Lord of the vineyard, shall I do? I will send my beloved son:] He sent unto them {him} His son {also unto them} saying. What [It may be] They will reverence [Him] my son. [when they see Him] But when {those} the husbandmen saw [Him] the son, they said [reasoned] among themselves. [saying] This is the heir: come let us kill

Him, and let us seize on [that] His {the} inheritance {shall [may] be ours}. And [so] they caught {took} Him, and cast *Him* out of the vineyard and slew [{killed}] *Him*. And When the lord therefore of the vineyard cometh, what will He {the lord of the vineyard} do unto those husbandmen? {he will come and destroy the husbandmen, and will give the vineyard unto others.}

[And when they heard *it*, they said, God forbid.] They say unto Him, He will miserably destroy those wicked men, and will let out His vineyard unto other husbandmen, which shall render Him the fruits in their seasons. [And He beheld them, and] Jesus saith unto them, [what is this then written,] Did ye never {and have ye not} read in the {this} scriptures, The stone which the builders rejected. The same is become the head of the corner: This is {was} the Lord's doing, and it is marvellous in our eyes? Therefore say I unto you, The kingdom of God shall be taken from you, and given to a nation bringing forth fruits thereof. And whosoever shall fall on [upon] this [that] stone shall be broken: but on whosoever [whomsoever] it shall fall, it will grind him to powder. And when the chief priests and Pharisees [and scribes] had heard His parables, they perceived that He spake of them. But when {and} they sought to lay hands {hold} on Him, {but} they feared the multitude, {people} because they took Him for a prophet. {For they knew that He had spoken the parable against them; And they left Him, and went their way.}

And Jesus answered and spake unto them again by parables, and said, The kingdom of heaven is like unto a certain king, which made a marriage for His son, and sent forth his servants to call them that were bidden to the wedding: and they would not come. Again He sent forth other servants saying, Tell them which are bidden, Behold, I have prepared My dinner: My oxen and *My* fatlings are killed, and all things *are* ready: come unto the marriage. But they made light of *it*. And went their ways one to his farm, another to his merchandise: And the remnant took His servants, and entreated *them* spitefully, and slew *them*. But when the King heard *thereof*, He was wroth: and He sent forth His armies, and destroyed those murderers, and burned up their city. Then saith He to His servants, The wedding is ready, but they which were bidden were not worthy. Go ye therefore into the highways, and as many as ye shall find, bid to the marriage. So those servants went out into the highways and gathered together all as many as they found, both bad and good: and the wedding was furnished with guests.

And when the King came into see the guests. He saw there a man, which had not on a wedding garment: And saith unto him, Friend, how earnest thou in hither not having a wedding garment? And he was speechless. Then said the King to the servants, Bind him hand and foot, and take him away, and cast *him* into outer darkness; there shall be weeping and gnashing of teeth. For many are called but few *are* chosen.)

(68) (38) **(Matthew 22:15–46)** {Mark 12:13–37} [Luke 20:19–47]

(Then went {they certain of} the Pharisees [The chief priests and the scribes the same hour sought to lay hands on Him; and they feared the people: for they preceived that He had spoken this parable against them.] [and they watched *Him,* and sent forth spies, which should feign themselves: just men,] and took counsel how [that] they might entangle [take hold of] {to catch} Him in *his* talk. {[words]} [So they might deliver Him unto power and authority of the governor.] And they sent out unto Him their disciples with the Herodians, [And they asked Him, saying,] Master, we know that Thou art true, [sayest] and teachest the way of God in truth, neither carest [acceptest] Thou for any *man:* for Thou regardest not the person of men [any]. Tell us therefore, what thinkest thou? Is it lawful [for us] to give tribute unto Caesar, or [no] not? {shall we give, or shall we not give?} But {He,} Jesus perceived their [craftiness] wickedness, {knowing their hypocrisy} and said, {[unto them]} Why tempt ye Me, ye hypocrites? {Bring Me a penny,} Shew Me the tribute money {that I may see it.} And they brought {it} unto Him a penny. And He saith unto them, Whose is this image and superscription? They [Answered and,] say unto Him, Caesar's. Then saith He {Jesus} unto them, {answering} Render therefore unto Caesar the things which are {that} [be] Caesar's; and unto God the things that are [which be] God's. [And] when they had heard *these* words, [they could not take hold of

His words before the people:] they marvelled [at His answer] and left Him, [and held their peace] and went their way.

Then the same day came to {come unto} Him [certain of] the Sadducees, which say [deny] that there is no [any] resurrection, and {[they]} asked Him, saying Master, Moses said {[wrote unto us]} If a man {s brother} [any] die, having {and leaving} no [without] children, {[that]} his brother {should take} shall marry his wife, and raise up seed unto his brother. Now therefore were [therefore] with us seven brethren: and the first, when he had married {took} a wife, deceased, [died] {dying} and, having no issue {left no seed} [without children], left his wife unto his brother: [And] Likewise the second {took her [to wife] and [he] died, neither left he any seed [childless] also, and the third, {likewise} [in like manner] [took her] {and} unto the seventh [also], {had her and left no seed} [and they left no children and died] and last of all the woman died also. Therefore in the resurrection {when they shall rise} whose wife shall she be [is she] of {them} the seven? For they [the seven] all had her {[to wife]}. Jesus answered and said unto them, Ye do [therefore] err, {because ye know} not the scriptures nor the power of God. For in the ressurrection they neither marry, nor are given in marriage: But they which shall be accounted worthy to obtain that world, and the resurrection from the dead.] For {when they shall rise from the dead} in the resurrection they neither marry, nor are given in marriage, [neither can they die any more:] but [for they] are as [equal unto] the angels of God {which are} in heaven, [and are the children of God, being the children of the resurrection.] But {and} [now] as touching the resurrection of the dead, [that the dead {they} are raised {rise}] have ye not [even] read {in the book of Moses, [when he calleth the Lord] how in [shewed at] the bush} that which was spoken unto you {him} by God, saying, I Am the God of Abraham, [and] the God of Isaac, and the God of Jacob? [For] {He} God is not the God of the dead, but {God} of the living. [for all live unto Him] {ye therefore greatly err.} when the multitude heard *this*, they were astonished at His doctrine.

But when the Pharisees had heard that He put the Sadducees to silence, they were gathered together. {And} then one {of the scribes came} of them, which was a lawyer, {and having heard them reasoning together and perceiving that He had answered them well} asked *Him a question,* tempting Him and saying, Master, which is the great {first} commandment {of all} in the law? Jesus {answered} said unto him, {The first of all commandments is, Hear O Israel, The Lord our God is one Lord: and} Thou shalt love the Lord thy God with all thy heart, and with all thy soul, and with all thy mind, {and with all thy strength.} This is the first and great commandment. And the second *is* {*namely* this} like unto it, thou shalt love thy neighbour as thyself. On these two commandments hang all the law and the prophets. {There is none other commandment greater than these.}

{And [then certain of] the scribes [answering] said unto Him, [Thou hast] well [said], Master Thou hast said the truth: for there is one God: and there is none other but He: and to love Him with all the heart, and with all the understanding, and with all the soul, and with all the strength, and to love *his* neighbour as himself, is more than all whole burnt offerings and sacrifices. And when Jesus saw that he answered discreetly, He said unto him, Thou art not far from the kingdom of God. And [they] no man after that durst [not] ask Him, *any questions* [*at all.*]}

While the Pharisees were gathered together, {And} Jesus {answered and} asked them, {while He taught in the temple} saying, {How say [they] the scribes that Christ is *the son* of David?}

What think ye of Christ? Whose son is He? They say unto Him, The Son of David. He saith unto them, How then doeth {For} David {himself said by the Holy Ghost} [in the book of Psalms] in spirit call Him Lord, saying, The LORD said unto my Lord, sit Thou on my right hand, till I make Thine enemie: Thy footstool? If David then call Him Lord, how {whence} is He then His son? And no man was able to answer Him a word, neither durst any *man* from that day forth ask Him any more *questions.* {And the common people heard Him gladly.} [Then in the audience of all the people He said unto His disciples Beware of the scribes, which desire to walk in long robes, and love greetings in the markets, and the highest seats in the synagogues, and the chief rooms at feasts; Which devour widows' houses, and for a shew make long prayers: the same shall receive greater damnation])

(69) (39) **(Matthew 23:1–39)** {Mark 12:38–40} [Luke 20:45–47]

({And} Then [in the audience of all the people] spake {He} Jesus {said un-} to {them} the multitude, and to His disciples {in His doctrine}, saying, {Beware of} The scribes and the Pharisees sit in Moses seat: All therefore whatsoever they bid you observe, *that* observe and do; but do not ye after their works: for they say, and do not. For they bind heavy burdens and grievous to be borne, and lay *them* on men's shoulders; but they *themselves* will not move them with one of their fingers. But all their works they do for to be seen of men: {which love to go in long clothing [robes]} they make broad their phylacteries, and enlarge the borders of their garments, and love the uppermost [highest] rooms at feasts, and the chief seats in the synagogues, and {love salutations} greetings in the markets {places}, and to be called of men, Rabbi, Rabbi. But be not ye called Rabbi: for one is your Master, *even* Christ; and all ye are brethren. And call *no man* your father upon the earth: for one is your Father, which is in heaven. Neither be ye called masters; for one is your Master, *even* Christ. But he that is greatest among you shall be your servant. And whosoever shall exalt himself shall be abased; and he that shall humble himself shall be exalted.

But woe unto you, scribes and Pharisees, hypocrites! For ye shut up the kingdom of heaven against men; for ye neither go in *yourselves*, neither suffer ye them that are entering to go in. Woe unto you, scribes and Pharisees, hypocrites! For {which} ye devour widow's houses, and for a pretence [shew] make long prayer {s}: therefore ye {these} shall receive the greater damnation. Woe unto you, scribes and Pharisees, hypocrites! for ye compass sea and land to make one proselyte, and when he is made, ye make him twofold more the child of hell than yourselves. Woe unto you, *ye* blind guides, which say, Whosoever shall swear by the temple, it is nothing; but whosoever shall swear by the gold of the temple, he is a debtor! *Ye* fools and blind: for whether *is* greater, the gift, or the alter that sanctifieth the gift? Whoso therefore shall swear by the alter, sweareth by it, and by all things thereon. And whoso shall swear by the temple, sweareth by it and by Him that dwelleth therein. And He that shall swear by heaven, sweareth by the throne of God. And by Him that sitteth thereon. Woe unto you, scribes and Pharisees, hypocrites! For ye pay tithe of mint and anise and cummin, and have omitted the weightier *matters* of the law, judgement, mercy, and faith: these ought ye to have done, and not to leave the other undone. *Ye* blind guides, which strain at a gnat, and swallow a camel. Woe unto you, scribes and Pharisees, hypocrites! For ye make clean the outside of the cup and of the platter, but within they are full of extortion and excess. *Thou* blind Pharisee, cleanse first that *which is* within the cup and platter, that the outside of them may be clean also. Woe unto, scribes and Pharisees, hypocrites! For ye are like unto whited sepulchres, which indeed appear beautiful outward, but are within full of dead *men's* bones, and of all uncleanness. Even so ye also outwardly appear righteous unto men, but within ye are full of hypocrisy and iniquity. Woe unto you, scribes and Pharisees hypocrites! Because ye build the tombs of the prophets, and garnish the sepulchres of the righteous. And say, If we had been in the days of our fathers, we would not have been partakers with them in the blood of the prophets. Wherefore ye be witnesses unto yourselves, that ye are the children of them which killed the prophets. Fill ye up then the measure of your fathers. *Ye* serpents, *ye* generation of vipers, how can ye escape the damnation of hell?

Wherefore, behold I send unto you prophets, and wise men, and scribes: and *some* of them ye shall kill and crucify; and *some* of them shall ye scourge in your synagogues. And presecute *them* from city to city: That upon you may come all the righteous blood shed upon the earth, from the blood of righteous Abel, unto the blood of Zacharias son of Barachias, whom ye slew between the temple and the alter. Verily I say unto you, All these things shall come upon this generation. O Jerusalem, Jerusalem, *thou* that killest the prophets, and stonest them which are sent unto thee, how often would I have gathered thy children together, even as a hen gathereth her chickens under *her* wings, and ye would not! Behold, your house is left unto you desolate. For I say unto you, ye shall not see Me henceforth, till ye shall say, Blessed is *He* that cometh in the name of the Lord.)

(70) **(40)** **(Matthew 24:1–25:46)** {Mark 12:41–13:37} [Luke 21:1–38]

({And [He] Jesus sat over against the treasury, and beheld [looked up, and saw] how the people {rich men} cast [ing their gifts] money into the treasury: and many that were rich cast in much. And [He saw also] there came a certain poor widow, and she [casting in thither] threw in two mites, which makes a farthing. And He called *unto Him* His disciples, and saith unto them, Verily [of a truth] I say unto you, That this poor widow hath cast more in, than all they which have cast into the treasury: For all *they* did cast in of their abundance; but she of her want did cast in all that she had, *even* all her living.} And {as He} Jesus went out. and departed from the temple: and His disciple; came to *Him* for to shew Him the buildings [and as some spake] of the temple [how it was adorned with goodly stones and gifts] {one of His disciples saith unto Him, Master, see what manner of stones and what buildings *are here!*} and [He] Jesus {answering} said unto them, See ye not all these things? {Seest thou these great buildings?} [which ye behold,] Verily I say unto you, There shall not be left here one stone upon another, [the days will come in the which] [there] that shall not be thrown down.

And as He sat upon the mount of Olives, {over against the temple} the disciples {Peter and James and John and Andrew} [they] the disciples came unto Him privately, {Asked} [Him] saying. [Master] Tell us, [But] when shall these things be? And what *shall* be the sign {when all these things shall be fulfilled} of Thy coming, and of the end of the world? And Jesus [He] answered {ing} and said {began to say,} unto them, Take heed {lest any man} that no man [ye be not] deceive [d] you. For many shall come in My name, saying, I am Christ; and shall deceive many [and the time draweth near: go ye not therefore after them.]. [But] and {when} ye shall hear of wars and [commotions] rumours of wars: See that ye be not troubled: [be not terrified:] for all *these things* {*such things*} must [first] {needs be ;} come to pass, but the end {shall} not {be} yet [by and by]. [**Then said He unto them,**] For nation shall rise against nation, and kingdom against kingdom: and there shall be famines, and pestilences {troubles} [and fearful sights], and [great] earthquakes, [shall be] in divers places [and great signs shall there be from heaven.] [But before] all these *are* the beginning of sorrows. {But take heed to yourselves; for} Then shall [they lay their hands on you] they deliver you up {to councils} to be afflicted [and persecute you,] [and in the synagogues ye shall be beaten:] [and into prisons,] and shall kill you: {and ye shall be [ing] brought before rulers and kings for My [name] sake, [and it shall turn to you] for a testimony against them.} {But when they shall lead you, and deliver you up, take no thought beforehand [settle *it* therefore in your hearts not to meditate] [before] what ye shall speak, neither do ye premeditate: [For I will give you a mouth and wisdom, which all your adversaries shall not be able to gainsay nor resist.] but whatsoever shall be given you in that hour, that speak ye: for it is not ye that speak but the Holy Ghost. Now the brother shall betray to death [and ye shall be betrayed by brethren], and the father [parents] the son: and children shall rise up against *their* parents [kinfolk] [and friends] and [some of you] shall [they] cause them to be put to death.} and ye shall be hated of all nations [{*men*}] for My name's sake. And then shall many be offended, and shall betray one another, and shall hate one another. And many false prophets shall rise, and shall deceive many. And because iniquity shall abound, the love of many shall wax cold. But he that shall endure unto the end, the same shall be saved. And this {the} gospel of the kingdom shall {must first} be preached {published} in {among} all the world for a witness unto all nations; and then shall the end come. [And when ye shall see Jerusalem compassed with armies, then know that the desolation thereof is nigh.] {But} When ye therefore shall see the abomination of desolation, spoken of by Daniel the prophet, stand {ing where it ought not,} in the holy place (whoso readeth, let him understand:) Then let them which {that} [are] be in Judaea flee into the mountains: [and let them which are in the midst of it depart out: and let not them that are in the countries enter there into. For these be the days of vengence that all thing which are written may be fulfilled.] [And] let him [them] {that} which is on the housetop not {go} come down {in} to take anything out of his house: {And} neither let him which {that} is in the field return {not turn} back {again for} to take {up} his clothes {garment}. [{But}] and woe unto them that are with child, and to them that give suck in those days! [For there shall be great distress in the land, and wrath upon this people. And they shall fall by the edge of the sword, and shall be lead away captive into all nations: anc Jerusalem shall be trodden down of the Gentiles, until the times of the Gentiles be fulfilled.] But pray ye that your flight be not in the winter, neither on the sabbath day: For then {in those days} shall be great tribulation {affliction}, such as was not since {from} the beginning of the world {creation} to {which God created unto} this time, no, nor {neither} ever shall be. And except those days should be shortened, there should no flesh be saved: but for the elect's sake {whom He hath chosen} those days {He hath} shall be shortened. {And} then if any man shall say unto you, Lo, here *is* Christ; or {lo He is} there; believe *it* {*him*} not. For there shall arise false Christs, and false prophets. And shall shew great signs and wonders: insomuch that, if *it were* possible, they shall deceive {seduce} the very elect. {But take heed} behold, I have {for} told you before {all things}. Wherefore if they shall say unto you, Behold, He is in the desert: go not forth: behold, *He is* in the secret chambers; believe *it* not. For as the lightning cometh out of the east, and shineth even unto the west; so shall also the coming of the Son of man be. For wheresoever the carcase is, there will the eagles be gathered together.

{But} Immediately after {that} the tribulation {in} those days [and there] shall [be signs in] the sun be darkened, and [in] the moon shall not give her light, and [in] the stars shall fall from {of} heaven [and upon the earth distress of nations with perplexity: the sea and the waves roaring: Men's hearts failing them for fear, and for looking after those things which are coming on the earth:] and [for] the powers of {are in} the heavens shall be shaken: And then shall [{they see}] appear the sign of the Son of man coming in the clouds of heaven with power and great glory. [And when these things begin to come to pass, then look up, and lift up your heads; for your redemption draweth nigh.] and {then} He shall send His angels with a great sound of a trumpet, and they shall gather together His elect from the four winds, from {the uttermost part of} one end of heaven to the other. **[And He spake to them a parable]** Now learn a parable of [behold] the fig tree [and all the trees;] when his {her} branch is yet tender, and [they now shoot] putteth forth leaves, ye [see and] know [of your own selves] that summer is [now] nigh {near} [at hand]: So {in like manner} likewise ye, when ye shall see all these things [{come to pass}], know [ye] that [the kingdom of God] it is near {nigh} [at hand even at the doors. Verily I say unto you, {that} This generation shall not pass [away], till all these things be fulfilled {done}. Heaven and earth shall pass away, but My words shall not pass away.

[And take heed to yourselves, lest at any time your hearts be overcharged with surfeiting, and drunkeness and cares of this life, and so that day come upon you unawares For as a snare shall it come on all them that dwell on the face of the whole earth.] But of that day and hour knoweth no *man* no, not the angels {which are in} of heaven, {neither the Son,} but My {the} Father only. But as the days of Noe *were*, so shall also the coming of the Son of man be. For as in the days that were before the flood they were eating and drinking, marrying and giving in marriage, until the day that Noe entered into the ark, and knew not until the flood came, and took them all away; so shall also the coming of the Son of man be. Then shall two be in the field; the one shall be taken, and the other left. Two *women* shall be grinding at the mill; the one shall be taken, and the other left.

Watch [{ye}] therefore :[and pray always that ye may be accounted worthy to escape all these things that shall come to pass, and to stand before the Son of man.] for ye know not {when} what hour your Lord {the master of the house} doth come {eth}. {At even, or at midnight, or at the cock crowing, or in the morning: lest coming suddenly He find you sleeping. And what I say unto you I say unto all, watch.} But know this, that if the goodman of the house had known in what watch the thie would come, he would have watched, and would not have suffered his house to be broken up. Therefore be ye also ready: for in such an hour as ye think not the Son of man cometh. Who then is a faithful and wise servant, whom His lord hath made ruler over His household, to give them meat in due season Blessed *is* that servant, whom his Lord when He cometh shall find so doing. Verily I say unto you, That He shall make him ruler over all his goods. But and if that evil servant shall say in his heart, my Lord delayeth his coming; And shall begin to smite *his* fellow servants, and to eat and drink with the drunken The Lord of that servant shall come in a day when he looketh not for *him,* and in an hour that he is not aware of. And shall cut him asunder, and appoint *him* his portion with the hypocrites: there shall be weeping and gnashing of teeth.

Then shall the kingdom of heaven be likened unto ten virgins, which took their lamp, and went forth to meet the Bridegroom. And five of them were wise, and five *were* foolish. They that *were* foolish took their lamps, and took no oil with them: But the wise took oil in their vessels with their lamps While the Bridegroom tarried, they all slumbered and slept. And at midnight there was a cry made, Behold, the Bridegroom cometh; go ye out to meet him. Then all those virgins arose, and trimmed their lamps. And the foolish said unto the wise, Give us of your oil; for our lamps are gone out. But the wise answered, saying, *Not so;* lest there be not enough for us and you: but go ye rather to them that sell, and buy for yourselves. And while they went to buy, the Bridegroom came; and they that were ready went in with Him to the marriage: and the door was shut. Afterward came also the other virgins, saying, Lord, Lord, open to us. But He answered and said, verily I say unto you, I know you not. Watch therefore, for ye know neither the day nor the hour wherein the Son of man cometh.

For *the kingdom of heaven is* as man traveling into a far country, *who* called His own servants, and delivered unto them His goods. And unto one he gave five talents, to another two, and to another one; to every man according to his several ability; and straightway He took His journey. Then he that had received the five talents went and traded with the same, and made *them* other five talents. And like wise he that had received two, he also gained other two. But he that had received one went and digged in the earth, and hid his lords money. After a long time the lord of these servants cometh, and reckoneth with them And he that *had received* five talents, came and brought other five talents, saying, Lord, Thou deliverest unto me five talents: behold, I have gained beside them five talents more. His lord said unto him, Well done, *thou* good and faithful servant: thou hast been faithful over a few things, I will make thee ruler over many things: enter thou into the joy of thy lord. He also that had received two talents came and said, Lord, thou deliverest unto me two talents: behold, I have gained two other talent beside them, His lord said unto him, Well done, good and faithful servant; thou hast been faithful over a few things, I will make you thee ruler over many things: enter thou into the joy of thy lord. Then he which had received one talent came and said, Lord, I knew thee that Thou art an hard man, reaping where Thou hast not sown, and gathering where Thou hast not strawed: And I was afraid, and went and hid thy talent in the earth: lo, *there* thou hast *that is* thine His lord answered and said unto him, *Thou* wicked and slothful servant, thou knewest that I reap where I sowed not, and gather where I have not strawed: Thou oughtest therefore to have put my money to the exchangers, and *then* at my coming I should have received mine own with usury. Take therefore the talent from him, and give *it* unto him which hath ten talents. For unto everyone that hath shall be given, and he shall have abundance: but from him that hath not shall be taken away even that which he hath. And cast ye the unprofitable servant into outer darkness: there shall be weeping and gnashing of teeth.

When the Son of man shall come in His glory, and all the holy angels with Him, then shall He sit upon the throne of His glory: And before Him shall be gathered all nations: and He shall separate them one from another, as a shepard divideth *his* sheep from the goats: And He shall set the sheep on His right hand, but the goats on the left. Then shall the King say unto them on His right hand, come ye blessed of my Father, inherit the kingdom prepared for you from the foundation of the world: For I was an hungred, and ye gave Me meat: I was thirsty, and ye gave Me drink: I was a stranger, and ye took Me in: Naked, and ye clothe Me: I was sick, and ye visited Me: I was in prison, and ye came unto Me. Then shall the righteous answer Him, saying, Lord, when saw we thee an hungred. and fed *thee?* or thirsty, and gave *thee* drink? When saw we thee a stranger, and took *Thee* in? or naked, and clothed *Thee?* Or when saw we Thee sick, or in prison, and came unto *Thee?* And the King shall answer and say unto them, Verily I say unto you, Inasmuch as ye have done *it* unto one of the least of these My brethren, ye have done *it* unto Me. Then shall He say also unto them on the left hand, depart from Me, ye cursed, into everlasting fire, prepared for the devil and his angels: For I was an hungred, and ye gave Me no meat: I was thristy, and ye gave Me no drink: I was a stranger, and ye took Me not in: Naked, and ye clothed Me not: sick and in prison, and ye visited Me not. Then shall they also answer Him, saying, Lord, when saw we Thee an hungred, or athirst, or a stranger, or naked, or sick, or in prison, and did not minister unto thee? Then shall He answer them, saying, Verily I say unto you, Inasmuch as ye did *it* not to one of the least of these, ye did it not to Me. And these shall go away into everlasting punishment: But the righteous into life eternal. [**And** in the day time He **was** teaching in the temple: **and** at night **He went out, and** abode in the mount that is called the mount of Olives **And all the people came early in the morning** to Him in the temple, **for to hear Him.**])

(71) (41) **(Matthew 26:1–5)** {Mark 14:1–2} [Luke 22:1–2]

([**Now** the feast of unleavened bread drew nigh, **which is called the Passover.**] **And it came to pass, when Jesus had finished all these sayings, He said unto His disciples,** Ye know that after two days is *the feast of* the passover, and the Son of man is betrayed to be crucified. {**And**} **Then assembled together the chief priests, and the scribes, and the elders of the people, unto** the palace of the high priest, **who was called Caiaphas.** {sought} **and consulted** {how} **that they might take** {**Him**} **Jesus by subtilty** {craft} **and kill** {put} *Him* {to death}. **But they said, not on the feast** *day,* **lest there be an uproar among** {of} **the people.** [For they feared the people.])]

(72) (42) **(Matthew 26:6–16)** {Mark 14:3–11} [Luke 22:3–6]

({**And**} **Now when** Jesus was {being} in Bethany, in the house of Simon the leper, **there came unto Him a woman having an alabaster box of very precious ointment** {of spikenard}, {she broke the box,} **and poured it on His head, as He sat** *at meat.* **But when His disciples saw** *it,* **they** {there were some that} **had indignation** {within themselves} {and} **saying, To what purpose** *is* {was} **this waste** {of the ointment made}? **For** {it} **this ointment might have been sold for**

229

much {more than three hundred pence,} and {have been} given to the poor {and they murmured against her.} {And} when Jesus understood *it*. He said unto them, {Let her alone;} Why trouble ye {her} the woman? For she hath wrought a good work upon {on} Me. For ye have the poor always with you; {and whensoever ye will ye may do them good:} but Me ye have not always. For in that she hath poured this ointment on My body, {she hath done what she could:} she did *it* for my burial {is come aforehand to anoint My body to the burying.} Verily I say unto you. Wheresoever this gospel shall be preached in {throughout} the whole world, *there* shall also this, that {she} this woman hath done, {shall} be told {spoken of} for a memorial of her. {And} Then [entered Satan into] one [of the number] of the twelve, called Judas [sumamed] Iscariot, [And he,] went [his way] unto [and communed with] the chief priests [and captains], And said *unto them,* What will ye give me, and I will deliver Him unto you? {and when they heard it, they were glad,} And they covenanted {promised} with him for {to give him money,} thirty pieces of silver. [And he promised] and from that time he sought opportunity to {how he might conveniently} betray Him. [unto them in the absence of the multitude.])

(73) (43) **{Mark 14:12–16}** (Matthew 26:17–19)

{And (Now) the first day (of the feast) of unleavened bread, when they killed the passover, His (the) disciples (came to Jesus saying) said unto Him, Where wilt Thou that we go and prepare (for thee) that Thou mayest (to) eat the passover? And He sendeth forth two of His disciples, and saith unto them, Go ye into the city, and there shall meet you (to such) a man bearing a pitcher of water: follow him. And wheresoever he shall go in, say ye to the goodman of the house (unto him). The Master saith (My time is at hand; I will keep the passover at thy house) Where is the guestchamber, where I shall eat the passover with My disciples? And he will shew you a large upper room furnished *and* prepared: there make ready for us. And His (the) disciples went forth (did as Jesus had appointed them:), and came into the city, and found as He had said unto them: and they made ready the passover.}

(74) (31) **<John 12:23–50>**

<And Jesus answered Them, Saying, The hour is come, that the Son on man should be glorified Verily, verily, I say unto you, Except a corn of wheat fall into the ground and die, it abideth alone: but if it die. it bringeth forth much fruit. He that loveth his life shall lose it; and he that hateth his life in this world shall keep it unto life eternal. If any man serve Me, let him follow Me: and where I am, there shall also My servant be: if any man serve Me, him will *my* Father honour. Now is my soul troubled; and what shall I say? Father, save Me from this hour, but for this cause came I unto this hour. Father, glorify Thy name. Then came there a voice from heaven, *saying,* I have both glorified *it,* and will glorify *it* again. The people therefore, that stood by, and heard *it,* said that it thundered: others said, An angel spoke to Him. Jesus answered and said, This voice came not because of Me, but for your sakes. Now is the judgement of this world: now shall the prince of this world be cast out. And I, if I be lifted up from the earth, will draw all *men* unto Me. This He said, signifying what death He should die. The people answered Him, We have heard out of the law that Christ abides for ever: and how sayest Thou, The Son of man must be lifted up? Who is this Son of man? Then Jesus said unto them, Yet a little while is the light with you. Walk while ye have the light, lest darkness come upon you: for he that walketh in darkness knoweth not whither he goeth. While ye have light, believe in the light, that ye may be the children of light. These things spake Jesus, and departed, and did hide Himself from them.

But though He had done so many miracles before them, yet they believed not on Him: That the saying of Esaias the prophet might be fulfilled, which he spake, Lord, who hath believed our report? And to whom hath the arm of the Lord been revealed? Therefore they could not believe, because that Esaias said again, He hath blinded their eyes, and hardened their heart; that they should not see with *their* eyes, nor understand with *their* heart, and be converted, and I should heal them. These things said Esaias, when he saw His glory, and spake of Him.

Nevertheless among the chief rulers also many believed on Him; but because of the Pharisees they did not confess *Him,* lest they should be put out of the synagogue: For they loved the praise of men more than the praise of God.

Jesus cried and said, He that believeth on Me, believeth not on Me, but on Him that sent Me.

And he that seeth Me seeth Him that sent Me. I am come a light into the world, that whosoever believeth on Me should not abide in darkness. And if any man hear My words, and believe not, I judge him not: for I came not to judge the world, but to save the world. He that rejecteth Me. and receiveth not My words, hath one that judgeth him: the word that I have spoken, the same shall judge him in the last day. For I have not spoken of Myself; but the Father which sent Me, He gave Me a commandment, what I should say. and what I should speak. And I know that His commandment is life everlasting: whatsoever I speak therefore, even as the Father said unto Me, so I speak.>

(75) (44) **[Luke 22:14–38]** (Matthew 26:20–29, 31–35) {Mark 14:17–25, 27–31} <John 13:1–38>

[And (Now) {before the feast of the passover} when {Jesus knew that His} the hour was was come, <that He should depart out of this world unto the Father, having loved His own which were in the world, He loved them unto the end,> {in the evening} {He cometh} He sat down, and (with) the twelve apostles with Him. <When Jesus had thus said, He was troubled in spirit (And as they {sat and} did eat, He {Jesus} said <testified>, Verily <verily,> I say unto you, that one of you {which eateth with Me} shall betray Me. And they were exceeding {began to be} sorrowful, and began every one of them to say unto Him, {one by one} Lord, is it I? {and another said is it I?} And He answered and said {unto them}, {It is one of the twelve,} he that dippeth his hand with Me in the dish, the same shall betray Me. The Son of man {indeed} goeth as it is written of Him: but woe unto that man by whom the Son of man is betrayed! It had been good {were it} for that man if he had not been born. Then Judas, which betrayed Him, answered and said, Master, is it I? He said unto him, Thou hast said.

<Then the disciples looked one to another, doubting of whom He spake. Now there was leaning on Jesus bosom one of His disci-

ples, whom Jesus loved. Simon Peter therefore beckoned to him, that he should ask who it should be of whom He spake. He then lying on Jesus breast saith unto Him, Lord, who is it? Jesus answered, He it is, to whom I shall give a sop, when I have dipped *it*. And when He had dipped the sop, He gave it to Judas Iscariot, the son of Simon. And after the sop Satan entered into him. Then said Jesus unto him, That thou doest, do quickly. Now no man at the table knew for what intent He spake this unto him. For some of them thought, because Judas had the bag, that Jesus had said unto him, Buy those things that we have need of against the feast; or, that he should give something to the poor.> <And supper being ended the devil having now put into the heart of Judas Iscariot, Simon's son, to betray Him;> He then having received the sop went immediately out: and it was night.>

And He said unto them, With desire I have desired to eat this passover with you before I suffer: For I say unto you, I will not any more eat there of, until it be fulfilled in the kingdom of God.

<Jesus knowing that the Father had given all things into His hands, and that He was come from God, and went to God; He riseth from supper, and laid aside His garments; and took a towel, and girded Himself. After that He poureth water into a bason, and began to wash the disciples' feet, and to wipe them with the towel wherewith He was girded. Then cometh He to Simon Peter: and Peter saith unto Him, Lord, dost Thou wash my feet? Jesus answered and said unto him, What I do thou knowest not now; but thou shalt know hereafter Peter saith unto Him, Thou shalt never wash my feet. Jesus answered him, If I wash thee not, thou hast no part with Me. Simon Peter saith unto Him, Lord, not my feet only, but also *my* hands and *my* head. Jesus saith to him, He that is washed needeth not save to wash *his* feet, but is clean every whit: and ye are clean, but not all. For He knew who should betray Him; therefore said He, Ye are not all clean. So after He had washed their feet, and had taken His garments, and was set down again, He said unto them, Know ye what I have done to you? Ye call Me Master and Lord: and ye say well; for so I am. If I then, *your* Lord and Master, have washed your feet; ye also ought to wash one another's feet. For I have given you an exam-

ple, that ye should do as I have done to you. Verily, verily, I say unto you, The servant is not greater than His lord; neither He that is sent greater than He that sent Him. If ye know these things, happy are ye if ye do them.

I speak not of you all: I know whom I have chosen: but that the scripture may be fulfilled, He that eateth bread with Me hath lifted up his heel against Me. Now I tell you before it come, that, when it is come to pass, ye may believe that I AM *He*. Verily, verily, I say unto you, He that receiveth whomsoever I send receiveth Me: and he that receiveth Me receiveth Him that sent Me.>

And He took the cup, and {when He had} gave {given} thanks (and {He} gave it to them), and said (saying), Take this and divide *it* among yourselves: For {verily} I say unto you, I will not drink (henceforth) {no more} of (this) the fruit of the vine, until (that day when I drink it new with you in) (My Father's) the kingdom of God shall come.

And (as they were {did eat} eating) He (Jesus) took bread, and (blessed *it*.) gave thanks, and brake *it*, and gave (*it*) unto them (the disciples), saying (and said) (Take eat) This is My body which is given for you: this do in remembrance of Me. **Likewise also the cup after supper, saying** (For) This cup is the new testament in My blood, which is shed for you (many for the remission of sins.) (Drink ye all of it:) {and they all drank of it.}

But, behold, the hand of him that betrayeth Me *is* with Me on the table. And truly the Son of man goeth, as it was determined: but woe unto that man by whom He is betrayed! **And they began to inquire among themselves, which of them it was that should do this thing.**

And there was also a strife among them, which of them should be accounted the greatest. And He said unto them, The kings of the Gentiles exercise lordship over them; and they that exercise authority upon them are called benefactors. But ye *shall* not *be* so: but he that is greatest among you, let him be as the younger; and he that is chief, as he that doth serve. For whether *is* greater, he that sitteth at meat, of he that serveth? *Is* not he that sitteth at meat? But I am among you as he that serveth.

Ye are they which have continued with Me in My temptations. And I appoint unto you a kingdom, as My Father hath appointed unto Me: That ye may eat and drink at My table in My kingdom, and sit on thrones judging the twelve tribes of Israel.

<Therefore when He was gone out, Jesus said, Now is the Son of man glorified, and God is glorified with Him. If God be glorified in Him, God shall also glorify Him in Himself, and shall straightway glorify Him. Little children, yet a little while I am with you. Ye shall seek Me: and as I said unto the Jews, Whither I go, ye can not come; so now I say unto you. A new commandment I give unto you, That ye love one another; as I have loved you, By this shall all *men* know that ye are My disciples, If ye have love one to another.>

And the Lord said, Simon, Simon, behold, Satan hath desired to have you, that he may sift you as wheat: But I have prayed for thee, that thy faith fail not: and when thou art converted, strengthen thy brethren.

<Simon Peter said unto Him, Lord, whither goest Thou? Jesus answered him, Whither I go, thou canst not follow Me now; but thou shalt follow Me afterwards. Peter said unto Him, Lord, why cannot I follow Thee now? I will lay down my life for Thy sake.> {And} (Then) {Jesus saith unto them, All ye shall be offended because of Me this night: for it is written, I will smite the shepard, and the sheep (of the flock) shall be scattered (abroad). But after that I am risen, I will go before you into Galilee. But [he] Peter (answered and) said unto Him, [Lord I am ready to go with Thee, both into prison, and to death.] Although all (men) shall be offended (because of Thee), yet will not I (never be offended). And [He] Jesus saith unto him, <Wilt thou lay down thy life for My sake?> Verily, <verily> I say [tell] unto thee, [Peter] That this day, even in this night, before the cock <[shall not]> crow twice <till>, thou shalt deny <hast denied> Me thrice [that thou knowest Me.] But he (Peter) spake (and said unto Him) the more vehemently, If [though] I should die with Thee (yet) I will not deny Thee in any wise, Likewise also said they all (the disciples).} When I sent you without purse, and scrip, and shoes, lacked ye any thing? And they said, Nothing. Then said He unto them, But now, he that hath a purse, let him take *it,* and likewise *his* scrip: and he that

hath no sword, let him sell his garment, and but one. For I say unto you, that this that is written must yet be accomplished in Me. And He was reckoned among the transgressors: for the things concerning Me have an end. **And they said, Lord, behold here are two swords. And He said, unto them,** It is enough.]

(76) (32) **<John 14:1–17:26>**

<Let not your heart be troubled: ye believe in God, believe also in Me. In My Father's house are many mansions: if *it were* not so. I would have told you. I go to prepare a place for you. And if I go and prepare a place for you, I will come again, and receive you unto Myself; that where I am, *there* ye may be also. And whither I go ye know, and the way ye know. **Thomas saith unto him, Lord, we know not whither thou goest; and how can we know the way? Jesus saith unto him,** I am the way, the truth, and the life, no man cometh unto the Father, but by Me. If ye had known Me, ye should have known My Father also: and from henceforth ye know, Him, and have seen Him. **Philip saith unto Him, Lord, shew us the Father, and it sufficeth us, Jesus saith unto him,** Have I been so long time with you, and yet hast thou not known Me. Philip? He that hath seen Me hath seen the Father; and how sayest thou *then,* Shew us the Father? Believest thou not that I am in the Father, and the Father in Me? The words that I speak unto you I speak not of Myself: but the Father that dwelleth in Me, He doeth the works. Believe Me that I *am* in the Father, and the Father in Me: or else believe Me for the very works' sake. Verily, verily, I say unto you, He that believeth on Me, the works that I do shall he do also; and greater works than these shall he do; because I go unto My Father. And whatsoever ye shall ask in My name, that will I do. That the Father may be glorified in the Son. If ye shall ask any thing in My name I will do *it*.

If ye love Me, keep My commandments. And I will pray the Father and He shall give you another Comforter, that He may abide with you for ever; Even the Spirit of truth; whom the world cannot receive because it seeth Him not, neither knoweth Him: but ye know Him; for He dwelleth with you, and shall be in you. I will not leave you comfortless: I will come to you. Yet a little while, and the world seeth Me no more; but ye see Me: because I live, ye shall live also. At that day ye shall know that I am in my Father and ye in Me, and I in you. He that hath My commandments, and keepeth them, he it is that loveth Me: and he that loveth Me shall be loved of My Father, and I will love him, and will manifest Myself to him. **Judas saith unto Him, not Iscariot, Lord, how is it that Thou wilt manifest Thyself unto us, and not unto the world? Jesus answered and said unto him,** If a man love Me, he will keep My words: and My Father will love him, and We will come unto him, and make Our abode with him. He that loveth Me not keepeth not My sayings: and the word which ye hear is not Mine, but the Father's which sent Me. These things have I spoken unto you, being *yet* present with you. But the Comforter, *which is* the Holy Ghost, whom the Father will send in My name, He shall teach you all things, and bring all things to your remembrance whatsoever I have said unto you. Peace I leave with you, My peace I give unto you: not as the world giveth, give I unto you. Let not your heart be troubled, neither let it be afraid. Ye have heard how I said unto you, I go away, and come *again* unto you. If ye loved Me, ye would rejoice, because I said, I go unto the Father: for My Father is greater than I. And now I have told you before it come to pass, that, when it is come to pass, ye might believe. Hereafter I will not talk much with you: for the prince of this world cometh, and hath nothing in Me. But that the world may know that I love the Father; and as the Father gave Me commandment, even so I do. Arise, let us go hence.

I Am the true vine, and My Father is the husbandmen. Every branch in Me that beareth not fruit He taketh away: and every *branch* that beareth fruit, He purgeth it, that it may bring forth more fruit. Now ye are clean through the word which I have spoken unto you. Abide in Me, and I in you. As the branch cannot bear fruit of itself, except it abideth in the vine: no more can ye, except ye abide in Me. I Am the vine, *ye are* the branches: He that abideth in Me, and I in him, the same bringeth forth much fruit: for without Me ye can do nothing. If a man abide not in Me, he is cast forth as a branch, and is withered; and men gather them, and cast *them* into the fire, and they are burned. If ye abide in Me and My words abide in you, ye shall ask what ye will, and it shall be done unto you. Herein is My Father glorified, that ye bear much fruit; so shall ye be My disciples. As the Father has loved Me, so I have loved you: continue ye in My love. If ye keep My commandments, ye shall abide in My love; even as I have kept My Father's commandments, and abide in His love. These things have I spoken unto you, that my joy might remain in you, and *that* your joy might be full. This is my commandment, That ye love one another, as I have loved you. Greater love has no man than this, that a man lay down his life for his friends. Ye are My friends, if ye do whatsoever I command you. Henceforth I call you not servants; for the servant knoweth not what his lord doeth: but I have called you friends; for all things I have heard of My Father I have made known unto you. Ye have not chosen Me, but I have chosen you, and ordained you, that ye should go and bring forth fruit, and *that* your fruit should remain: that whatsoever ye shall ask of the Father in My name, He may give it you. These things I command you, that ye love one another. If the world hate you, ye know that it hated Me before *it h*ated you. If ye were of the world, the world would love his own: but because ye are not of the world, but I have chosen you out of the world, therefore the world hateth you. Remember the word that I said unto you, the servant is not greater than his lord. If they have persecuted Me, they will also persecute you; if they have kept My sayings, they will keep yours also. But all these things will they do unto you for My name's sake, because they know not Him that sent Me. If I had not come and spoken unto them, they had not had sin: but now they have no cloke for their sin. He that hateth Me hateth My Father also. If I had not done among them the works which none other man did, they had not had sin: but now have they both seen and hated both Me and My Father. But *this cometh to pass,* that the word might be fulfilled that is written in their law, They hated Me without a cause. But when the Comforter is come, whom I will send unto you from the Father, *even* the Spirit of truth which proceedeth from the Father, He shall testify of Me: And ye also shall bear witness, because ye have been with Me from the beginning.

These things have I spoken unto you, that ye should not be offended. They shall put you out of the synagogues; yea, the time cometh, that whosoever killeth you will think that he doeth God service And these things will they do unto you, because they have not known the Father, nor Me. But these things have I told you, that when the time shall come, ye may remember that I told you of them. And these things I said not unto you at the beginning, because I was with you. But now I go My way to Him that sent Me; and none of you asketh Me, Whither goest thou? But because I have said these things unto you, sorrow hath filled your heart. Nevertheless I tell you the truth; It is expedient for you that I go away: for if I go not away, the Comforter will not come unto you; but if I depart, I will send Him unto you. And when He is come, He will reprove the world of sin, and of righteousness, and of judgement; Of sin, because they believe not on Me; Of righteousness, because I go to My Father, and ye see Me no more; Of judgement, because the prince of this world is judged. I have yet many things to say unto you, but ye cannot bear them now. Howbeit when He the Spirit of truth, is come, He will guide you into all truth: for He shall not speak of Himself; but whatsoever He shall hear, *that* shall He speak: and He will shew you things to come. He shall glorify Me: for He shall receive of Mine, and shall shew *it* unto you. All things that the Father hath are Mine: therefore said I, that He shall take of Mine, and shall shew *it* unto you. A little while, and ye shall not see Me: and again, a little while, and ye shall see Me, because I go to the Father. **Then said** *some* **of the disciples among themselves, What is this that He saith unto us, A little while, and ye shall not see Me: and again, a little while, and ye shall see Me: Because I go to the Father? They said therefore, What is this that He saith. A little while? We cannot tell what He saith. Now Jesus knew that they were desirous to ask Him, and said unto them,** Do ye inquire among yourselves of that I said, A little while, and ye shall not see Me: and again, a little while, and ye shall see Me? Verily, verily, I say unto you, That ye shall weep and lament, but the world shall rejoice: and ye shall be sorrowful, but your sorrow shall be turned into joy. A woman when she is in travail hath sorrow, because her hour is come: but as soon as she is delivered of the child, she remembereth no more the anguish, for joy that a man is born into the world. And ye now therefore have sorrow: but I will see you again, and your heart shall rejoice, and your joy no man taketh from you. And in that day ye shall ask Me nothing. Verily, verily, I say unto you, Whatsoever ye shall ask the Father in My name, He will give *it* you. Hitherto have ye asked nothing in My name: ask, and ye shall receive, that your joy may be full. These things have I spoken unto you in proverbs: but the time cometh, when I shall no more speak unto you in proverbs, but I shall shew you plainly of the Father. At that day ye shall ask in My name: and I say not unto you, that I will pray the Father for you: For the Father Himself loveth you, because ye have loved Me, and have believed that I came out from God. I came forth from the Father, and am come into the world: again, I leave the world, and go to the Father. **His disciples said unto Him, Lo, now speakest Thou plainly, and speakest no proverb. Now are we sure that Thou knowest all things, and needest not that any man should ask Thee: by this we believe that Thou camest forth from God. Jesus answered them,** Do you now believe? Behold, the hour cometh, yea, is now come, that ye shall be scattered, every man to his own, and shall leave Me alone: and yet I am not alone, because the Father is with Me. These things I have spoken unto you, that in Me ye might have peace. In the world ye shall have tribulation but be of good cheer; I have over come the world.

These words spake Jesus, and lifted up His eyes to heaven, and said, Father the hour is come; glorify thy Son, that thy Son also may glorify Thee: As Thou hast given Him power over all flesh, that He should give eternal life to as many as Thou hast given Him. And this is life eternal, that they might know Thee the only true God, and Jesus Christ, whom Thou hast sent. I have glorified Thee on the earth: I have finished the work which Thou gavest Me to do. And now, O Father, glorify Thou Me with Thine own self with the glory which I had with Thee before the world was. I have manifested Thy Name unto the men which Thou gavest Me out of the world: Thine they were, and Thou gavest them Me; and they kept Thy word. Now they have known that all things whatsoever Thou hast given Me are of Thee. For I have given unto them the words which Thou gavest Me; and they have received *them*, and have known surely that I came out from Thee, and they have believed that Thou didst send

Me. I pray for them: I pray not for the world, but for them which Thou hast given Me; for they are Thine. And all Mine Are Thine, and Thine are Mine: and I am glorified in them. And now I am no more in the world, but these are in the world, and I come to Thee. Holy Father, keep through Thine own name those whom Thou hast given Me, that they may be one, as We *are*. While I was with them in the world, I kept them in Thy name: those that you gavest Me I have kept, and none of them is lost, but the son of perdition; that the scripture might be fulfilled. And now I come to Thee; and these things I speak in the world, that they might have My joy fulfilled in themselves. I have given them Thy word and the world hath hated them because they are not of the world, even as I am not of the world. I pray not that Thou shouldest take them out of the world, but that Thou shouldest keep them from the evil. They are not of the world, even as I am not of the world. Sanctify them through Thy truth: Thy word is truth. As Thou hast sent Me into the world, even so have I also sent them into the world. And for their sakes I sanctify Myself, that they also might be sanctified through the truth. Neither pray I for these alone, but for them also which shall believe on Me through their word; That they all may be one; as Thou, Father, *art* in Me and I in Thee, that they also may be one in Us: that the world may believe that Thou hast sent Me. And the glory which Thou gavest Me I have given them; that they may be one, even as We are one. I in them, and Thou in Me, that they may be made perfect in one; and that the world may know that Thou hast sent Me, and hast loved them, as Thou hast loved Me. Father, I will that they also, whom Thou hast given Me, be with me where I am; that they may behold My glory, which Thou hast given Me: for Thou lovest Me before the foundation of the world. O righteous Father, the world hath not known Thee, but I have known Thee, and these have known that Thou hast sent Me. And I have declared unto them Thy name, and will declare *it:* that the love wherewith Thou hast love Me may be in them, and I in them.>

(77) (45) **<John 18:1>** (Matthew 26:30) {Mark 14:26} [Luke 22:39]

< When Jesus had spoken these words (And {when} they had sung an hymn) He (they) went [came] (out) [as He was wont] forth {(into the mount of Olives)} [and] with His disciples [also followed Him.] over the brook Cedron, where was a garden into the which he entered, and His disciples. >

(78) (46) **(Matthew 26:36–46)** {Mark 14:32–42}

({And they} Then cometh {came} Jesus with them unto a place called {which was named} Gethsemane and {He} saith unto {His} the disciples, Sit ye here, while I {shall} go and pray yonder. And He took {taketh} with Him Peter and {James and John} the two sons of Zebedee and began to be sorrowful {sore amazed} and {to be} very heavy. {And} Then saith He unto them, My soul is exceeding sorrowful, even unto death: tarry ye here, and watch with Me. And He went a little further, {forward a little} and fell on His face, {on the ground}, and prayed {that if it were possible, the hour might pass from Him.}, saying, {and He said} {Abba} O My Father, if it be {all things are} possible, {unto thee:} let {take away} this cup pass from Me: nevertheless not as {what} I will, but as {what} thou *wilt*. And He cometh unto {them} the disciples, and findeth them asleep {sleeping}, and saith unto Peter, {Simon, sleepest thou?} What, could {est} ye not watch with Me one hour? Watch and pray, that {lest} ye enter not into temptation the spirit indeed {truly} *is* willing {ready}, but the flesh *is* weak. {And} He went away again the second time, and prayed, {and spake the same words} saying, O My Father, if this cup may not pass away from Me, except I drink it, Thy will be done. And {when} He came {returned} and found them asleep again: for their eyes were heavy {neither wist they what to answer Him,}. And He left them, and went {cometh} away again, and prayed, the third time, saying the same words. Then cometh He to His disciples, and saith unto them, Sleep on now, and take *your* rest {it is enough}: behold, the hour is {come} at hand, and {behold} the Son of man is betrayed into the hands of sinners. Rise {up}, let us be going: behold, {lo} he is at hand that doth betray Me.)

(79) (47) **{Mark 14:43–52}** (Matthew 26:47–56) [Luke 22:47–53] <John 18:2–11>

{<And Judas also, which betrayed Him, knew the place: for Jesus ofttimes resorted thither with His disciples. Judas then, having received a band of *men* and officers from the chief priests and Pharisees, cometh thither with lanterns and torches and weapons. Jesus therefore, knowing all things that should come upon Him, went forth, and said unto them, Whom seek ye? They answered Him, Jesus of Nazareth, Jesus saith unto them, I Am He. And Judas also, which betrayed Him, stood with them, As soon then as He had said unto them, I Am He, they went backward, and fell to the ground. Then asked He them again, Whom seek ye? And they said, Jesus of Nazareth. Jesus answered, I have told you that I am He: if therefore ye seek Me, let these go their way: That the saying might be fulfilled, which He spake, Of them which Thou gavest Me have I lost none. >

And immediately, while He yet spake (lo) [behold] cometh [he that was called] Judas, one of the twelve, and with him a great multitude with swords and staves, from the chief priests and the scribes and the elders (of the people). And (Now) he that betrayed Him had given (gave) them a token (sign), saying, Whomsoever I shall kiss, that same is He; take (hold) Him (fast), and lead *Him* away safely. And as soon as he was come (and forthwith) [went before them] he goeth (came) straightway [and drew near] to Him (Jesus), [to kiss Him] and saith (said), (Hail) Master, master; and kissed Him. (And Jesus said unto him, Friend, wherefore art thou come?) [But Jesus said unto him, Judas betrayest thou the Son of man with a kiss?]

When they which were about Him saw what would follow, they said unto Him, Lord, shall we smite with the sword?] And (Then came) they (and) laid their hands on Him (Jesus), and took Him. And (behold), <then> one of them <Simon Peter> (which were with Jesus) that stood by <having a sword> (stretched out *his* hand, and) drew<it> (his) a sword, and smote (struck) a (the) servant of the high priest ('s), and cut off (smote) his [right] ear. <The servant's name was Malchus> [And Jesus answered and said, Suffer ye thus far. And He touched his ear, and healed him.] And (then) Jesus answered and said unto (him <Peter,> Put up again thy sword into his place <sheath>: for all they that take the sword shall perish with the sword. Thinkest thou that I cannot now pray to My Father, and He shall presently give Me more than twelve legions of angels? <the cup which My Father hath given Me. shall I not drink it?> But how then shall the scriptures be fulfilled, that thus it must be? In that same hour [then] said Jesus [un] to) them (the multitude) [the chief priests, and captains of the temple, and the elders, which were come to Him,] Are [be] ye come out, as against a thief, with swords, and with staves (for) to take Me? [When]

I was (sat) daily with you in the temple teaching, and ye took Me not: (laid no hold on Me.) [ye stretched forth no hands against Me: but this is your hour, and the power of darkness,] but {all this was done, that) the scriptures (of the prophets) (might) must be fulfilled. And (then) they all (the disciples) forsook Him, and fled. And there followed Him a certain young man, having a linen cloth cast about *his* naked *body;* and the young men laid hold on him: And he left the linen cloth, and fled from them naked.}

(80) (48) **{Mark 14:53–15:1}** (Matthew 26:57–27:2) [Luke 22:54–71] <John 18:12–27>

(<Then the band and the captain and officers of the Jews took Jesus, and bound Him, and led Him away to Annas first: for he was father-in-law to Caiaphas, which was the high priest that same year. Now Caiaphas was he, which gave counsel to the Jews, that it was expedient that one man should die for the people.> And [Then took] they (that had laid hold on) [Him, and] led Jesus away [and brought Him] to (Caiphas) the high priest ['s house]: and with him were assembled all the chief priests and elders and (where) the scribes. (But) Peter followed Him afar off, <and so did another disciple: that disciple was known unto the high priest, and went in with Jesus> even into (unto the palace of the high priest ('s): [And when they had kindled a fire in the midst of the hall, and were set down together.] and he [Peter] <stood at the door without, Then went out that other disciple, which was known unto the high priest, and spake unto her that kept the door, and brought in Peter> (went in) and he sat [down among them], with the servants (to see the end), and warmed himself at the fire. <The high priest then ask Jesus of His disciples, and of His doctrine. Jesus answered him, I spoke openly to the wortd, t ever taught in the synagogue, and in the temple, whither the Jews always resort; and in secret have I said nothing Why askest thou Me? Ask them which heard Me, what. I have said unto them: behold they know what I said. And when He had thus spoken, one of the officers which stood by struck Jesus with the palm of his hand, saying, Answerest thou the high priest so? Jesus answered him, If I have spoken evil, bear witness of the evil: but if well, why smitest thou Me? And (now) the chief priest) and elders) and all the council sought for (false) witness against Jesus to put Him to death; (But) and found none. For (yea, though) many bare false witness (es came *yet* found they none.) against Him, but their witness agreed not together. And (At the last) there arose (came) certain (two) and bare false witness (es) against Him, saying (and said), we heard Him (this *fellow* said) say I will (am able to) destroy this (the) temple (of God) that is made with hands, and (to) within three days I will build (it) another made without hands. But neither so did their witness agree together. And the high priest stood up (arose) in the midst, and asked (said unto Him) Jesus, saying, Answerest thou nothing? What is it which these witness against thee? But He (Jesus) held His peace, and answered nothing. (And) Again the high priest asked Him (answered) and said unto Him. Art (I adjure thee by the living God, that Thou tell us whether) Thou (be) the Christ the Son of the Blessed (God)? And Jesus said, [He said unto them] (saith unto him) [If I tell you, ye will not believe: and if I also ask you, ye will not answer Me, nor let Me go.] [ye say that I am] (Thou hast said:) I AM: and (nevertheless I say unto you. Hereafter) ye shall see the Son on man sitting on the right hand of] the] power, [of God] and coming in the clouds of heaven. Then the high priest rent his clothes, and saith (saying) (He hath spoken blasphemy;) what need (have) we (of) any further witnesses? (Behold, now) [for] ye [we ourselves] have heard [of] (His) [own mouth] the blasphemy: what think ye? And they all (answered and said) condemned Him to be (He is) guilty of death.

[And the men that held Jesus mocked Him,] And (then did they) some began to spit on Him (in His face), [and when they had blindfolded Him,] and to cover His face, and to buffet (ed) Him, and to say (ing) unto [and asked] Him, [saying] Prophesy (unto us, Thou Christ): and (others the servants did strike (smote) Him with the palms of their hands [on the face] (who is he [it] that smote thee?) [And many other things blasphemously spake they against Him.]

And (Now) as Peter was beneath (sat without) in the palace, there (a damsel came) cometh one of the [But a certain] maids of the high priest [beheld him]: And when she saw Peter [as he sat by the fire,] warming himself, [and] she [earnestly] looked upon him, and said (saying), And thou [this man] also wast [was] with [Him] Jesus of Nazareth (Galilee). But [And] he denied (before them all) [Him] <And the servants and officers stood there, who had made a fire of coals; for it was cold; and they warmed themselves: and Peter stood with them, and warmed himself.> <One of the servants of the high priest, being his kinsman whose ear Peter cut off, saith, did not I see thee in the garden with Him?> [Woman] I know [Him] not, neither understand I what thou sayest. And (when) he went (was gone) out into the porch; and the cock crew. And [after a little while] a [(another)] maid saw him again, and began to say [(said)] (un) to them that stood by (were there), This (fellow [thou art] is (was also) *one* [also] of them [with Him] (Jesus of Nazareth). And he denied it again (with an oath, I know not the man). And a little (while) after, [about the space of one hour another confidently affirmed] (unto him) they that stood by said again to Peter, surely [of a truth] thou [this fellow] [(also)] *art one of them [was with Him]*: for thou [*he is*] *art a Galilaean, also of them.*] and thy speech agreeth *thereto* (bewrayeth thee). But he [Peter said] (then) began to curse and to swear, *saying,* I know not [what thou sayest,] this (the) man of whom ye speak. And (immediately. [while he yet spake,] the second time the cock crew. And the Lord turned and looked upon Peter,] And Peter called to mind (remembered) the word [of the Lord] Jesus (which) [how He] said unto him. Before the cock crow twice, thou shalt deny Me thrice. (And he [Peter] went out) and when he thought thereon, he wept (bitterly.)

And when straightway in the morning [as soon as it was day (was come)] (all) the chief priests held a consultation (took counsel) (against Jesus to put Him to death:) (and) with the elders (of the people) and scribes and the whole council and (when they had) bound (Him) Jesus and carried Him away, and delivered Him to (Pontius) Pilate (the governor.))

(81) **(49) (Matthew 27:3–32)** {Mark 15:2–21} [Luke 23:1–26] <John 18:28–19:17>

(Then Judas, which had betrayed Him, when he saw that he was condemned, repented himself, and brought again the thirty pieces of silver to the chief priests and elders. Saying, I have sinned in that I have betrayed the innocent blood. And they said, What *is that* to us? See thou *to that*. And he cast down the pieces of silver in the temple, and departed, and went and hanged himself. And the chief priests took the silver pieces, and said, It is not lawful for to put them into the treasury, because it is the price of blood. And they took counsel, and bought with them the potters field, to bury strangers in. Wherefore that field was called, the field of blood, unto this day. Then was fulfilled that which was spoken by Jeremy the prophet, saying, And they took the thirty pieces of silver, the price of Him that was valued, whom they of the children of Israel did value; and gave them for the potter's field, as the Lord appointed me. [And the whole multitude of them arose, <Then led they Jesus from Caiphas unto the hail of judgement: and it was early; and they themselves went not into the judgement hall, lest they should be defiled; but that they might eat the passover.> and led him unto Pilate <Pilate then went out unto them, and said, What accusation bring ye against this Man.> <They answered and said unto him, If He were not a malefactor, we would not have delivered him up unto thee. Then said Pilate, unto them, Take ye Him, and judge Him according to your law. The Jews therefore said unto him, It is not lawful for us to put any man to death: That the saying of Jesus might be fulfilled, which He spake, signifying what death He should die.> [And they began to accuse Him, saying, We found this fellow pre-verting the nation, and forbidding to give tribute to Caesar, saying that He himself is Christ a King.] <Then Pilate entered into the judgement hall again, and called Jesus,> And Jesus stood before the governor: and the governor {Pilate} asked Him, <said unto Him.>, saying, Art thou the king of the Jews? And {He} Jesus {answering [ed]} said unto him, Thou sayest. <Sayest thou this thing of thyself, or did others tell it thee of Me?> <Pilate answered Him, Am I a Jew? Thine own nation and the chief priests have delivered thee unto me: what hast thou done? Jesus answered, My kingdom is not of this world: if My kingdom were of this world, then would My servants fight, that I should not be delivered to toe Jews; bet now is my kingdom not from hence. Pilate therefore said unto Him, Art thou a King then? Jesus answered, Thou sayest that I am a King. To this end was I born, and for this cause <came I into the world, that I should bear witness unto the truth. Every one that is of the truth heareth My voice. Pilate saith unto Him, What is truth? And when he had said this, he went out again unto the Jews and saith unto them, I find not fault at all.> And when He was accused {many things} of the chief priests and elders, {but} He answered nothing. {And} Then said {asked} Pilate unto Him, {again} {answerest} Hearest thou not {nothing} {behold} how many things they witness against thee? {But} And He {Jesus yet} answered him to never a word {nothing}; insomuch {so} that the governor {Pilate} marvelled greatly. [Then said Pilate to the chief priests and to the people, I find no fault in this man. And they were the more fierce, saying, He stirreth up the people, teaching through out all Jewry, beginning from Galilee to this place. When Pilate heard of Galilee, he asked whether the man were a Galilaean. And as soon as he knew that He belonged unto Herod's jurisdiction, he sent Him to Herod, who himself also was at Jerusalem at that time.

And when Herod saw Jesus, he was exceeding glad: for he was desirous to see him of a long season, because he had heard many things of Him; and he hoped to have seen some miracle done by Him. Then he questioned with Him in many words: but He answered him nothing. And the chief priests and scribes stood and vehemently accused Him. And Herod with his men of war set Him at nought, and mocked Him, and arrayed Him in a gorgeous robe, and sent Him again to Pilate.

And the same day Pilate and Herod were made friends together: for before they were at enmity between themselves.

And Pilate, when he had called together the chief priests and the rulers and the people. Said unto them, Ye have brought this man unto me, as one that perverteth the people: and, behold, I having examined *Him* before you have found no fault in this man touching those things whereof ye accuse Hin No, nor yet Herod for I sent you to him; and, lo, nothing worthy of death is done unto Him. I will therefore chastise Him, and release *Him*. <But ye have a custom, that I should release unto you one at the passover:> (for of a necessity he must release one unto them at the feast.)]

Now at that feast {he} the governor was wont to release {ed} unto {them} the people {one} a prisoner, whom {soever} they would {desired}. And they had then a notable prisoner, called {there was one named} Barabbas. {which lay bound with them that had made insurrection with him, who had committed murder in the insurrection. And the multitude crying aloud began to desire *him* to do as he had ever done unto them.} Therefore when they were gathered together. {But} Pilate {answered said unto them, {saying} Whom will ye <therefore> that I release unto you <{the king of the Jews?}: {for the chief priests had delivered Him for envy.} Barabbas or Jesus which is called Christ? <Then cried they all again, saying, Not this man, but Barabbas. Now Barabbas was a robber.> For he knew that for envy they had delivered Him. {But the chief priests moved the people, that he should rather release Barabbas unto them,}

When he <Pilate therefore heard that saying, he brought Jesus forth, and> was sat down on the judgement seat <in a place that is called the Pavement, but in the Hebrew Gabbatha.>, <And it was the preparation of the passover, and about the sixth hour: and he said unto the Jews, Behold your King! But they cried out, Away with Him, away with Him, Crucify Him. Pilate saith unto them, shall I crucify your King? The chief priests answered we have no king but Caesar.> his wife sent unto him saying, Have thou nothing to do with that just man: for I have suffered many things this day in a dream because of Him. But the chief priests and elders persuaded the multitude that they should ask Barabbas and destroy Jesus. The governor answered and said unto them, Whether of the twain will ye that I release unto you? [And] They [cried out all at once, saying,] [Away with this *man*, and release unto us,] Barabbas. [(Who for a certain sedition made in the city, and for murder, was cast into prison.)] {And} Pilate [therefore, willing to release Jesus,] {answered} saith [spake] {said again} unto [to] them, What shall I do {will ye} then with {that I shall do unto Him whom ye call the King of the Jews?} Jesus which is called Christ? {And} [But] they all {cried out again} say [ing] unto him, Let Him be crucified [crucify Him.] And {then} the governor {Pilate} said; {unto them} Why, what evil hath He done? [I have found no cause of death in Him: I will therefore chastise, and let Him go!] But {And they cried out the {exceedingly} more [were instant with loud voices], saying, Let Him [requiring that He might] be crucified {crucify Him}. [And the voices of them and of the chief priests prevailed]

When Pilate saw that he could prevail nothing, but *that* rather a tumult was made [Pilate gave sentence that it should be as they required], he took water, and washed *his* hands before the multitude saying, I am innocent of the blood of this just person: see *ye to it*. Then answered all the people, and said, His blood *be* on us, and on our children.

{And so Pilate, willing to content the people,} [And] Then [he] released [unto them him] he Barabbas [him that for sedition and murder was cast into prison, whom they had desired;] unto them: [but he delivered Jesus to their will] and, <then Pilate took Jesus and> when he had scourged {*Him*} Jesus, <And the soldiers platted a crown of thorns, and put it on His head, and they put on Him a purple robe. And said, Hail King of the Jews! And they smote Him with their hands. Pilate therefore went forth again, and saith unto them, Behold I bring Him forth to you, that ye may know that I find no fault in Him. Then came Jesus forth, wearing the crown of thorns, and the purple robe. And *Pilate* saith unto them, Behold the Man! When the chief priests therefore and officers saw Him, they cried out, saying, Crucify Him, crucify Him, Pilate saith unto them, Take ye Him, and crucify Him: for I find no fault in Him. The

Jews answered him, We have a law, and by our law He ought to die, because He made Himself the Son of God.

When Pilate therefore heard that saying, he was the more afraid; And went again into the judgement hall, and saith unto Jesus, Whence art Thou? But Jesus gave him no answer. Then saith Pilate unto him, Speakest Thou not unto me? Knowest Thou not that I have power to release Thee? Jesus answered, Thou couldest have no power at all against Me, except it were given thee from above: therefore he that delivered Me unto thee hath the greater sin. And from thence forth Pilate sought to release Him: but the Jews cried out, saying, If thou let this man go, thou art not Caesar's friend: whosoever maketh himself a king speakest against Caesar.> <Then> he delivered *Him* <therefore unto them> to be crucified. Then the soldiers of the governor took Jesus {led Him away} into the common hall called Praetorium}, and {they called together} gathered unto him the whole band of *soldiers*. And they stripped Him, and {they clothed} put on Him a scarlet robe {with purple}.

And when they had platted a crown of thorns, {And} they put *it* upon {about} His head, and a reed in His right hand: and they bowed {ing} the knee {s worshipped} before Him, {and began to salute Him,} and {when they had} mocked Him, saying, Hail, King of the Jews! And they spit upon Hin and took the reed, and smote Him {on} the head. And after that they had mocked Him, <And> they took the {purple} robe off from Him <Jesus>, and put His own raiment {clothes} on Him, and [as they] led Him away to crucify Him <And He bearing His cross went forth>. And as they came out, {And} they found [laid hold upon one] a man of Cyrene {Cyrenian}, Simon by name: {who passed by,} {coming out of the country, the father of Alexander and Rufus,} him they compelled to bear His [the] cross, [that he might bear it after Jesus] <into a place called the place of a skull which is called in the Hebrew Golgotha>)

(82) **(50) <John 19:18–37>** (Matthew 27:34–56) {Mark 15:22–41} [Luke 23:27–49]

<[And there followed Him a great company of people, and of women, which also bewailed and lamented Him. But Jesus turn-

ing unto them said, Daughters of Jerusalem, weep not for Me. but weep for yourselves, and for your children. For, behold. the days are coming, in the which they shall say, Blessed are the barren, and the wombs that never bare, and the paps which never gave suck. Then shall they begin to say to the mountains fall on us: and to the hills. Cover us. For if they do these things in a green tree, what shall be done in the dry?] [And when they were come to the place which is called Calvary. [And] (They [the soldiers also mocked Him, coming to Him, and] gave [offering] Him vinegar {wine} to drink mingled with gall {myrrh} [and saying, if Thou be the king of the Jews save thyself.] and when He had tasted *thereof,* {but} He would not drink) {received it not.} Where (and) they crucified Him, and [there were also] two other (thieves) [male factors] with Him [to be put to death], on either side one, [(one on the {His} righthand, and another on the {His} left.)] {And the scripture was fulfilled, which saith and He was numbered with the transgressors.} and Jesus in the midst.

And Pilate wrote a title {the [superscription]}, [also {was written]} and put *it* (set up over His [Him] head) (His accusation) on the cross. And the writing was, [{THIS IS)] JESUS OF NAZARETH THE KING OF THE JEWS. This title then read many of the Jews for the place where Jesus was crucified was nigh to the city: and it was written in [letters of] Hebrew, *and* Greek, *and* Latin. Then said the chief priests of the Jews to Pilate, Write not, The king of the Jews, but that He said I am king of the Jews. Pilate answered, What I have written I have written.

{And it was the third hour,} Then the soldiers, when [there] they had crucified {Him} Jesus, [Then said Jesus, Father, forgive them for they know not what they do.] [And] {they} took (parted) His garments [raiment], and made four parts, to every soldier a part; and also His coat: now the coat was without seam, woven from the top throughout. They said therefore among themselves, Let us not rend it, but cast (ing) lots for it {upon them}, whose it shall be {what every man should take.}: that the scripture (it) might be fulfilled (which was spoken by the prophet) which saith, They parted My raiment (garments) among them, and for (upon) My vesture they did cast lots. (And sitting down they watched Him there :) These Things therefore the soldiers did.

Now there stood by the cross of Jesus His mother, and His mother's sister, Mary the *wife* of Cleophas, and Mary Magdalene. When Jesus therefore saw His mother, and the disciple standing by whom He loved, He saith unto His mother, Woman behold thy son! Then saith He to the disciple, Behold thy mother! And from that hour disciple that took her unto his own *home.* (And they that passed by reviled {railed on} Him, wagging their heads, and saying, {Ah} Thou that destroyest the temple, and buildest it in three days, save thyself. If thou be the Son of God come down from the cross. [And] Likewise also the chief priests, mocking [with them derided] *Him,* {among themselves} with the scribes and elders, said, He saved others: [let Him save] Himself He cannot save. If He be {let [Christ]} the king of Israel [the chosen of God,] let Him {descend} now come down from the cross, and we will {that we may see and} believe Him. He trusted in God: let Him deliver Him now, if He will have Him: for He said, I am the Son of God. {And they} The thieves also, which {that} were crucified with Him, cast the same in His teeth {reviled Him} [one of the malefactors which were hanged riled on Him, saying, If Thou be Christ save thyself and us. But the other answering rebuked him, saying, Dost not thou fear God, seeing thou art in the same condemnation? And we indeed justly for we receive the due reward of our deeds: but this man hath done nothing amiss. And he said unto Jesus, Lord, remember me when Thou comest into Thy Kingdom, And Jesus said unto him, Verily I say unto thee. To day shalt thou be with Me in paradise.]

[And] Now from the {and when} (it was about) the sixth hour [and] there was [a] darkness ovei all the {whole} land [earth] until the nineth hour. [and the sun was darkened,] And about {at} the nineth hour Jesus cried with a loud voice, saying, Eli {Eloi}, Eli {Eloi}, la-ma sabach-thani? That is to say {which is being interpreted}, My God, My God, why hast Thou forsaken Me? {and} Some of them that stood there, when they heard *that* {it}, said, This man {behold, He} calleth for Elias.)

After this Jesus knowing that all things were now accomplished, that the scripture might be fulfilled, saith I thirst. Now there was set a vessel full of vinegar: and (straightway) they (one of them ran) (took) filled a spunge {full} with vinegar, and put it upon hyssop (reed) (and gave Him to drink) and put it to His mouth. (The rest said {saying}, let be, let us see whether Elias will come to save (take} Him {down}. {And} when Jesus therefore had received the vinegar, He said {cried with a loud voice} It is finished: [Father, into Thy hands I commend My Spirit: and having said thus.] and He bowed His head, and [He] gave (yielded) up the ghost {And (behold) the veil of the temple was rent in [the midst] twain from the top to the bottom.} (and the earth did quake. and the rocks rent: And the graves were opened: and many bodies of the saints which slept arose. And came out of the graves after His resurrection, and went into the holy City, and appeared unto many.)

{And [Now] when the centurion (and they that were with him). which stood over against Him. (watching Jesus.) saw (the earthquake, and those things that were done, they feared greatly. [what was done] that He so cried out, and gave up the ghost, he [glorified God saying.] said. Truly [Certainly] this Man was the Son of God [a righteous Man.] [And all the people that came together to that sight, beholding the things which were done, smote their breasts, and returned. And all His acquaintance, and] There were also [the] (many) women [that followed Him from Galilee,] looking on afar off ft there) beholding these things.] Among whom (which)was Many' Magdalene and Mary the mother of James the less of Joses, {the mother of Zebedee's children {and Salome:} (who also, when He was in Galilee followed Him ministered unto Him) and many other women which came up with Him unto Jerusalem.)}

The Jews therefore, because it was the preparation, that the bodies should not remain upon the cross on the sabbath day. (for that sabbath day was an high day) besought Pilate that their legs might be broken, and that they might be taken away Then came the soldiers and brake the legs of the first, and of the other which was crucified with Him. But when they came to Jesus, and saw that He was dead already, they brake not His legs: But one of the soldiers with a spear pierced His side, and forthwith came there out blood and water And He that saw *it* bare record and his record is true: and he knoweth that he saith true, that ye might believe. For these things were done, that the scripture should be fulfilled. A bone of Him shall not be broken. And again another scripture saith. They shall loot on Him whom they pierced.>

(83) **(51) (Matthew 27:57–28:1)** {Mark 15:42–16:3} [Luke 23:49–24:1] <John 19:38–20:1>

([And the sabbath drew on] {And now} when the even was come. {because it was the prepation that is, the day before the sabbath.} [Behold,] <after this> there came [was] a rich man of Arimathaea, named Joseph, {an honourable counseller, which also {himself] waited for the kingdom of God.} [*he was* a good man and a just.] [(The same had not consented to the counsel deed of them.)] who also himself was Jesus disciple <being a>. <but secretly for the fear of the Jews.> He {came, and} [this man] went {in boldly} to {unto} Pilate, and begged {craved} <besought> <that he might take away> the body of Jesus. {And Pilate, marvelled if He were already dead: and calling *unto him* the centurion he asked him whether He had been any while dead. And when he knew it of the centurion}

Then Pilate {he} commanded {gave} <him> the body to be delivered {to Joseph.} {And he brought fine linen.} <And there came also Nicodemus. which at the first came to Jesus by night, and brought a mixture of myrrh and aloes, about an hundred pound *weight*. Then took they the body of Jesus.> and when Joseph [he] had taken the body. {took Him [it] down,} {And} he wrapped <wound> {Him} it <with the spices as was the manner of the Jews is to bury> in a clean {the} linen cloth. <Now in the place where He was crucified there was a garden> and laid {Him} it in [a] his own new tomb {a sepulchre} <in the garden>, which he had {was} hewn out in {of a} the rock [stone]: [wherein never man before was, <yet> laid.] <There laid they Jesus therefore because of the Jews preparation day; for the sepulchre was nigh a hand> and he rolled a great stone {un} to the door of the sepulchre, and departed. And there was Mary Magdalene, and the other Mary. {the mother of Joses beheld where He was laid.}.

[And the women also, which came with Him from Galilee, followed after, and beheld the sepulchre, and how His body was laid.] sitting over against the sepulchre. [And they returned, and prepared spices and ointments, and rested the sabbath day according to the commandment.]

Now the next day, that followed the day of preparation, the chief preists and Pharisees came together unto Pilate. Saying. Sir. we remember that that deceiver said, while He was yet alive. After three days I will rise again. Command therefore that the sepulchre be made sure until the third day. lest His disciples come by night, and steal Him away and say unto the people, He is risen from the dead: so the iast error shall be worse than the first. Pilate said unto them. Ye have a watch: go your way, make *it* as sure as ye can. So they went, and made the sepulchre sure, sealing the stone and setting a watch.

In the end of {when} the sabbath {was past}. [very early in the morning <when it was yet dark>], [Now] as it began to dawn {at the rising of the sun} toward [upon] the first day of the week [they] came <cometh> Mary Magdalene and the other Mary {the mother of James an Salome had brought [bringing the jsweet spices. [which they hao prepared,] [and certain others with them] that they might come and anoint Him.} {[un]} to see the sepulchre)

(84) **(52)** **[Luke 24:2–53]**

(Mt. 28:2–20) {Mr. 16:3–20} <Jn. 20:2–21:25> ((Acts 1:1–11))

[(And behold, there was a great earthquake: for the angel of the Lord descended from heaven, and came and rolled back the stone from the door, and sat upon it. His countenance was like lightning and his raiment white as snow: And for fear of him the keepers did shake, and became as dead *men*.) {And they said among themselves, Who shall roll us away the stone from the door of the sepulchre?} And they found the stone rolled away from the sepulchre (And {he} the angel answered and said unto the women. Fear not ye {Be not affrighted}: for I know that ye seek Jesus {of Nazareth}. which was crucified. He is not here: for He is risen, as He said. Come {behold}. see the place where the Lord lay) {they laid Him}. And they entered {ing} in {to the sepulchre.} and found not the body of the Lord Jesus.

And it came to pass, as they were much perplexed thereabout. {they saw a young man sitting on the right side, clothed in a long white garment: and they were affrighted} behold two men stood by them in shining garments: And as they were afraid {affrighted}, and bowed down *their* faces to the earth, they said unto them, Why seek ye the living among the dead? He is not here, but is risen remember how He spake unto you, when He was yet in Galilee Saying. The Son of man must be de-livered into the hands of sinful men. and be crucified, and the third day rise again. And they remembered His words, and (they departed {went out} quickly) returned {fled} from the sepul-chre. ({for they trembled} with fear and great joy {were amazed}) {neither said they any thing to any *man* for they were afraid.} (<Then she> did run to bring His disciples word.) (And as they went to tell His disciples, behold. Jesus met them, saying. All hail. And they came and held Him by the feet, and worshipped Him Then said Jesus unto them, Be not afraid, go tell My brethren that they go into Galilee and there shall they see me.

Now when they were going behold, some of the watch came into the city, and shewed unto the chief priests all the things that were done. And when they were assembled with the elders, and had taken counsel, they gave large money unto the soldiers, saying, Say ye, His disciples came by night, and stole Him *away* while we slept And if this come to the governor's ears, we will persuade him, and secure you. So they took the money, and did as they were taught: and this saying is commonly reported among the Jews until this day.) told all these things unto the eleven, and to all the rest.

{Now when Jesus was risen early the first day of the week. He appeared first to Mary Magdalen out of whom He had cast seven devils} It was Mary Magdalene and Joanna and Mary *the mother of* James, {and she went and told them that had been with Him. as they mourned and wept.} and other *women that were* with them, which told these things unto the apostles And {they, when they had heard that He was alive, and had been seen of her,} their words seemed to them as idle tales, and they belie them not. {After that He appeared in another form unto two of them, as they walked, and went into the country. And they went and told it unto the residue neither believed they them.} Then arose <therefore went forth> Peter. <and that other disciple> and ran <came> unto the sepulchre: <So they ran both together and the other disciple did out run Peter and came first to the sepulcher.> and <he> stooping down <*and looking in.*> he beheld <saw> the linen clothes laid <lying> by themselves <yet went he not in Then cometh Simon Peter following him. and went into the sepulchre, and seeth the linen clothes lie And the napkin, that was about His head not tying with the linen clothes but wrapped together in a place by itself Then went in also that other disciple, which came first to the sepulchre and he saw, and believed. For as yet they knew not the scripture, that He must rise again from the dead. Then the disciples went away again unto their own home> and departed, wondering in himself at that which was come to pass <But Mary stood without at the sepulchre weeping and as she wept, she stooped down, *and looked* into the sepulchre, and seeih two angels in white sitting, the one at the head, and the other at the feet where the body of Jesus had lain. And they say unto her. Woman, why weepest thou? She saith unto them. Because they have taken away my Lord, and I know not where they have laid Him. And when she had thus said, she turned herself back and saw Jesus standing and knew not that it was Jesus. Jesus saith unto her. Woman, why weepest thou whom seekest thou? She, supposing him to be the gardener saith unto him Sir if thou have borne Him hence tell me where thou hast laid Him. and I will take Him away. Jesus saith unto her, Mary, she turned herself, and saith unto Him. Rabboni; which is to say. Master Jesus saith unto her. Touch Me not: for I am not yet ascended to My Father: but go to My brethren, and say unto them, I ascend unto My Father, and your Father: and to My God. and your God, Mary Magdalene came and told the disciples that she had seen the Lord, and that He had spoken these things unto her.>

And. behold, two of them went that same day to a village called Emmaus which was from Jerusalem *about* three-score furlongs And they talked together of all these things which had happened. And it came to pass. that, while they communed *together* and reasoned. Jesus Himself drew near, and wen with them But their eyes were holden that they should not know Him. And He said unto them, What manner of communications are these that ye have one to another, as ye walk, and are sad? And one of them, whose name was Cleopas. Answering said unto Him, Art thou only a stranger in Jerusalem and hast not known the things which are come to pass there in these days? And He said unto them. What things? And they said unto Him. Concerning Jesus of Nazareth, which was a prophet mighty in deed and word before God and all the people. And how the chief priests and the rulers delivered Him to be condemned to death, and have crucified Him. But we trusted that it had been He which should have redeemed Israel And beside all this today is the third day since these things were done. Yea and certain women also of our company made us astonished, which were early at the sepulchre; And when they found not His body, they came, saying, that they had also seen a vision of angels, which said that He was alive. And certain of them which were with us went to the sepulchre and found it even so as the women had said, but Him they saw not. Then He said unto them. O fools, and slow of heart to believe all that the prophets have spoke Ought not Christ to have suffered these things, and to enter into His glory. And beginning at Moses and all the prophets, He expounded unto them in all the scriptures the things concerning Himself And they drew nigh unto the village, whither they went and He made as though He would have gone further But they constrained Him. saying, abide with us for it is toward evening, and the day is far spent. And He went in to tarry with them. And it came to pass, as He sat at meat with them, He took bread. and blessed *it*, and brake, and gave unto them. And their eyes were opened, and they knew Him: and He vanished out of their sight. And the one said to another, Did not our heart burn within us, while He talked with us, by the way, and while He opened to us the scriptures? And they rose up the same hour and returned to Jerusalem, and found the eleven gathered together, and them that were with them, saying. The Lord is risen indeed, and hath appeared to Simon. And they told what things *were done* in the way. And how He was known of them in breaking of bread.

{Afterward} <Then the same day at evening, being the first day of the week, when the doors were shut where the disciples were assembled for fear of the Jews.> and as they thus spake. {He appeared unto the eleven as they sat at meat}. Jesus Himself <came and> stood in the midst of them and saith unto them, Peace be unto you {and upbraided them with their unbelief and hardness of heart, because they believed not them which had seen Him after He was risen.} But they were terrified and affrighted, and supposed that they had seen a spirit. And He said unto them, Why are ye troubled? And why do thoughts arise in your hearts? Behold My hands and My feet, that it is I Myself: handle Me, and see; for a spirit hath not flesh and bones, as ye see Me have. And when He had thus spoken, <had so said> He shewed <unto> them *His* hands, and *His* feet <and His side>. And while they yet believed not for joy. and wondered <Then were the disciples glad, when they saw the Lord.> He said unto them. Have ye here any meat? And they gave Him a piece of a broiled fish, and of a honeycomb. And He took *it* and did eat before them And He said unto them, These *are* the words which I spake unto you, while I was yet. with you, that all things must be fulfilled, which were written *in* the law of Moses and *in* the prophets, and *in* the Psalms, concerning Me.

<But Thomas one of the twelve, called Didymus. was not with them when Jesus came. The other disciples therefore said unto him. We have seen the Lord. But he said unto them. Except I shall see in His hands the print of the nails, and put my finger into the print of the nails, and thrust my hand into His side, I will not believe.

And after eight days again His disciples were within, and Thomas with them—then came Jesus the doors being shut and stood in the midst, and said, Peace *be* unto you. Then saith He to Thomas. Reach hither thy finger, and behold My hands, and reach hither thy hand, and thrust it into my side: and be not faithless, but believing. And Thomas answered and said unto Him My Lord and My God. Jesus saith unto him. Thomas because thou hast seen Me, thou hast believed: blessed *are* they that have not seen, and *yet* have believed.

And many other signs truly did Jesus in the presence of His disciples, which are not written in this book. But these things are written, that ye might believe that Jesus is the Christ, the Son of God: and that believing ye might have life through His name.>

(Then the eleven disciples went away into Galilee into a mountain where Jesus had appointed them. And went they saw Him. they worshipped Him but some doubted. And Jesus came and spake unto them, saying. All power is given unto Me in heaven and in earth. Go ye therefore, and teach all nations, baptizing them in the name of the Father, and of the Son. and of the Holy Ghost: Teaching them to observe all things whatsoever I have commanded you: and. lo. I am with you always, even unto the end of the world. Amen)

<After these things Jesus shewed Himself again to the disciples at the sea of Tiberas; and on this wise shewed He *himself.* There were together Simon Peter and Thomas called Didymus. and Nathanael of Cana in Galilee, and the sons of Zebedee, and two other of His disciples Simon Peter saith unto them. I go a fishing. They say unto him, We also go with thee They went forth, and entered into a ship immediately: and that night they caught nothing. But when the mourning was now come, Jesus stood on the shore: but the disciples knew not that it was Jesus. Then Jesus said unto them, Children, have ye any meat? They answered Him, no. And He said unto them. Cast the net on the right side of the ship, and ye shall find. They cast therefore, and now they were not able to draw it for the multitude of fishes Therefore that disciple whom Jesus loved saith unto Peter, it is the Lord Now when Simon Peter heard that it was the Lord, he girt *his* fisher's coat *unto him.* {for he was naked.) and did cast himself into the sea. And the other disciples came in a little ship; (for they were not far from land, but as it were two hundred cubits) dragging the net with fishes As soon then as they were come to land, they saw a fire of coals there, and fish laid thereon and bread. Jesus saith unto them, Bring of the fish which ye have now caught. Simon Peter went up, and drew the net to iand full of great fishes, and hundred and fifty and three and for all there were so many, yet was not the net broken Jesus saith unto them Come *and* dine. And none of the disciples durst ask Him Who art Thou? Knowing that it was the Lord. Jesus then cometh. and taketh bread and giveth them, and fish likewise This is now the third time that Jesus shewed himself to His disciples, after that He was risen from the dead.

So when they had dined, Jesus saith to Simon Peter. Simon, son of Jonas, lovest thou Me more than these? He saith unto Him, Yea Lord, thou knowest that I love thee. He saith unto him. feed My lambs. He saith to him again the second time, Simon, son of Jonas lovest Thou Me? He saith unto Him, Yea Lord; Thou knowest that I love thee He saith unto him. Feed My sheep. He saith unto him the third time. Simon, son of Jonas, lovest thou Me? Peter was grieved because he said unto him the third time, Lovest Thou Me? And he said unto him. Lord, thou knowest all things: thou knowest that I love thee Jesus saith unto him. Feed my sheep. Verily, verily I say unto thee. When thou wast young, thou girdest thyself, and walkedst whither thou wouldest: but when thou shalt be old, thou shalt stretch forth thy hands, and another shall gird thee, and carry thee wither thou wouldest not. This spake he. signifying by what death he should glorify God. And when he had spoken this, he saith unto him Follow Me. Then Peter, turning about, seeth the disciple whom Jesus loved following: which also leaned on His breast at supper, and said, Lord, which is he that betrayeth thee? Peter seeing him saith to Jesus. Lord, and what shall this man *do*? Jesus saith unto him, If I will that he tarry till I come, what is that to thee? Follow thou Me. Then went this saying abroad among the brethren, that that disciple should not die: yet Jesus said not unto him. He shall not die: but, If I will that he tarry till I come, what is that to thee? This is the disciple which testifieth of these things, and we know that his testimony is true.>

Then opened He their understanding, that they might understand the scriptures. And <then> said <Jesus> unto them, Thus it is written, and thus it behooved Christ to suffer, and to rise from the dead the third day: <Peace be unto you: as My Father hath sent Me. even so send I you, And when He had said this He breathed on *them*, and saith unto them, Receive ye the Holy Ghost: Whose soever sins ye remit, they are remitted unto them, and whose soever *sins*, ye retain they are retained.> And that repentance and remission of sins should be preached in His name among all nations, beginning at Jerusalem. And ye are witnesses of these things.

{Go ye into all the 'world, and preach the gospel to every creature. He that believeth and is baptized shall be saved: but he that believeth not shall be damned. And these signs shall follow them that believe in My name shall they cast out devils; they shall speak with new tongues; They shall take up serpents; and if they drink any deadly thing, it shall not hurt them; they shall lay hands on the sick, and they shall recover.}

And behold, I send the promise of My Father upon you but tarry ye in the city of Jerusalem, until ye be endued with power from on high.

((The former Treatise have I made. O Theophilus, of all that Jesus began both to do and teach. Until the day in which He was taken up. after that He through the Holy Ghost had given commandment: unto the apostles whom He had chosen To whom also He shewed Himself alive after His passion by many infallible proofs, being seen of them forty days, and speaking of the things pertaining to the kingdom of God: And. being assembled together with *them,* commanded them that they should not depart from Jerusalem, but wait for the promise of the Father, which, *saith He,* ye have heard of Me For John truly baptized with water; but ye shall be baptized with the Holy Ghost not many days hence. When they therefore were come together, they asked of Him. saying. Lord, wilt Thou at this time restore again the kingdom to Israel? And He said unto them, It is not for you to know the times or the seasons, which the Father hath put in His own power. But ye shall receive power after that the Holy Ghost is come upon you: and ye shall be witnesses unto Me both in Jerusalem, and in all Judaea, and in Samaria, and unto the uttermost part of the earth.)) {So then after the Lord ((when He)) had spoken unto them.} ((these things)) And He led them out as far as to Bethany, and He lifted up His hands, and blessed them. And it came to pass, while He blessed them. ((while they beheld)) He was parted from them ((He was taken up.)) and carried up into heaven ((and a cloud {received} Him out of their sight.)) {and sat on the right hand of God.} And they worshipped Him ({And while they looked stedfastly toward heaven as He went up. behold, two men stood by them in white apparel Which also said, Ye men of Galilee, why stand ye gazing up into heaven? This same Jesus which is taken up from you into heaven, shall so come in like manner as ye have seen Him go into heaven.)) and {they went forth} returned to Jerusalem with great joy {and preached every where, the lord working with *them,* and confirming the word with signs following.} And were continually in the temple, praising and blessing God. <And there are also many other things which Jesus did. the which, if they should be written every one. I suppose that even the world itself could not contain the books that should be written. Amen.>]

ABOUT THE AUTHOR

One who walked in darkness for 21 years, who Has become a believer in the way, of faith. The Master passion of life, now learning of YHVH for Several decades, and eternity to come. This learning Is the reason this book has come about. We look Through a glass darkly, but soon to be face to face. The Godhead has inspired this work, to Him be all The honor and glory. With "bara" (nothing of) Comparison, yours sincerely, an unprofitable servant.

CPSIA information can be obtained
at www.ICGtesting.com
Printed in the USA
BVHW090148021120
592244BV00003B/17

9 781098 038656